THE COMMON MAN

by

G. K. CHESTERTON

NEW YORK

SHEED AND WARD

1950

FIRST PUBLISHED 1950
BY SHEED AND WARD, INC.
NEW YORK

PRINTED IN THE UNITED STATES OF AMERICA

CONTENTS

Contents

THE COMMON MAN

THE explanation, or excuse, for this essay is to be found in a certain notion, which seems to me very obvious, but which I have never, as it happens, seen stated by anybody else. It happens rather to cut across the common frontiers of current controversy. It can be used for or against Democracy, according to whether that swear-word is or is not printed with a big D. It can be connected, like most things, with religion; but only rather indirectly with my own religion. It is primarily the recognition of a fact, quite apart from the approval or disapproval of the fact. But it does involve the assertion that what has really happened, in the modern world, is practically the precise contrary of what is supposed to have happened there.

The thesis is this : that modern emancipation has really been a new persecution of the Common Man. If it has emancipated anybody, it has in rather special and narrow ways emancipated the Uncommon Man. It has given an eccentric sort of liberty to some of the hobbies of the wealthy, and occasionally to some of the more humane lunacies of the cultured. The only thing that it has forbidden is common sense, as it would have been understood by the common people. Thus, if we begin with the seventeenth and eighteenth centuries, we find that a man really has become more free to found a sect. But the Common Man does not in the least want to found a sect. He is much more likely, for instance, to want to found a family. And it is exactly *there* that the modern emancipators are quite likely to begin to frustrate him ; in the name of Malthusianism or Eugenics or Sterilisation or at a more advanced stage of progress, probably, Infanticide. It would be a model of modern liberty to tell him that he might preach anything, however wild, about the Virgin Birth, so long as he avoided anything like a natural birth ; and that he was welcome to build a tin chapel to preach a twopenny creed, entirely based on the text, " Enoch begat Methuselah ", so long as he himself is forbidden to beget anybody. And, as a matter of historical fact, the sects which enjoyed this sectarian freedom, in the seventeenth or eighteenth centuries, were generally founded by merchants or manufacturers of the comfortable, and sometimes of the luxurious classes. On the other hand, it is strictly to the lower classes, to use the liberal modern title for the poor, that such schemes as Sterilisation are commonly directed and applied.

It is the same when we pass from the Protestant world of the seventeenth and eighteenth centuries to the Progressive world of the nineteenth and twentieth. Here the form of freedom mostly claimed, as a boast and a dogma, is the freedom of the Press. It is no longer merely a freedom of pamphlets but a freedom of papers ; or rather, it is less and less a freedom at all, and more and more a monopoly. But the important point is that the process, the test and the comparison are the same as in the first example. Modern emancipation means this : that anybody who can afford it can publish a newspaper. But the Common Man would not want to publish a newspaper, even if he could afford it. He might want, for instance, to go on talking politics in a pothouse or the parlour of an inn. And that is exactly the sort of really popular talk about politics which modern movements have often abolished : the old democracies by forbidding the pothouse, the new dictatorships by forbidding the politics.

Or again, it is the boast of recent emancipated ethics and politics not to put any great restraints upon anybody who wants to publish a book, especially a scientific book, full of

The Common Man

psychology or sociology; and perhaps unavoidably full of perversions and polite pornography. As that modern tendency increased, it was less and less likely that the police would interfere very much with a man publishing the sort of book that only the wealthy could publish with sumptuous artistic plates or scientific diagrams. It is much more probable, in most modern societies, that the police would be found interfering with a man singing a song, of a coarse and candid description, bawling out a ballad of the grosser sort, or even using the more restrained medium of prose with a similar lack of restraint. Yet there is a great deal to be said for song, or even speech, of the old ribald sort, as compared with writing of the new sort, when it is at once analytic and anarchic. The old obscenity had a gusto and a great virility even in its violence, which is not easily rendered in a diagram or a table of statistics; and the old was always normal and never had any of the horrors of abnormality. The point is that, here again, the Common Man does not generally want to write a book, whereas he may occasionally want to sing a song. He certainly does not want to write a book on psychology or sociology—or to read it. But he does want to talk, to sing, to shout, to yell and howl on due and suitable occasions; and, rightly or wrongly, it is when he is thus engaged that he is much more likely to fall foul of a policeman than when he is (as he never is) writing a scientific study of a new theory of sex. The upshot of uplift, in the modern sense, is the same in practice as in the previous examples. In the actual atmosphere of the age, men will still be arrested for using a certain kind of language, long after they cannot be arrested for writing a certain kind of literature.

It would be easy to give other examples; but these contemporary examples are already too continuous to be a coincidence. It is equally true, for instance, that the liberating movement of the eighteenth century, the life in the American and French Revolutions, while it did really vindicate many virtues of republican simplicity and civic liberty, also accepted as virtues several things that were obviously vices : that had been recognised as vices long before, and are now again beginning to be recognised as vices so long afterwards. Where even ambition had once been a pardonable vice, avarice became an utterly unpardonable virtue. Liberal economics too often meant merely giving to those already rich the liberty to grow richer, and magnificently granting to the poor the permission to remain rather poorer than before. It was much more certain that the usurer was released to practise usury than that the peasant was released from the practices of the usurer. It was much more certain that the Wheat Pit was as big as the Bottomless Pit, than that the man who grew wheat would ever be found anywhere except at the bottom.

There was a sense in which " liberal economics " were a proclamation of freedom, for the few who were rich enough to be free. Nobody thought there was anything queer about talking of prominent public men " gambling " in the Wheat Pit. But all this time, there were laws of all kinds against normal human gambling ; that is, against games of chance. The poor man was prevented from gambling, precisely because he did not gamble so much as the rich man. The beadle or the policeman might stop children from playing chuck-farthing; but it was strictly because it was only a farthing that was chucked. Progress never interfered with the game of chuck-fortune, because much more than a farthing was being chucked. The enlightened and emancipated age especially encouraged those who chucked away other people's fortunes instead of their own. But anyhow, the comparison remains continuous and clear. Progress, in the sense of the progress that has progressed since the sixteenth century, has upon every

The Common Man

matter persecuted the Common Man ; punished the gambling he enjoys and permitted the gambling he cannot follow; restrained the obscenity that might amuse him and applauded the obscenity that would certainly bore him ; silenced the political quarrels that can be conducted among men and applauded the political stunts and syndicates that can only be conducted by millionaires ; encouraged anybody who had anything to say against God, if it was said with a priggish and supercilious accent ; but discouraged anybody who had anything to say in favour of Man, in his common relations to manhood and motherhood and the normal appetites of nature. Progress has been merely the persecution of the Common Man.

Progress has a hagiology, a martyrology, a mass of miraculous legends of its own, like any other religion ; and they are mostly false and belong to a false religion. The most famous is the fancy that the young and progressive person is always martyred by the old and ordinary person. But it is false. It is the old and ordinary person who is almost always the martyr. It is the old and ordinary person who has been more and more despoiled of all his old and ordinary rights. In so far as this progress progresses, it is far more likely that six million men will be forbidden to go to sleep, because six men say that certain breathing exercises are a substitute for slumber, than that any of the six million somnambulists will wake up sufficiently to clout the six men over their highbrowed but half-witted heads. There is no normal thing that cannot now be taken from the normal man. It is much more likely that a law will be passed to forbid the eating of grain (notoriously the parent of poisons like beer and whisky) than that it will be even faintly suggested, to men of that philosophy, that the economic evil is that men cannot grow grain, and that the ethical evil is that men are still despised for growing it. Given the purely progressive principle, and nothing else as a guide to our future, it is entirely possible that they may be hanged or buried alive for growing it. But of course, in a scientific age, they will be electrocuted—or perhaps only tortured by electricity.

Thus far my thesis is this : that it is not the Uncommon Man who is persecuted; but rather the Common Man. But this brings me into direct conflict with the contemporary reaction, which seems to say, in effect, that the Common Man had much better be persecuted. It is quite certain that many modern thinkers and writers honestly feel a contempt for the Common Man ; it is also quite certain that I myself feel a contempt for those who feel this contempt. But the actual issue must be faced more fully ; because what is called the reaction against democracy is at this moment the chief result of democracy. Now on this quarrel I am democratic, or at least defiant of the attacks of democracy. I do not believe that most modern people have seen the real point of the advantage or disadvantage of popular rule ; and my doubt can be very largely suggested and summarised under this title of the Common Man.

To put it briefly ; it is now the custom to say that most modern blunders have been due to the Common Man. And I should like to point out what appalling blunders have in fact been due to the Uncommon Man. It is easy enough to argue that the mob makes mistakes; but as a fact it never has a chance even to make mistakes until its superiors have used their superiority to make much worse mistakes. It is easy to weary of democracy and cry out for an intellectual aristocracy. But the trouble is that every intellectual aristocracy seems to have been utterly unintellectual. Anybody might guess beforehand that there would be blunders of the ignorant. What nobody could have guessed, what nobody could have dreamed of in a nightmare, what no morbid mortal imagination could ever have dared to imagine, was the mistakes of the well-

The Common Man

informed. It is true, in a sense, to say that the mob has always been led by more educated men. It is much more true, in every sense, to say that it has always been misled by educated men. It is easy enough to say the cultured man should be the crowd's guide, philosopher and friend. Unfortunately, he has nearly always been a misguiding guide, a false friend and a very shallow philosopher. And the actual catastrophes we have suffered, including those we are now suffering, have not in historical fact been due to the prosaic practical people who are supposed to know nothing, but almost invariably to the highly theoretical people who knew that they knew everything. The world may learn· by its mistakes; but they are mostly the mistakes of the learned.

To go back no further than the seventeenth century, the quarrel between the Puritans and the populace was originally due to the pride of a few men in being able to read a printed book, and their scorn for people who had good memories, good traditions, good stories, good songs, and good pictures in glass or gold or graven stone, and therefore had less need of books. It was a tyranny of literates over illiterates. But it was the literates who were narrow, sullen, limited and often oppressive; it was the illiterates who were, at least relatively, gay and free and fanciful and imaginative and interested in everything. The Uncommon Men, the elect of the Calvinist theory, did undoubtedly lead the people along the next stretch of the path of progress; but what it led to was a prison. The book-reading rulers and statesmen managed to establish the Scottish Sabbath. Meanwhile, a thousand traditions, of the sort they would have trampled out, yet managed to trickle down from the medieval poor to the modern poor, and lingering as legends in countless cottages and farmhouses, were collected by Scott (often repeated orally by people who could not read or write) to combine in the construction of the great

The Common Man

Scottish Romances, which profoundly moved and partly inspired the Romantic Movement throughout the world.

When we pass to the eighteenth century, we find the same part played by a new and quite contrary party; differing from the last in everything except in being the same sort of rather dried up aristocracy. The new Uncommon Men, now leading the people, are no longer Calvinists, but a dry sort of Deists drying up more and more like Atheists ; and they are no longer pessimists but the reverse ; only their optimism is often more depressing than pessimism. There were the Benthamites, the Utilitarians, the servants of the Economic Man ; the first Free-Traders. They have the credit of having first made clear the economic theories of the modern state; and the calculations on which were mainly based the politics of the nineteenth century. It was they who taught these things scientifically and systematically to the public, and even to the populace. But what were the things, and what were the theories ? Perhaps the best and broadest of them was a most monstrous and mythical superstition of Adam Smith ; a theological theory that providence had so made the world that men might be happy through their selfishness ; or, in other words, that God would overrule everything for good, if only men could succeed in being sufficiently bad. The intellectuals in this epoch taught definitely and dogmatically that if only men would buy and sell freely, lend or borrow freely, sweat or sack freely, and in practice, steal or swindle freely, humanity would be happy. The Common Man soon found out how happy ; in the Slums where they left him and in the Slump to which they led him.

We need not continue, through the last two centuries, all the tale of the frenzy and folly inflicted by the fickleness of the educated class on the relative stability of the uneducated. The fickle intellectuals next rushed to the other extreme, and became Socialists, despising small property as they had despised

8

The Common Man

popular tradition. It is quite true that these intellectuals had a lucid interval in which they proclaimed some primary truths along with many priggish falsehoods. Some of them did rightly exalt liberty and human dignity and equality, as expressed in the Declaration of Independence. But even that was so much mishandled that there is now a disposition to deny the truth along with the falsehood. There has been a reaction against Democracy; or, in plain words, the prigs are now too bored even to go on with their normal routine about the Common Man; the familiar routine of oppressing him in practice and adoring him in theory.

I do not adore him, but I do believe in him; at least I believe in him much more than I believe in them. I think the actual history of the relations between him and them, as I have narrated it, is enough to justify my preference. I repeat that they have had all the educational advantages over him; they have always led him; and they have always misled him. And even in becoming reactionaries, they remain as raw and crude as when they were revolutionaries. Their anti-democracy is as much stuffed with cant as their democracy. I need only allude to the detestable new fashion of referring to ordinary men as morons. First, it is pedantry, the dullest form of vanity ; for a moron is only the Greek for a fool ; and it is mostly sham pedantry, for most of those who mention morons hardly know they are talking Greek, still less why on earth they should. It also involves this moral evil : that a man who says that men are mostly fools knows at least that he has often made a fool of himself; whereas the morons are thought of like monkeys; as if they were a fixed tribe or caste. The Common Man may well be the victim of a new series of tyrannies, founded on this scientific fad of regarding him as a monkey. But it is doubtful whether he can be much more persecuted for having the instincts of a moron, than he has already been for having the instincts of a man.

A MIDSUMMER NIGHT'S DREAM

THE GREATEST of Shakespeare's comedies is also, from a certain point of view, the greatest of his plays. No one would maintain that it occupied this position in the matter of psychological study if by psychological study we mean the study of individual characters in a play. No one would maintain that Puck was a character in the sense that Falstaff is a character, or that the critic stood awed before the psychology of Peaseblossom. But there is a sense in which the play is perhaps a greater triumph of psychology than *Hamlet* itself. It may well be questioned whether in any other literary work in the world is so vividly rendered a social and spiritual atmosphere. There is an atmosphere in *Hamlet*, for instance, a somewhat murky and even melodramatic one, but it is subordinate to the great character, and morally inferior to him ; the darkness is only a background for the isolated star of intellect. But *A Midsummer Night's Dream* is a psychological study, not of a solitary man, but of a spirit that unites mankind. The six men may sit talking in an inn ; they may not know each other's names or see each other's faces before or after, but night or wine or great stories, or some rich and branching discussion may make them all at one, if not absolutely with each other, at least with that invisible seventh man who is the harmony of all of them. That seventh man is the hero of *A Midsummer Night's Dream*.

A study of the play from a literary or philosophical point of view must therefore be founded upon some serious realisation of what this atmosphere is. In a lecture upon *As You Like It*, Mr. Bernard Shaw made a suggestion which is an admirable

example of his amazing ingenuity and of his one most interesting limitation. In maintaining that the light sentiment and
optimism of the comedy were regarded by Shakespeare merely
as the characteristics of a more or less cynical pot-boiler, he
actually suggested that the title "As You Like It" was a taunting
address to the public in disparagement of their taste and the
dramatist's own work. If Mr. Bernard Shaw had conceived of
Shakespeare as insisting that Ben Jonson should wear Jaeger
underclothing or join the Blue Ribbon Army, or distribute little
pamphlets for the non-payment of rates, he could scarcely have
conceived anything more violently opposed to the whole spirit
of Elizabethan comedy than the spiteful and priggish modernism of such a taunt. Shakespeare might make the fastidious
and cultivated Hamlet, moving in his own melancholy and
purely mental world, warn players against an over-indulgence
towards the rabble. But the very soul and meaning of the
great comedies is that of an uproarious communion between
the public and the play, a communion so chaotic that whole
scenes of silliness and violence lead us almost to think that some
of the "rowdies" from the pit have climbed over the foot-
lights. The title "As You Like It", is, of course, an expression
of utter carelessness, but it is not the bitter carelessness which
Mr. Bernard Shaw fantastically reads into it ; it is the god-like
and inexhaustible carelessness of a happy man. And the simple
proof of this is that there are scores of these genially taunting
titles scattered through the whole of Elizabethan comedy. Is
"As You Like It " a title demanding a dark and ironic explanation in a school of comedy which called its plays "What you
Will", " A Mad World, My Masters ", "If It Be Not Good,
the Devil Is In It", "The Devil is an Ass", "An Humorous
Day's Mirth", and "A Midsummer Night's Dream"? Every
one of these titles is flung at the head of the public as a drunken
lord might fling a purse at his footman. Would Mr. Shaw

maintain that "If It Be Not Good, the Devil Is In It", was the opposite of "As You Like It", and was a solemn invocation of the supernatural powers to testify to the care and perfection of the literary workmanship? The one explanation is as Elizabethan as the other.

Now in the reason for this modern and pedantic error lies the whole secret and difficulty of such plays as *A Midsummer Night's Dream*. The sentiment of such a play, so far as it can be summed up at all, can be summed up in one sentence. It is the mysticism of happiness. That is to say, it is the conception that as man lives upon a borderland he may find himself in the spiritual or supernatural atmosphere, not only through being profoundly sad or meditative, but by being extravagantly happy. The soul might be rapt out of the body in an agony of sorrow, or a trance of ecstasy; but it might also be rapt out of the body in a paroxysm of laughter. Sorrow we know can go beyond itself; so, according to Shakespeare, can pleasure go beyond itself and become something dangerous and unknown. And the reason that the logical and destructive modern school, of which Mr. Bernard Shaw is an example, does not grasp this purely exuberant nature of the comedies is simply that their logical and destructive attitude have rendered impossible the very experience of this preternatural exuberance. We cannot realise *As You Like It* if we are always considering it as we understand it. We cannot have *A Midsummer's Night Dream* if our one object in life is to keep ourselves awake with the black coffee of criticism. The whole question which is balanced, and balanced nobly and fairly, in *A Midsummer Night's Dream*, is whether the life of waking, or the life of the vision, is the real life, the *sine quâ non* of man. But it is difficult to see what superiority for the purpose of judging is possessed by people whose pride it is not to live the life of vision at all.

A Midsummer Night's Dream

At least it is questionable whether the Elizabethan did not know more about both worlds than the modern intellectual ; it is not altogether improbable that Shakespeare would not only have had a clearer vision of the fairies, but would have shot very much straighter at a deer and netted much more money for his performances than a member of the Stage Society.

In pure poetry and the intoxication of words, Shakespeare never rose higher than he rises in this play. But in spite of this fact, the supreme literary merit of *A Midsummer Night's Dream* is a merit of design. The amazing symmetry, the amazing artistic and moral beauty of that design, can be stated very briefly. The story opens in the sane and common world with the pleasant seriousness of very young lovers and very young friends. Then, as the figures advance into the tangled wood of young troubles and stolen happiness, a change and bewilderment begins to fall on them. They lose their way and their wits for they are in the heart of fairyland. Their words, their hungers, their very figures grow more and more dim and fantastic, like dreams within dreams, in the supernatural mist of Puck. Then the dream-fumes begin to clear, and characters and spectators begin to awaken together to the noise of horns and dogs and the clean and bracing morning. Theseus, the incarnation of a happy and generous rationalism, expounds in hackneyed and superb lines the sane view of such psychic experiences, pointing out with a reverent and sympathetic scepticism that all these fairies and spells are themselves but the emanations, the unconscious masterpieces, of man himself. The whole company falls back into a splendid human laughter. There is a rush for banqueting and private theatricals, and over all these things ripples one of those frivolous and inspired conversations in which every good saying seems to die in giving birth to another. If ever the son of a man in his wanderings was at home and drinking by the fireside, he is at home in the house of Theseus. All the dreams have been forgotten, as a melancholy dream remembered throughout the morning might be forgotten in the human certainty of any other triumphant evening party ; and so the play seems naturally ended. It began on the earth and it ends on the earth. Thus to round off the whole midsummer night's dream in an eclipse of daylight is an effect of genius. But of this comedy, as I have said, the mark is that genius goes beyond itself ; and one touch is added which makes the play colossal. Theseus and his train retire with a crashing finale, full of humour and wisdom and things set right, and silence falls on the house. Then there comes a faint sound of little feet, and for a moment, as it were, the elves look into the house, asking which is the reality. " Suppose we are the realities and they the shadows." If that ending were acted properly any modern man would feel shaken to his marrow if he had to walk home from the theatre through a country lane.

It is a trite matter, of course, though in a general criticism a more or less indispensable one to comment upon another point of artistic perfection, the extraordinarily human and accurate manner in which the play catches the atmosphere of a dream. The chase and tangle and frustration of the incidents and personalities are well known to every one who has dreamt of perpetually falling over precipices or perpetually missing trains. While following out clearly and legally the necessary narrative of the drama, the author contrives to include every one of the main peculiarities of the exasperating dream. Here is the pursuit of the man we cannot catch, the flight from the man we cannot see ; here is the perpetual returning to the same place, here is the crazy alteration in the very objects of our desire, the substitution of one face for another face, the putting of the wrong souls in the wrong bodies, the fantastic disloyalties of the night, all this is as obvious as it is important.

A Midsummer Night's Dream

It is perhaps somewhat more worth remarking that there is about this confusion of comedy yet another essential characteristic of dreams. A dream can commonly be described as possessing an utter discordance of incident combined with a curious unity of mood ; everything changes but the dreamer. It may begin with anything and end with anything, but if the dreamer is sad at the end he will be sad as if by prescience at the beginning ; if he is cheerful at the beginning he will be cheerful if the stars fall. *A Midsummer Night's Dream* has in a most singular degree effected this difficult, this almost desperate subtlety. The events in the wandering wood are in themselves, and regarded as in broad daylight, not merely melancholy but bitterly cruel and ignominious. But yet by the spreading of an atmosphere as magic as the fog of Puck, Shakespeare contrives to make the whole matter mysteriously hilarious while it is palpably tragic, and mysteriously charitable, while it is in itself cynical. He contrives somehow to rob tragedy and treachery of their full sharpness, just as a toothache or a deadly danger from a tiger, or a precipice, is robbed of its sharpness in a pleasant dream. The creation of a brooding sentiment like this, a sentiment not merely independent of but actually opposed to the events, is a much greater triumph of art than the creation of the character of Othello.

It is difficult to approach critically so great a figure as that of Bottom the Weaver. He is greater and more mysterious than Hamlet, because the interest of such men as Bottom consists of a rich subconsciousness, and that of Hamlet in the comparatively superficial matter of a rich consciousness. And it is especially difficult in the present age which has become hag-ridden with the mere intellect. We are the victims of a curious confusion whereby being great is supposed to have something to do with being clever, as if there were the smallest reason to suppose that Achilles was clever, as if there were not

15

on the contrary a great deal of internal evidence to indicate that he was next door to a fool. Greatness is a certain indescribable but perfectly familiar and palpable quality of size in the personality, of steadfastness, of strong flavour, of easy and natural self-expression. Such a man is as firm as a tree and as unique as a rhinoceros, and he might quite easily be as stupid as either of them. Fully as much as the great poet towers above the small poet the great fool towers above the small fool. We have all of us known rustics like Bottom the Weaver, men whose faces would be blank with idiocy if we tried for ten days to explain the meaning of the National Debt, but who are yet great men, akin to Sigurd and Hercules, heroes of the morning of the earth, because their words were their own words, their memories their own memories, and their vanity as large and simple as a great hill. We have all of us known friends in our own circle, men whom the intellectuals might justly describe as brainless, but whose presence in a room was like a fire roaring in the grate changing everything, lights and shadows and the air, whose entrances and exits were in some strange fashion events, whose point of view once expressed haunts and persuades the mind and almost intimidates it, whose manifest absurdity clings to the fancy like the beauty of first-love, and whose follies are recounted like the legends of a paladin. These are great men, there are millions of them in the world, though very few perhaps in the House of Commons. It is not in the cold halls of cleverness where celebrities seem to be important that we should look for the great. An intellectual salon is merely a training-ground for one faculty, and is akin to a fencing class or a rifle corps. It is in our own homes and environments, from Croydon to St. John's Wood, in old nurses, and gentlemen with hobbies, and talkative spinsters and vast incomparable butlers, that we may feel the presence of that blood of the gods. And this creature so hard to describe, so easy to remember, the august and memorable fool, has never been so sumptuously painted as in the Bottom of *A Midsummer Night's Dream*.

Bottom has the supreme mark of this real greatness in that like the true saint or the true hero he only differs from humanity in being as it were more human than humanity. It is not true, as the idle materialists of today suggest, that compared to the majority of men the hero appears cold and dehumanised; it is the majority who appear cold and dehumanised in the presence of greatness. Bottom, like Don Quixote and Uncle Toby and Mr. Richard Swiveller and the rest of the Titans, has a huge and unfathomable weakness, his silliness is on a great scale, and when he blows his own trumpet it is like the trumpet of the Resurrection. The other rustics in the play accept his leadership not merely naturally but exuberantly; they have to the full that primary and savage unselfishness, that uproarious abnegation which makes simple men take pleasure in falling short of a hero, that unquestionable element of basic human nature which has never been expressed, outside this play, so perfectly as in the incomparable chapter at the beginning of *Evan Harrington* in which the praises of The Great Mel are sung with a lyric energy by the tradesmen whom he has cheated. Twopenny sceptics write of the egoism of primal human nature; it is reserved for great men like Shakespeare and Meredith to detect and make vivid this rude and sub-conscious unselfishness which is older than self. They alone with their insatiable tolerance can perceive all the spiritual devotion in the soul of a snob. And it is this natural play between the rich simplicity of Bottom and the simple simplicity of his comrades which constitutes the unapproachable excellence of the farcical scenes in this play. Bottom's sensibility to literature is perfectly fiery and genuine, a great deal more genuine than that of a great many cultivated critics of literature—

" the raging rocks, and shivering shocks shall break the locks of prison gates, and Phibbus' car shall shine from far, and make and mar the foolish fates", is exceedingly good poetical diction with a real throb and swell in it, and if it is slightly and almost imperceptibly deficient in the matter of sense, it is certainly every bit as sensible as a good many other rhetorical speeches in Shakespeare put into the mouths of kings and lovers and even the spirits of the dead. If Bottom liked cant for its own sake the fact only constitutes another point of sympathy between him and his literary creator. But the style of the thing, though deliberately bombastic and ludicrous, is quite literary, the alliteration falls like wave upon wave, and the whole verse, like a billow mounts higher and higher before it crashes. There is nothing mean about this folly ; nor is there in the whole realm of literature a figure so free from vulgarity. The man vitally base and foolish sings " The Honeysuckle and the Bee " ; he does not rant about " raging rocks " and " the car of Phibbus". Dickens, who more perhaps than any modern man had the mental hospitality and the thoughtless wisdom of Shakespeare, perceived and expressed admirably the same truth. He perceived, that is to say, that quite indefensible idiots have very often a real sense of, and enthusiasm for letters. Mr. Micawber loved eloquence and poetry with his whole immortal soul ; words and visionary pictures kept him alive in the absence of food and money, as they might have kept a saint fasting in a desert. Dick Swiveller did not make his inimitable quotations from Moore and Byron merely as flippant digressions. He made them because he loved a great school of poetry. The sincere love of books has nothing to do with cleverness or stupidity any more than any other sincere love. It is a quality of character, a freshness, a power of pleasure, a power of faith. A silly person may delight in reading masterpieces just as a silly person may delight in picking flowers. A fool may be in love with a poet as he may be in love with a woman. And the triumph of Bottom is that he loves rhetoric and his own taste in the arts, and this is all that can be achieved by Theseus, or for the matter of that by Cosimo di Medici. It is worth remarking as an extremely fine touch in the picture of Bottom that his literary taste is almost everywhere concerned with sound rather than sense. He begins the rehearsal with a boisterous readiness, " Thisby, the flowers of odious savours sweete." " Odours, odours," says Quince, in remonstrance, and the word is accepted in accordance with the cold and heavy rules which require an element of meaning in a poetical passage. But " Thisby, the flowers of odious savours sweete ", Bottom's version, is an immeasurably finer and more resonant line. The " i " which he inserts is an inspiration of metricism.

There is another aspect of this great play which ought to be kept familiarly in the mind. Extravagant as is the masquerade of the story, it is a very perfect æsthetic harmony down to such *coup-de-maître* as the name of Bottom, or the flower called Love in Idleness. In the whole matter it may be said that there is one accidental discord ; that is in the name of Theseus, and the whole city of Athens in which the events take place. Shakespeare's description of Athens in *A Midsummer Night's Dream* is the best description of England that he or any one else ever wrote. Theseus is quite obviously only an English squire, fond of hunting, kindly to his tenants, hospitable with a certain flamboyant vanity. The mechanics are English mechanics, talking to each other with the queer formality of the poor. Above all, the fairies are English ; to compare them with the beautiful patrician spirits of Irish legend, for instance, is suddenly to discover that we have, after all, a folk-lore and a mythology, or had it at least in Shakespeare's day. Robin Goodfellow, upsetting the old women's ale, or pulling the

stool from under them, has nothing of the poignant Celtic
beauty ; his is the horse-play of the invisible world. Perhaps
it is some debased inheritance of English life which makes
American ghosts so fond of quite undignified practical jokes.
But this union of mystery with farce is a note of the medieval
English. The play is the last glimpse of Merrie England, that
distant but shining and quite indubitable country. It would be
difficult indeed to define wherein lay the peculiar truth of
the phrase " merrie England ", though some conception of it
is quite necessary to the comprehension of *A Midsummer
Night's Dream*. In some cases at least, it may be said to lie in
this, that the English of the Middle Ages and the Renaissance,
unlike the England of today, could conceive of the idea of a
merry supernaturalism. Amid all the great work of Puritanism
the damning indictment of it consists in one fact, that there
was one only of the fables of Christendom that it retained
and renewed, and that was the belief in witchcraft. It cast away
the generous and wholesome superstition, it approved only of
the morbid and the dangerous. In their treatment of the great
national fairy-tale of good and evil, the Puritans killed St.
George but carefully preserved the Dragon. And this seven-
teenth-century tradition of dealing with the psychic life still
lies like a great shadow over England and America, so that
if we glance at a novel about occultism we may be perfectly
certain that it deals with sad or evil destiny. Whatever else
we expect we certainly should never expect to find in it spirits
such as those in *Aylwin* as inspirers of a tale of tomfoolery like
the *Wrong Box* or *The Londoners*. That impossibility is the
disappearance of " merrie England " and Robin Goodfellow.
It was a land to us incredible, the land of a jolly occultism
where the peasant cracked jokes with his patron saint, and only
cursed the fairies good-humouredly, as he might curse a
lazy servant. Shakespeare is English in everything, above all

in his weaknesses. Just as London, one of the greatest cities in the world, shows more slums and hides more beauties than any other, so Shakespeare alone among the four giants of poetry is a careless writer, and lets us come upon his splendours by accident, as we come upon an old City church in the twist of a city street. He is English in nothing so much as in that noble cosmopolitan unconsciousness which makes him look eastward with the eyes of a child towards Athens or Verona. He loved to talk of the glory of foreign lands, but he talked of them with the tongue and unquenchable spirit of England. It is too much the custom of a later patriotism to reverse this method and talk of England from morning till night, but to talk of her in a manner totally un-English. Casualness, incongruities, and a certain fine absence of mind are in the temper of England; the unconscious man with the ass's head is no bad type of the people. Materialistic philosophers and mechanical politicians have certainly succeeded in some cases in giving him a greater unity. The only question is, to which animal has he been thus successfully conformed?

ON READING

THE highest use of the great masters of literature is not literary; it is apart from their superb style and even from their emotional inspiration. The first use of good literature is that it prevents a man from being merely modern. To be merely modern is to condemn oneself to an ultimate narrowness; just as to spend one's last earthly money on the newest hat is to condemn oneself to the old-fashioned. The road of the ancient centuries is strewn with dead moderns. Literature, classic and enduring literature, does its best work in reminding us perpetually of the whole round of truth and balancing other and older ideas against the ideas to which we might for a moment be prone. The way in which it does this, however, is sufficiently curious to be worth our fully understanding it to begin with.

From time to time in human history, but especially in restless epochs like our own, a certain class of things appears. In the old world they were called heresies. In the modern world they are called fads. Sometimes they are for a time useful; sometimes they are wholly mischievous. But they always consist of undue concentration upon some one truth or half-truth. Thus it is true to insist upon God's knowledge, but heretical to insist on it as Calvin did at the expense of his Love; thus it is true to desire a simple life, but heretical to desire it at the expense of good feeling and good manners. The heretic (who is also the fanatic) is not a man who loves truth too much; no man can love truth too much. The heretic is a man who loves his truth more than truth itself. He prefers the half-truth that he has found to the whole truth

On Reading

which humanity has found. He does not like to see his own precious little paradox merely bound up with twenty truisms into the bundle of the wisdom of the world.

Sometimes such innovators are of a sombre sincerity like Tolstoi, sometimes of a sensitive and feminine eloquence like Nietzsche, and sometimes of an admirable humour, pluck, and public spirit like Mr. Bernard Shaw. In all cases they make a stir, and perhaps found a school. But in all cases the same fundamental mistake is made. It is always supposed that the man in question has discovered a new idea. But, as a fact, what is new is not the idea, but only the isolation of the idea. The idea itself can be found, in all probability, scattered frequently enough through all the great books of a more classic or impartial temper, from Homer and Virgil to Fielding and Dickens. You can find all the new ideas in the old books ; only there you will find them balanced, kept in their place, and sometimes contradicted and overcome by other and better ideas. The great writers did not neglect a fad because they had not thought of it, but because they had thought of it and of all the answers to it as well.

In case this point is not clear, I will take two examples, both in reference to notions fashionable among some of the more fanciful and younger theorists. Nietzsche, as every one knows, preached a doctrine which he and his followers regard apparently as very revolutionary ; he held that ordinary altruistic morality had been the invention of a slave class to prevent the emergence of superior types to fight and rule them. Now, modern people, whether they agree with this or not, always talk of it as a new and unheard-of idea. It is calmly and persistently supposed that the great writers of the past, say Shakespeare for instance, did not hold this view, because they had never imagined it ; because it had never come into their heads. Turn up the last act of Shakespeare's *Richard III*

23

and you will find not only all that Nietzsche had to say put
into two lines, but you will find it put in the very words of
Nietzsche. Richard Crookback says to his nobles :

> Conscience is but a word that cowards use,
> Devised at first to keep the strong in awe.

As I have said, the fact is plain. Shakespeare had thought
of Nietzsche and the Master Morality ; but he weighed it at
its proper value and put it in its proper place. Its proper place
is the mouth of a half-insane hunchback on the eve of defeat.
This rage against the weak is only possible in a man morbidly
brave but fundamentally sick; a man like Richard, a man like
Nietzsche. This case alone ought to destroy the absurd fancy
that these modern philosophies are modern in the sense that
the great men of the past did not think of them. They thought
of them ; only they did not think much of them. It was not
that Shakespeare did not see the Nietzsche idea ; he saw it, and
he saw through it.

I will take one other example: Mr. Bernard Shaw in his striking
and sincere play called "Major Barbara", throws down
one of the most violent of his verbal challenges to proverbial
morality. People say, "Poverty is no crime." "Yes," says
Mr. Bernard Shaw, "poverty is a crime, and the mother of
crimes. It is a crime to be poor if you could possibly rebel or
grow rich. To be poor means to be poor-spirited, servile or
tricky." Mr. Shaw shows signs of an intention to concentrate
on this doctrine, and many of his followers do the same. Now,
it is only the concentration that is new, not the doctrine.
Thackeray makes Becky Sharp say that it is easy to be moral
on £1,000 a year, and so difficult on £100. But, as in the case
of Shakespeare I have quoted, the point is not merely that
Thackeray knew of this conception, but that he knew exactly

what it was worth. It not only occurred to him, but he knew where it ought to occur. It ought to occur in the conversation of Becky Sharp; a woman shrewd and not without sincerity, but profoundly unacquainted with all the deeper emotions which make life worth living. The cynicism of Becky, with Lady Jane and Dobbin to balance it, has a certain breezy truth. The cynicism of Mr. Shaw's Undershaft, preached alone with the austerity of a field preacher, is simply not true at all. It is simply not true at all to say that the very poor are as a whole more insincere or more grovelling than the very rich. Becky's half-truth has become first a crotchet, then a creed, and then a lie. In the case of Thackeray, as in that of Shakespeare, the conclusion which concerns us is the same. What we call the new ideas are generally broken fragments of the old ideas. It was not that a particular notion did not enter Shakespeare's head; it is that it found a good many other notions waiting to knock the nonsense out of it.

MONSTERS AND THE MIDDLE AGES

I DO NOT remember to have read anywhere an adequate and comprehensive account of the fabulous monsters so much written of in the Middle Ages. Such studies as I have seen suffered from the three or four strange and senseless blunders which throttle all our thought on such subjects.

The primary blunder, of course, is that comic one to which students like Mr. Frazer have lent, or rather pawned, their authority. I mean the absurd notion that in matters of the imagination men have any need to copy from each other. Poems and poetic tales tend to be a little alike, not because Hebrews were really Chaldeans, nor because Christians were really Pagans, but because men are really men. Because there is, in spite of all the trend of modern thought, such a thing as man and the brotherhood of men. Anyone who has really looked at the moon might have called the moon a virgin and a huntress without ever having heard of Diana. Anyone who had ever looked at the sun might call it the god of oracles and of healing without having heard of Apollo. A man in love, walking about in a garden, compares a woman to a flower, and not to an earwig; though an earwig also was made by God, and has many superiorities to flowers in point of education and travel. To hear some people talk, one would think that the love of flowers had been imposed by some long priestly tradition, and the love of earwigs forbidden by some fearful tribal taboo.

The second great blunder is to suppose that such fables, even when they really are borrowed from older sources, are used in an old, tired and customary spirit. When the soul

Monsters and the Middle Ages

seen properly described. In one of the oldest of the legends of St. George and the Dragon, St. George did not kill the Dragon, but led it captive and sprinkled it with holy water. Something of the same sort happened to that whole department of the human mind which creates violent and unnatural images. Take the griffin for example. In our time the griffin, like most other medieval symbols, has been made a mean and farcical thing for fancy-dress balls : in twenty pictures from *Punch*, for instance, we can see the griffin and the turtle as supporters of the civic arms of London. For the modern "citizen" the arrangement is excellent ; the griffin, which eats him, does not exist; the turtle, which he eats, does exist. But not only was the griffin not always trivial, but he was not always even bad. He was a mystical incorporation of two animals held wholly sacred : the lion of St. Mark, the lion of generosity, valour, victory ; the eagle of St. John, the eagle of truth, of aspiration, of intellectual liberty. Thus the griffin was often used as the emblem of Christ ; as combining the eagle and the lion in that mysterious and complete compound in which Christ combined the divine and human. But even if you thought of the griffin as good, you were not less afraid of him. Perhaps more.

But the stongest case is that of the unicorn, which I intended to figure prominently in this article but which seems to have evaded my thought in a most miraculous manner, and which up to this time I seem to have practically omitted. He is a terrible creature, the unicorn ; and though he seems to live rather vaguely in Africa, I could never be surprised if he came walking up one of the four white roads that lead to Beaconsfield ; the monster whiter than the roads, and his horn higher than the church spire. For all these mystical animals were imagined as enormously big as well as incalculably fierce and free. The stamping of the awful unicorn would shake the

endless deserts in which it dwelt; and the wings of the vast
griffin went over one's head in heaven with the thunder of a
thousand cherubim. And yet the fact remains that if you had
asked a medieval man what the unicorn was supposed to *mean*,
he would have replied " chastity ".

When we have understood that fact we shall understand
a great many other things, but above all the civilisation out
of which we come. Christianity did *not* conceive Christian
virtues as tame, timid, and respectable things. It *did* conceive
of these virtues as vast, defiant, and even destructive things,
scorning the yoke of this world, dwelling in the desert, and
seeking their meat from God. Till we have understood that
no one will really understand even the " Lion and the Unicorn "
over a pastry cook's shop.

WHAT NOVELISTS ARE FOR

A LONG time ago, when I happened to be living in Rye
in Sussex, I had the honour of being visited by two very
distinguished men ; they were both Americans, indeed, they
were brothers ; but the type of their success seemed oddly
different. One was Henry James, the novelist, who lived next
door ; the other was William James, the philosopher, who had
just crossed the Atlantic and seemed as breezy as the sea. In
fact, there was an almost fantastic contrast between the two
men : the one so solemn about social details often considered
trivial ; the other so hearty about abstract studies generally
considered dry. Henry James talked about toast and teacups
with the impressiveness of a family ghost ; while William
James talked about the metabolism and the involution of values
with the air of a man recounting his flirtations on the steamer.
But though I had and have the greatest possible regard for
them both, I cannot but think that a certain relative completeness, and incompleteness, in the contrast between them reveals
a certain truth about two different types of letters.

I was recently rereading one of the late Harvey Wickham's
exceedingly clever studies of modern thought ; including the
study of William James. I think the critic was mainly just
about the philosophy, but not quite just about the philosopher.
I do not myself think that Pragmatism can ever stand up as a
serious rival to the permanent philosophy of Truth and the
Absolute. But I do think that William James did really stand
up as a rattling good fighter and cleaner-up of the particular
sort of solemn nonsense most current in his time. He may have
only indirectly served the cause of belief in belief. But he did

The Common Man

a lot to serve the cause of unbelief in unbelief; a very wholesome object. But that is not my main point. It seems to me that where William James failed was exactly where Henry James succeeded; in making a whole scheme out of fine shades and doubtful cases. Now that can be done with a novel; for it only claims to be exceptional. It cannot be done with philosophy; for it must claim to be universal.

Pragmatism fails because it is a cosmos made out of odds and ends. But stories are better for being made out of odds and ends; especially if the ends are very odd. Recalling at random some Henry James stories, there was one about an intelligent youth who unaccountably became a sort of tame cat in the house of a couple of rich but unspeakably dull people. But it is not because he is a snob or a plate-licker; but because he is really touched by a devotion and delusion of the old couple, about their dead daughter, whose life they continue in a sort of waking dream, in which the young man figures as her lover. It is beautifully and delicately done; and it does not seem impossible. Now if we apply to this any moral philosophy on earth, however modern, however mad, we shall all shrink from laying it down as a general rule that young men ought to cadge on old men, that they ought to encourage delusions; that this *ménage* is a model for the normal home. But that is exactly what a novelist is for. He is not bound to justify human beings, but only to humanise them. It is for him and not the philosopher to deal with all this chapter of accidents; in which " things work out differently in practice ". William James's mistake was that he did not put his notions into novels, like his brother; where such opportunism is quite appropriate. He tried to make a cosmic system out of these accidents and this opportunism; and the system is not systematic. The comparison carries a faint hint that novelists may be some use after all.

THE SONG OF ROLAND

MOST OF us remember reading, in the school histories of our childhood, that at the Battle of Hastings Taillefer the Jongleur went in front of the Norman Army, throwing his sword in the air and singing the Song of Roland. They were naturally histories of a very Victorian sort, which passed lightly over the Roman Empire and the Crusades on the way to serious things, such as the genealogy of George I or the administration of Addington. But that one image emerged in the imagination as something alive in its dead surroundings; like finding a familiar face in a faded tapestry. The song he sang was presumably not the noble and rugged epic which Major Scott Moncrieff has done so solid and even historic a service to letters in rendering in its entirety. The Jongleur must at least have selected extracts or favourite passages, or the battles would have been unduly delayed. But the tale has the same moral as the translation; since both have the same inspiration. The value of the tale was that it did suggest to the childish mind, through all the deadening effects of distance and indifference, that a man does not make such a gesture with a sword unless he feels something, and that a man does not sing unless he has something to sing about. Dull avarice and an appetite for feudal lands do not inspire such jugglery. In short the value of the tale was that it hinted that there is a heart in history, even remote history. And the value of the translation is that if we are really to learn history we must, in a double sense of the word, learn it by heart. We must learn it at length and as it were at large; lingering over chance spaces of contemporary work, for love of its detail, and one might almost say for love of its dullness. Even a random reader like myself, only dipping here and there into such things, so long as they are really things of the period, can often learn more from them than from the most careful constitutional digests or political summaries by modern men more learned than himself. A modern man, educated on the modern histories, may find here the things he does not expect. I have here only space for one example, out of many that I could give to show what I mean. Most of the stock histories tell the young student something of what Feudalism was in legal form and custom; that the subordinates were called vassals, that they did homage, and so on. But they do it somehow in such a way as to suggest a savage and sullen obedience; as if a vassal were no more than a serf. What is left out is the fact that the homage really was homage; a thing worthy of a man. The first feudal feeling had something ideal and even impersonal, like patriotism. The nations were not yet born; and these smaller groups had almost the soul of nations. The reader will find the word "vassalage" used again and again on a note which is not only heroic but even haughty. The vassal is obviously as proud of being a vassal as anybody could be of being a lord. Indeed the feudal poet uses the word "vassalage" where a modern poet would use the word "chivalry". The Paladins charging the Paynim are spurred on by vassalage. Turpin the Archbishop hacks the Moslem chieftain rib from rib; and the Christians, beholding his triumph, cry aloud in their pride that he has shown great vassalage; and that with such an Archbishop the Cross is safe. There were no Conscientious Objections in their Christianity.

This is a type of the truths that historical literature ought to make us feel; but which mere histories very seldom do. The one example I have already given, of the Jongleur at

The Song of Roland

Hastings, is a complexity of curious truths that might be conveyed and which very seldom are. We might have learned, for instance, what a Jongleur was; and realised that this one may have had feelings as deep and fantastic as the Jongleur celebrated in the twelfth-century poem, who died gloriously of dancing and turning somersaults before the image of Our Lady; that he was of the trade taken as a type by the mystical mirth of St. Francis, who called his monks the Jugglers of God. A man must read at least a little of the contemporary work itself before he thus finds the human heart inside the armour and the monastic gown; the men who write the philosophy of history seldom give us the philosophy, still less the religion, of the historical characters. And the final example of this is something which is also illustrated by the obscure minstrel who threw up his sword as he sang the Song of Roland, as well as by the Song of Roland itself. Modern history, mainly ethnological or economic, always talks of a thing like the Norman adventure in the somewhat vulgar language of success, but it is well to note, in the real Norman story, that the very bard in front of their battle-line was shouting the glorification of failure. It testifies to a truth in the very heart of Christendom that even the court poet of William the Conqueror was celebrating Roland the conquered.

That high note of the forlorn hope, of a host at bay and a battle against odds without end, is the note on which the great French epic ends. I know nothing more moving in poetry than that strange and unexpected end; that splendidly inconclusive conclusion. Charlemagne, the great Christian emperor, has at last established his empire in quiet, has done justice almost in the manner of a day of judgment, and sleeps as it were upon his throne with a peace almost like that of Paradise. And there appears to him the angel of God crying aloud that his arms are needed in a new and distant land, and that he must take up again the endless march of his days. And the great king tears his long white beard and cries out against his restless life. The poem ends, as it were with a vision and vista of wars against the barbarians ; and the vision is true. For that war is never ended which defends the sanity of the world against all the stark anarchies and rending negations which rage against it for ever. That war is never finished in this world ; and the grass has hardly grown on the graves of our own friends who fell in it.

THE SUPERSTITION OF SCHOOL

IT IS an error to suppose that advancing years bring retrogressing opinions. In other words, it is not true that men growing old must be growing reactionary. Some of the difficulties of recent times have been due to the obstinate optimism of the old revolutionary. Magnificent old men like Kropotkin and Whitman and William Morris went to their graves expecting Utopia if they did not expect Heaven. But the falsehood, like so many falsehoods, is a false version of a half-truth. The truth, or half-truth, is not that men must learn by experience to be reactionaries; but that they must learn by experience to expect reactions. And when I say reactions I mean reactions; I must apologise, in the world of current culture, for using the word in its correct sense.

If a boy fires off a gun, whether at a fox, a landlord or a reigning sovereign, he will be rebuked according to the relative value of these objects. But if he fires off a gun for the first time it is very likely that he will not expect the recoil, or know what a heavy knock it can give him. He may go blazing away through life at these and similar objects in the landscape; but he will be less and less surprised by the recoil; that is, by the reaction. He may even dissuade his little sister of six from firing off one of the heavy rifles designed for the destruction of elephants; and will thus have the appearance of being himself a reactionary. Very much the same principle applies to firing off the big guns of revolution. It is not a man's ideals that change; it is not his Utopia that is altered; the cynic who says, "You will forget all that moonshine of

37

idealism when you are older ", says the exact opposite of the truth. The doubts that come with age are not about the ideal, but about the real. And one of the things that are undoubtedly real is reaction : that is, the practical probability of some reversal of direction, and of our partially succeeding in doing the opposite of what we mean to do. What experience does teach us is this : that there is something in the make-up and mechanism of mankind, whereby the result of action upon it is often unexpected, and almost always more complicated than we expect.

These are the snags of sociology ; and one of them is concerned with Education. If you ask me whether I think the populace, especially the poor, should be recognised as citizens who can rule the state, I answer in a voice of thunder, " Yes". If you ask me whether I think they ought to have education, in the sense of a wide culture and familiarity with the classics of history, I again answer, "Yes". But there is, in the achievement of this purpose, a sort of snag or recoil that can only be discovered by experience and does not appear in print at all. It is not allowed for on paper, even so much as is the recoil of a gun. Yet it is at this moment an exceedingly practical part of practical politics ; and, while it has been a political problem for a very long time past, it is a little more marked (if I may stain these serene and impartial pages with so political a suggestion) under recent conditions that have brought so many highly respectable Socialists and widely respected Trade Union officials to the front.

The snag in it is this : that the self-educated think far too much of education. I might add that the half-educated always think everything of education. That is not a fact that appears on the surface of the social plan or ideal ; it is the sort of thing that can only be discovered by experience. When I said that

The Superstition of School

I wanted the popular feeling to find political expression, I meant the actual and autochthonous popular feeling as it can be found in third-class carriages and bean-feasts and bank-holiday crowds; and especially, of course (for the earnest social seeker after truth), in public-houses. I thought, and I still think, that these people are right on a vast number of things on which the fashionable leaders are wrong. The snag is that when one of these people begins to "improve himself" it is exactly at that moment that I begin to doubt whether it is an improvement. He seems to me to collect with remarkable rapidity a number of superstitions, of which the most blind and benighted is what may be called the Superstition of School. He regards School, not as a normal social institution to be fitted in to other social institutions, like Home and Church and State; but as some sort of entirely supernormal and miraculous moral factory, in which perfect men and women are made by magic. To this idolatry of School he is ready to sacrifice Home and History and Humanity, with all its instincts and possibilities, at a moment's notice. To this idol he will make any sacrifice, especially human sacrifice. And at the back of the mind, especially of the best men of this sort, there is almost always one of two variants of the same concentrated conception: either "If I had not been to School I should not be the great man I am now", or else "If I had been to school I should be even greater than I am". Let none say that I am scoffing at uneducated people; it is not their uneducation but their education that I scoff at. Let none mistake this for a sneer at the half-educated; what I dislike is the educated half. But I dislike it, not because I dislike education, but because, given the modern philosophy or absence of philosophy, education is turned against itself, destroying that very sense of variety and proportion which it is the object of education to give. No man who worships education has got the best out of education; no man who sacrifices everything to education is even educated. I need not mention here the many recent examples of this monomania, rapidly turning into mad persecution, such as the ludicrous persecution of the families who live on barges. What is wrong is a neglect of principle; and the principle is that without a gentle contempt for education, no gentleman's education is complete.

I use the casual phrase casually; for I do not concern myself with the gentleman but with the citizen. Nevertheless, there is this historic half-truth in the case for aristocracy; that it is sometimes a little easier for the aristocrat, at his best, to have this last touch of culture which is a superiority to culture. Nevertheless, the truth of which I speak has nothing to do with any special culture of any special class. It has belonged to any number of peasants, especially when they were poets; it is this which gives a sort of natural distinction to Robert Burns and the peasant poets of Scotland. The power which produces it more effectively than any blood or breed is religion; for religion may be defined as that which puts the first things first. Robert Burns was justifiably impatient with the religion he inherited from Scottish Calvinism; but he owed something to his inheritance. His instinctive consideration of men as men came from an ancestry which still cared more for religion than education. The moment men begin to care more for education than for religion they begin to care more for ambition than for education. It is no longer a world in which the souls of all are equal before heaven, but a world in which the mind of each is bent on achieving unequal advantage over the other. There begins to be a mere vanity in being educated; whether it be self-educated or merely state-educated. Education ought to be a searchlight given to a man to explore everything, but very specially the things most distant from himself. Education tends to be a spotlight; which is centred

The Superstition of School

entirely on himself. Some improvement may be made by turning equally vivid and perhaps vulgar spotlights upon a large number of other people as well. But the only final cure is to turn off the limelight and let him realise the stars.

THE ROMANCE OF A RASCAL

IT WAS Thackeray, I think, somewhere in the dizzy mazes of his *Roundabout Papers*, who made a remark which throws some light on literary fashions and the fate of Smollett's *Peregrine Pickle*. He described very vividly the fervour he felt as a boy for the Waverley Novels; and how those great romances filled the boyhood of those, like himself, who were to make the literature of that most romantic epoch which we call in England the Victorian era. He adds an interesting comment to this effect : " Our fathers used to talk about *Peregrine Pickle*, telling us (the sly old boys) that it was capital fun. But I think I was rather bewildered by it."

That, I fear, may be the immediate effect upon many either of Thackeray's period or even of our own period, where it has inherited the great literary tradition, which many learnt in youth from Thackeray, and which Thackeray learnt in youth from Scott. Most of those who grew up under such standards of fiction, as did the present writer, may be disposed to say at first that they find Smollett's novel rather bewildering. Not quite so bewildering as some of the most modern novels, of course. But many people seem to have a singular literary test, by which they like being bewildered by a new book, but dislike being bewildered by an old one. As I shall point out presently, this is very largely because the new book is not so new as it pretends to be. And the old book is not so very old, as the real stages of history go. In short, the real moral of all these things is the astonishing rapidity with which moods and standards change and change again; often changing back from the third condition to the first. There is nothing so mystifying as the rapidity with which new literary methods harden, except the brittleness with which they break. Each traveller who turns the corner thinks it will lead him into a straight road of progress ; but really it leads him, in about ten minutes, to another corner which turns into another and equally crooked road. The point about a book like *Peregrine Pickle* can be fixed fairly precisely, by considering what are the changes that separated him from Thackeray, or that separate Thackeray from us.

In that little phrase from the *Roundabout Papers* there are, to begin with, some interesting and even amusing points. For instance, we are always told that the Victorian parent, or, even more, the early nineteenth-century parent, was a Puritan who forbade his family the idle as well as the improper forms of light literature ; a Heavy Father who sat very heavily even on ordinary love-stories or romantic plays. Even so eighteenth-century a type as Macaulay identified the opinion of most sober and responsible parents with so extraordinary a parent as Sir Anthony Absolute in the comic play. " A circulating library is an evergreen tree of diabolical knowledge." Even a modern so steeped in the eighteenth century as Mr. Max Beerbohm has described the typical papa of a generation that might well have been that of Thackeray's papa, as a gloomy and ponderous person who talked to his children about nothing but Hell. Surely that one little glimpse from Thackeray's own essays might lead one to guess that there is something wrong in all this. It is difficult to imagine the Puritan papa, who commonly talked about Hell, winding up with a recommendation to read *Peregrine Pickle*. It is difficult to suppose that a race of Sir Anthony Absolutes, disapproving of all novels, would have gone out of their way to select this novel, out of all earthly novels, on the ground that it was " capital fun ". The parent must have been a very sly old boy indeed if he really thrust

The Common Man

Peregrine Pickle on the attention of a little boy, whose head was full of ideals of chivalry, like those of Quentin Durward and Ivanhoe.

The truth is that the elements were too mixed, and, above all, the fashions too fugitive, for any of these generalisations. Men who lose traditions abandon themselves to conventions ; but the conventions are more fleeting than fashions. There were papas who would have been almost as much shocked at their daughters reading *Pride and Prejudice* as at their reading *Peregrine Pickle*. But they were the papas and not the grand-papas. There was a sort of household where Hell was the brightest topic of chat ; but it was not the old-fashioned household but rather the new-fashioned household. It came in with the Methodists, who were regarded as innovators and rebels. That episode of extreme severity, which was the beginning of the highly expurgated Victorian fiction, need not here be traced to its historical causes. Broadly speaking, it came from the rapid increase of wealth and power among the Noncon-formists of the north, who vetoed the frankness both of the old gentry and the old peasantry of the south. The point here is that the work of these Puritans, from Lancashire or Yorkshire, was so very rapidly done that men forgot that it was so very recent. All this has to be understood before anybody, looking back through the nineteenth century, can do justice to the work of Smollett. The point of it is that not only did the changes come, but each generation accepted them as if they had always been unchangeable. Thus, in the case just mentioned, Thackeray began to write novels long after Dickens ; he was still an artist, or art student, when he offered to illustrate *Pickwick*. Dickens, in the flood of his popularity that followed *Pickwick*, had already accepted and popularised what we call the Victorian conventions. This has been somewhat harshly expressed by Mr. Aldous Huxley, when he said that a

44

writer like Dickens writes as if he were a child, while a writer like Smollett writes as if he were a grown man. But indeed there is a considerable link between a writer like Smollett and a writer like Aldous Huxley. For the road has taken another sharp turn backwards; and the interlude of Victorian innocence is again out of sight. There is one instance of this, which dominates and largely explains the whole story of *Peregrine Pickle*.

When Thackeray called *Vanity Fair* "a novel without a hero", or even when he made the relatively realistic *Pendennis* a novel with a rather unheroic hero, he was doubtless by that time so accustomed to Victorian fiction as to feel that he was doing something new, and even "cynical". For Victorian fiction had already returned to the old romantic idea that the hero should be heroic, even if it did not understand him so well as did the old romances. Nicholas Nickleby vanquishes Squeers as St. George vanquishes the dragon; and John Ridd is a knight without fear or reproach, like Ivanhoe. But in fact Thackeray was only slightly reacting towards what had been universal in the time of that sly old boy, his papa.

All novels like *Peregrine Pickle*, all novels up to the time of *Pickwick*, were written frankly on a far more cynical convention: that the hero should not be heroic. The enterprising Mr. Pickle is certainly not heroic. He is many things that are good; not only brave, but often warm-hearted and considerate; and, above all, capable of recognising better men than himself. But, for the rest, by Victorian and even by normal standards, he is simply a coarse and rapacious rascal; nor does Smollett really pretend that he is anything else. This tendency to follow with delight the tricks and triumphs of somebody little better than a swindler comes from the historical origin of this type of story, which began in what is called the *picaresque* novel. It is the romance of a wanderer,

The Common Man

apt to turn from the romance of a peddler to that of a highway robber. It is a curious coincidence that Smollet translated *Gil Blas*, in which this new cynical romance made its first triumph ; and also translated *Don Quixote*, in which the road was cleared for it by the rout of the old romances which had made their heroes impossibly heroic. But about this sort of rambling tale, of the Romance of a Rascal, there are certain modern misunderstandings to be avoided. It would be a complete misunderstanding of men like Tobias Smollet to suppose that because the heroes are immoral the authors are even unmoral. It is a peculiar characteristic of all that stalwart school, which represented this *picaresque* element in England, that they do believe in heroism for anybody except heroes. Both in Fielding and Smollett and others we find a sort of fixed habit of thought, by which virtue is represented, and is even preached, and is often preached vehemently and in terms of authority ; but never by the principal character, who is a young man of the world apparently not expected either to preach it or to practise it. Parson Adams is a serious picture of a good man, and Joseph Andrews is only a bad joke ; but Joseph gives his name to the book. Fielding is more concerned with Tom Jones than with Alworthy ; but he agrees with Mr. Alworthy and not with Tom Jones. And if anyone wishes to note exactly how this habit expresses itself in Smollett, let him turn to the typical scene in which *Peregrine Pickle* provokes a duel with Mr. Gauntlet. By all possible standards Peregrine is to behave like a vulgar and low-minded cad, actually sneering at the poverty of the soldier whom he has insulted, and being ignominiously defeated by the man he has so coarsely despised. Certainly no Victorian romancer would have dragged his hero through the mud of such a meeting. And yet the whole incident brings out in glowing colours all that is really good and lovable about Peregrine Pickle. He does vividly realise that the other man is more virtuous than himself; he acts as impetuously on the moral as on the immoral impulse; he apologises after defeat, which is more difficult than apologising before it. In other words, Mr. Gauntlet, like Parson Adams, stands for something fixed and recognised; a virtue which the other characters venerate even while they violate. In this incident Peregrine is represented in the course of an hour or so as behaving almost incredibly badly and then almost incredibly well; and yet it is quite credible. Why do we thus feel that there is something solid in it after all? First, no doubt, because Smollett was a real novelist, and the character of Peregrine Pickle was a real character. He does convey what later sentiment would have called the contradiction: that Peregrine was a scoundrel, but a warm-hearted scroundrel; that he was very near to being a swindler, but always an impetuous swindler. But it is due, almost as much, to the sense of firmness produced by the fact that vice and virtue are still treated as facts. Our sense of sincerity is founded on the fact that Tobias Smollett, as well as Peregrine Pickle, did really believe in right and wrong, and thought the principal character wrong and the secondary character right.

It is here that we find the chief difference between old writers like Smollett and many modern writers who set themselves successfully to produce the same convincing smell of dirt, the same unmistakable ugliness in the details of life, the same slippery and sometimes slimy irresponsibility about sex, the same heroic persistency in avoiding heroism. The difference is that Smollett's hero, or villain, does know exactly where he is in the moral world, even if it is where he ought not to be. The modern adventurer of the same type occupies all his adventures in trying to discover where he is. He is not so much breaking laws with bravery and cunning, as trying to learn the laws, with constant bewilderment and despair.

The Common Man

Virtue does not rebuke him ; the best that can be said for him is that vice generally bores him. Therefore he is not wholly successful in copying the older writers in their two gifts of lucidity and grossness ; because he lacks the third angle of the triangle : their confidence.

Considered as a series of chapters, *Peregrine Pickle* is simply a chapter of accidents. Curiously enough the splash it made in its own day, especially in the sparkling world of wit and fashion, was almost entirely due to what almost anybody would now call the dullest part of the book. The insertion called " Memoirs of a Lady of Quality " · was supposed to have some scandalous allusiveness to aristocratic society at the time ; but it is not typical of the author, or even of the book. Nor can we in practice class this patchy and parenthetical style with the similar irregularity of a book like *Pickwick*. Most people, at least most mature people, have read *Pickwick*. Comparatively few, even among the most aged people, have read *Peregrine Pickle*. There cannot be very many sly old boys still going about the street, and advising modern youth to read it and find it capital fun. To many it must now be introduced as a new book rather than an old one ; and the method of approach is sharply divergent. In writing of Dickens, we are writing for our fellow Dickensians, and can prove any point or illustrate any theory by examples they know as well as we. I do not think it is unfair to say that if I were to begin by referring the average reader to the well-known attitude of Mr. Metaphor, or the incident of Mr. Hornbeck, he would hardly be so suddenly illumined as by a reference to Mr. Stiggins or Mr. Weller. In cases like this, where an historic work by a man of genius is not now widely popular, or in immediate contact with the reading public, the cause and the problem can almost always be found in certain changes of taste which, rapid as they are, do correspond largely to changes of ideas. A man who opens *Peregrine Pickle* must not expect what he gets from a good Victorian novel, or a good modern novel; and only by some explanation of principles can he ever discover that it may contain things quite as good. It is well, therefore, to emphasise some general qualities that are even better. The novel of Smollett's time was better than the novel of the Victorian time, in so far as it recognised more clearly that good and evil exist and are entangled even in the same man. The novel of Smollett's time was better than the novel of our own time, in so far as it recognised that, even when they are entangled in the same man, they can still be distinguished and are very different, and at war till death.

PAYING FOR PATRIOTISM

SOMEBODY was recently remonstrating with me in connection with certain remarks that I have made touching the history of English misgovernment in Ireland. The criticism, like many others, was to the effect that these are only old unhappy far-off things and battles long ago; that the present generation is not responsible for them; that there is, as the critic said, no way in which he or I could have assisted or prevented them; that if anyone was to blame, he had gone to his account; and we are not to blame at all. There was mingled with his protest, I think, a certain suggestion that an Englishman is lacking in patriotism when he resurrects such corpses in order to connect them with crime.

Now the queer thing is this: that I think it is I who am standing up for the principle of patriotism; and I think it is he who is denying it. As a matter of fact, I am one of the few people left, of my own sort and calling, who do still believe in patriotism; just as I am among the few who do still believe in democracy. Both these ideas were exaggerated extravagantly and, what is worse, erroneously, or entirely in the wrong way, during the nineteenth century; but the reaction against them today is very strong, especially among the intellectuals. But I do believe that patriotism rests on a psychological truth; a social sympathy with those of our own sort, whereby we see our own potential acts in them; and understand their history from within. But if there truly be such a thing as a nation, that truth is a two-edged sword, and we must let it out both ways.

Therefore I answer my critic thus. It is quite true that it was not I, G. K. Chesterton, who pulled the beard of an Irish

Paying for Patriotism

chieftain by way of social introduction ; it was John Planta-genet, afterwards King John ; and I was not present. It was not I, but a much more distinguished literary gent, named Edmund Spenser, who concluded on the whole that the Irish had better be exterminated like vipers ; nor did he even ask my advice on so vital a point. I never stuck a·pike through an Irish lady for fun, after the siege of Drogheda, as did the God-fearing Puritan soldiers of Oliver Cromwell. Nobody can find anything in my handwriting that contributes to the original drafting of the Penal Laws ; and it is a complete mistake to suppose that I was called to the Privy Council when it decided upon the treacherous breaking of the Treaty of Limerick. I never put a pitchcap on an Irish rebel in my life ; and there was not a single one of the thousand floggings of '98 which I inflicted or even ordered. If that is what is meant, it is not very difficult to see that it is quite true.

But it is equally true that I did not ride with Chaucer to Canterbury, and give him a few intelligent hints for the best passages in the *The Canterbury Tales*. It is equally true that there was a large and lamentable gap in the company seated at the Mermaid ; that scarcely a word of Shakespeare's most poetical passages was actually contributed by me ; that I did not whisper to him the word " incarnadine " when he was hesitating after " multitudinous seas " ; that I entirely missed the opportunity of suggesting that Hamlet would be effectively ended by the stormy entrance of Fortinbras. Nay, aged and infirm as I am, it were vain for me to pretend that I lost a leg at the Battle of Trafalgar, or that I am old enough to have seen (as I should like to have seen), ablaze with stars upon the deck of death, the frail figure and the elvish face of the noblest sailor of history.

Yet I propose to go on being proud of Chaucer and Shakes-peare and Nelson ; to feel that the poets did indeed love the language that I love and that the sailor felt something of what we also feel for the sea. But if we accept this mystical corporate being, this larger self, we must accept it for good and ill. If we boast of our best, we must repent of our worst. Otherwise patriotism will be a very poor thing indeed.

THE PANTOMIME

MR. MAURICE BARING, the chief Puppet-Master of the Puppet-Show of Memory, has included in a recent reprint, I am glad to see, an item that I have loved long since and lost awhile, in the form of a scene from the old Drury Lane sort of Harlequinade, recast in the manner of the mystical plays of Maeterlinck. It was probably written when Maeterlinck was very much the fashion, and when people had long been saying that the Harlequinade was hopelessly old-fashioned. In one sense it would be difficult to say which of the two is more old-fashioned now. But, to judge by current criticism and conversation, there are many who remember Pantaloon and Harlequin who hardly even remember Pélleas and Mélisande. It is a queer thing to note the extent to which the world has become silent about Maeterlinck; though it may be the more impressive to the remaining followers of so eloquent an admirer of silence. Whatever be the cause, it certainly was not that his work was devoid of a very individual imaginative quality. Personally, I should guess that he had shared the fate of many modern attempts to refound mysticism on something less real rather than something more real than this world. But the matter only arises here in relation to this little literary jest about the Pantomime, which I always felt to be one of Mr. Baring's most charming fancies. Of course it is a very good burlesque of Maeterlinck; it is also in a sense a very good burlesque of the Pantomime; and the latter is the more delicate achievement. Every healthy person wishes to make fun of a serious thing; but it is generally almost impossible to make fun of a funny thing. But

The Common Man

in this case the notion of fun or burlesque must not be confused in either case with any idea of hostility, or even of satire. Parody does not consist merely of contrast; at its best it rather consists of a superficial contrast covering a substantial congruity. The bitter sort of burlesque may exist, and have a right to exist; but it is doubtful whether in this particular form the bitterest is the best. The one sort of parodist will naturally parody the sort of style he dislikes. But the other sort of parodist will always prefer to parody the style he likes. I remember in my boyhood, when Swinburne was our (rather too bubbly) champagne, I for one wrote almost as many conscious travesties of Swinburne as unconscious copies of him.

Now in this case of the Pantomime the paradox has a sort of moral. For I know that the real reason why I return with unwearied joy to Mr. Baring's little Maeterlinckian Harlequinade is because the atmosphere of the harlequinade really was for me, if not exactly Maeterlinckian, at least in some mysterious sense mystical. I need not dwell on the points in the parody which were witty considered as contrasts as well as coincidences. The policeman repeats at intervals, like the tolling of a funeral bell (a lost and wandering bell attached to no church and uttering in its hollow throat an awful agnosticism), " It was not on my beat." The Pantaloon, one of the shivering old men of Maeterlinck, babbles not of green fields but of grey and ghostly sausages, as of things he will never find, or is not certain that he ever did find. But my point here is that, in spite of the comic contrast between the hilarity of the Pantomime and the hopelessness of the Maeterlinckian atmosphere, there really is something that, for me at least, melts the two into a sort of mystical unity; so that the top-heavy house of the Harlequinade is even here like my home. For I am quite certain, as a fact of psychology, that I did even in childhood regard the knockabout part of the Pantomime with its pokers and sausages, as being none the less a poetical part of the Pantomime; and as unmistakably within the frontiers of fairyland as the palace of the Fairy Queen. Never on earthly anvil, never in earthly fireplace, did that red poker gleam: never those clattering milkcans brim with an earthly cream. The Policeman was perfectly right about both scenes and in both senses. He was not on his beat. He was a stray and estranged policeman; a policeman stolen by the fairies; a constable wandering far away from his constabulary duties, if he ever had any. The joke depended on the very Victorian accident that the costume of a London policeman seemed both commonplace and comic; and yet, although he was comic, he was not really commonplace. He was not merely befooled but bewitched; and his blue uniform revisited the glimpses of a blue moon. Still, it is curious to reflect how completely different the whole drama would have seemed if he had been any sort of foreign *gendarme*, with a cocked hat and a sword.

Now my interest in the matter is this; that I know many will say that this sense of glamour is an effect of distance, like the colour of blue hills or crimson clouds; and that in this romantic aspect it is only a puppet-show of memory. They would say that I saw it in this mystical manner through the intervening veils of time, through the mists of Maeterlinck, through the mockeries of Mr. Baring, and, above all, through that depth of delicate melancholy with which the remote past is remembered. But I am certain that this is not so. Apart from the fact that the memory of childish joys does not make me melancholy (it is perhaps a fine shade of theology) and apart from the fact that I suspect that Mr. Baring himself remembers the thing very much as I do, I am quite sure that I am remembering a reality that was real then as well as now. You could as soon persuade me that the taste of toffee was an illusion that only came to me in later years, or that I think I liked roast chestnuts then only because I like them now, as convince me that I did not have, even as a child, an overwhelming impression that this farcical world was fantastic, not merely in the sense of being comic, but also in the sense of being mystic. Though the scene might superficially seem completely constructed out of objects made as much as possible prosaic, I had an instant inward certainty that they were all poetic. The sky above those staggering chimneys was not the sky above the chimneys in the street outside ; its stars would have been strange stars ; for I had looked round another corner of the cosmos. To wander in the streets of that strange town would have been as unearthly an experience as to wander in the Blue Forest round Bluebeard's Sapphire Palace, or along the Golden Orange-Groves in the gardens of Prester John. Not verbally, but quite vividly, I knew then, exactly as I know now, that there is something mysterious and perhaps more than mortal about the power and call of imagination. I do not think this early experience has been quite rightly understood, even by those modern writers who have written the most charming and fanciful studies of childhood ; and I am not so presumptuous as to think that I can scientifically succeed where I think they have somehow vaguely failed. But I have often fancied that it might be worth while to set down a few notes or queries about this difficult and distant impression. For one thing, the ordinary phrases used about childish fancies often strike me as missing the mark, and being in some subtle way, quite misleading. For instance, there is the very popular phrase, " Make-believe." This seems to imply that the mind makes itself believe something ; or else that it first makes something and then forces itself to believe in it, or to believe something about it. I do not think there is even this slight crack of falsity in the crystal clearness and directness

The Pantomime

of the child's vision of a fairy-palace—or a fairy-policeman. In one sense the child believes much less, and in another much more than that. I do not think the child is deceived; or that he attempts for a moment to deceive himself. I think he instantly asserts his direct and divine right to enjoy beauty; that he steps straight into his own lawful kingdom of imagination, without any quibbles or questions such as arise afterwards out of false moralities and philosophies, touching the nature of falsehood and truth. In other words, I believe that the child has inside his head a pretty correct and complete definition of the whole nature and function of art; with the one addition that he is quite incapable of saying, even to himself, a single word on the subject. Would that many other professors of aesthetics were under a similar limitation. Anyhow, he does not say to himself, " This is a real street, in which mother could go shopping." He does not say to himself, " This is an exact realistic copy of a real street, to be admired for its technical correctness." Neither does he say, " This is an unreal street, and I am drugging and deceiving my powerful mind with something that is a mere illusion." Neither does he say, " This is only a story, and nurse says it is very naughty to tell stories." If he says anything, he only says what was said by those men who saw the white blaze of the Transfiguration, " It is well for us to be here."

This is the beginning of all sane art criticism: wonder combined with the complete serenity of the conscience in the acceptance of such wonders. The purity of the child largely consists in its entire absence cf morality in the sense of Puritan morality, and all the modern and muddled moralities that have sprung from it, scientific and provincial and equivocal, especially the confusions about different meanings of words like " fact " and " fable " and falsehood. The problem is very close to the real problem about images. A child knows that

The Common Man

a doll is not a baby; just as clearly as a real believer knows that a statue of an angel is not an angel. But both know that in both cases the image has the power of both opening and concentrating the imagination. Stevenson, whom I shall always count a fountain of fine inspiration, and certainly a man gifted with the eye that sees the daydreams of childhood in broad daylight, was nevertheless not quite sound on this example, possibly because he was not quite sound on the other. He talks too often of the child having his head in a cloud of confusion and indifference to fact or fancy. I believe that our difficulty with the child has the directly opposite cause. It comes because the child is perfectly clear about the difference, not only between truth and falsehood but between fiction and falsehood. He understands the two essential types of truth : the truth of the mystic, which turns a fact into a truth where it should be turned into a truth, because the alternative is a triviality ; and the truth of the martyr, which treats a truth as a fact, where it should be treated as a fact, because the alternative is a lie. In other words, the child knows perfectly well without being told the difference between saying he has seen the policeman cut in two in the pantomime, and saying he has seen his little brother break the jug in the nursery, when he really broke it himself. It is we who have grown confused about these categories, and cannot realise the swiftness and clarity with which the child accepts what we call the convention of art. Looking at the street down which the clown pursues the policeman with a poker he would never dream of saying in the ordinary sense, indeed he would never dream of saying at all, " That is a real street." But still less would he ever dream of saying, " That is an unreal street." He has a better understanding of dreams—and visions.

In the case of the Pantomime there is one plain fact which clenches this conviction for me. I know I knew that the scenery and costume were "artificial", because I deeply rejoiced that they were artificial. I liked the notion that things were made of painted wood or plastered by hand with gold and silver. These were the vestments and ornaments of the ritual ; but they were not the rite, still less the revelation. I liked the magic-box called a stage, because there, for some reason, the light that never was on sea or land was on paint and pasteboard. But I knew perfectly well that it was paint and pasteboard. It would be impossible for anybody not to know that who had a toy-theatre of his own. In the Pantomime of my childhood, with its somewhat simpler scenery, there were tricks of mere stage carpentry which I enjoyed as much as if I were working them myself. There was one way of representing tossing waves, by rank behind rank of escaloped blue walls as groundpieces, moved in opposite directions so that the crests seemed to cross and dance. I knew how it was done, because my father did it himself before my very eyes, in my own toy-theatre at home. But it gave me such ecstasy that even now when I think of it for an instant my heart leaps up like the wave. I knew it was not water, but I knew it was sea ; and in that flash of knowledge I had passed far beyond those who suffer the fixed and freezing illusion, uttered by the pessimistic poet, that " the sea's a lot of water that happens to be there." In imagination there is no illusion ; no, not even an instant of illusion. For no split second even then did I believe that people had cut in two a live man—even if he was only a policeman. If I had believed it, I should have felt very different. What I felt was that it was *right* ; that it was a good and enlarging and inspiriting thing to see ; that it was an excellent thing to look down on the strange street where such things could be seen ; in short, I could say then, with a quite undivided mind, that it was a very good Christmas present to go to the Pantomime.

READING THE RIDDLE

AN INFINITE number of years ago, when I was the chief weakness of a publisher's office, I remember that there was issued from that establishment a book of highly modern philosophy: a work of elaborate evolutionary explanation of everything and nothing; a work of the New Theology. It was called "The Great Problem Solved" or some such title. When this book had been out for a few days it began to promise an entirely unexpected success. Booksellers sent to ask about it, travellers came in and asked for it, even the ordinary public stood in a sort of knot outside the door, and sent in their bolder spirits to make inquiries.

Even to the publisher this popularity seemed remarkable; to me (who had dipped into the work, when I should have been otherwise employed) it appeared utterly incredible.

After some little time, however, when they had examined "The Great Problem Solved", the lesser problem was also solved. We found that people were buying it under the impression that it was a detective story. I do not blame them for their desire, and most certainly I do not blame them for their disappointment. It must have exasperated them, it would certainly infuriate me, to open a book expecting to find a cosy, kindly, human story about a murdered man found in a cupboard, and find instead a lot of dull, bad philosophy about the upward progress and the purer morality. I would rather read any detective book than that book. I would rather spend my time in finding out why a dead man was dead than in slowly comprehending why a certain philosopher had never been alive.

Reading the Riddle

But this little incident has always stuck to me as a symbol of what is really wrong with modern popular religion. Why is a work of modern theology less startling, less arresting to the soul, than a work of silly police fiction ? Why is a work of modern theology less startling, less arresting to the soul than a work of old theology ? When those unfortunate clients bought "The Great Problem Solved", perhaps it was inevitable that they should feel slightly cooled and lowered in their vitality ; perhaps no philosophical work can really be so good as a good detective story. But at any rate there need not have been such an absolute abyss between them. People need not have felt that they had paid for the most exciting kind of book and got the least exciting kind of book. It cannot be right that religion should be the dullest of subjects. There must be something wrong if the most important human business is also the least exciting. There must be something wrong if everything is not interesting.

A man called Smith goes out for a walk, and stops by a bookstall, where he sees a book called "The Great Problem Solved". If Smith finds that this book solves a problem in crime, he is entranced. If Smith finds that it solves a problem in chess, he is interested. If Smith finds that it solves the problem in the last issue of *Answers*, he is genuinely excited. But if Smith finds that it solves the problem of Smith, that it explains the stones under his feet, and the stars over his head, that it tells him suddenly why it really is that he likes chess or detective stories, or anything else ; if I say, Smith finds that the book explains Smith—then we are told he finds it dull. It may be a democratic prejudice, but I do not believe this. I think that Smith likes modern chess problems more than modern philosophical problems for the very simple reason that they are better. I think he likes a modern detective story better than a modern religion simply because there are some good modern detective stories and no good modern religions. In short, he buys "The Great Problem Solved" as a police novel, because he knows that in a police novel, in some shape or form, the great problem will be solved. And he does not buy it as a book of modern philosophy, because he knows that in a book of modern philosophy, the great problem will certainly not be solved. This title as the title of a police romance is a sensation, but as the title of a metaphysical work it is a swindle. Those early friends of mine bought the book when they thought that it solved the mystery of Berkeley-square, but dropped it like hot bricks when they found that it professed only to solve the mystery of existence. But if those people had really believed for a moment that it did solve the mystery of existence they would not have dropped it like hot bricks. They would have walked over hot bricks for ten miles to find it.

That forgotten book may stand as a type of all the new theological literature. What is wrong with it is not that it professes to state the paradox of God, but that it professes to state the paradox of God as a truism. You may or may not be able to reveal the divine secret ; but at least you cannot let it leak out. If ever it comes, it will be unmistakable, it will kill or cure. Judaism, with its dark sublimity, said that if a man saw God he would die. Christianity conjectures that (by an even more catastrophic fatality) if he sees God he will live for ever. But whatever happens will be something decisive and indubitable. A man after seeing God may die ; but at least he will not be slightly unwell, and then have to take a little medicine and then have to call in a doctor. If any of us ever do read the riddle, we shall read it in brutal black and blazing white, exactly as we do read the riddle of some sixpenny mystery of murder. If we ever do find the solution, we shall know that it is the right solution.

This dark and drastic quality there has been certainly in all real religions. The ordinary detective story has one deep quality in common with Christianity; it brings home the crime in a quarter that is unsuspected. In any good detective story the last shall be first and the first shall be last. The judgment at the end of any silly sensational story is like the judgment at the end of the world; it is unexpected. As the sensational story always makes the apparently blameless banker, the seemingly spotless aristocrat, the author of the incomprehensible crime, so the author of Christianity told us that in the end the bolt would fall with a brutal novelty, and he that exalted himself would be abased.

The actual records of great religions are so terribly theatrical that Mr. Bernard Shaw recently said that the story of the Crucifixion in the Gospels was too dramatic to be true. This is sufficiently characteristic of the Fabian political philosophy, which has never lived in the heart of any heroic politics. The story of Danton and Robespierre (to take an accidental example) with its " speeches ", " eternal daring ", " If we do this our names are never forgotten among men ", " The blood of Danton chokes you ", " There is a God "—shows what men do say. These things were said, and said suddenly, because the heart of man was high. When man is at his utmost he is in a state indescribable ; he tells the truth or dies.

It is not in your lot or mine to live in a great or an ecstatic age. Men talk of the noise and unrest of our age ; but I think that all that age is really very sleepy ; all the wheels and the traffic send one to sleep. The shrieking pistons and the shattering hammers are one enormous and most soothing lullaby. But even in our quiet life I think we can feel the great fact that is the core of all religion. However quiet may be the skies, or however cool the meadows, we always feel that if we did know what they meant the meaning would be something mighty and shattering. About the weakest weed there is still a sensational difference between understanding and not understanding. We stare at a tree in an infinite leisure; but we know all the time that the real difference is between a stillness of mystery and an explosion of explanation. We know all the time that the question is whether it will always continue to be a tree or turn suddenly into something else.

A TALE OF TWO CITIES[1]

A TALE OF TWO CITIES was written in the later part of Dicken's literary development, and in one respect stands absolutely alone among all his works. It is, I think, the one solitary instance, from which a critic in distant days could possibly deduce that this very great literary man had ever read any literature at all. This generalisation may be subject to certain partial modifications, to be considered when we consider the course of his life; but as a matter of proportion, which is the essential of truth, it is true. In a thousand ways, ranging from the most depressing destitution to the most pantomimic parade and luxury, Dickens showed that he had studied life, and could turn life into literature. In a thousand moods, ranging from the rankest vulgar farce to the most stagey and melodramatic morality, he showed that he had within himself the powers and passions and appetites to stock the whole world with stories. But very seldom indeed, in enjoying the world of Dickens, do we feel that there was really any writer but Dickens in the world. Like all very creative men, he unfixes the dates of history, and stands as a sort of immortal anachronism. It is sometimes with a sort of start that we remember that his Hogarthian farce and tragedy went on long after Keats had written " La Belle Dame Sans Merci " and well into the time when Tennyson was writing the poems of his best period, which was his Pre-Raphaelite period. Dickens, in practice and in private life, was a very great admirer of Tennyson. Forster, his biographer, says that his literary tastes touching his contemporaries varied very much, but that

[1] Reprinted by permission of Messrs. Macmillan & Co., Ltd.

he never failed in his admiration of Tennyson. But I do not honestly believe that anybody could guess, from any printed word—from the first words about Mr. Pickwick and Mr. Blotton of Aldgate, to the last broken and doubtful sentences that hint at the identity of Datchery or the destruction of Drood—that Dickens had taken any particular pleasure in "The Lady of Shalott", or "Sir Galahad". It is partly a tribute to the strength of Dickens that his mind was so teeming with images that he never needed to borrow mere ideas. It is partly, also a real weakness in his position, that he had never valued the great culture of the past, and therefore could not fully understand its developments all around him in the culture of the present. But, for good or evil, it is true that in ninety-nine cases out of a hundred nobody (to use a popular phrase) ever made a bulge in Dickens; nobody even made a dent in him. He remained, with all his gifts and glories, solidly and almost insolently himself. The one example, among all works of his authorship, in which we feel even faintly the presence, or perhaps the shadow, of another author, is *A Tale of Two Cities;* and that other author is Thomas Carlyle.

As I have said, the normal human conditions necessary to his normal human life, involved some modification of this statement. He was very largely what is called a self-taught man, which means that he was taught, not by himself, but by other people; by other people acting as they really act in the real world, and not as they pose before pupils they are paid to teach. His domestic circumstances from the first were very insecure, so that he saw more of books than of school-books; he learned more from tattered volumes left about in a tavern than from grammars provided primly in an educational establishment. But it is quite true that among the tattered volumes in the tavern, or elsewhere, there were some with titles not yet entirely forgotten: titles like *Robinson Crusoe* and *Tom Jones* and *Roderick Random* and *Tristram Shandy*. In this sense it is true that he, like every other human being who ever wrote or even read, owed something to what had already been written. And indeed the great comic classics, which were the glory of eighteenth-century England, did leave a certain trend or track in his mind, which is an utterly trackless waste as regards all the things that anybody could ever have tried to teach him in school. It is evident, however, from the very nature of the story itself, that school in his case must have been almost as intermittent as truancy.

Charles Dickens was born in Portsea, adjoining Portsmouth, in 1812, and was promptly carried away from it at the age of two. He then became a Londoner for a few years, equally infantile; and then his wandering family settled down in Chatham, which was about the nearest approach it ever made to settling down anywhere. Thus we find first the two facts, that are both determining and important : one, that his family was one of very varied economic fortunes, such as leads to frequent change of abode, and has indeed made the modern poorer middle class almost as nomadic as Arabs ; and the other, that such background as a child of genius will always feel and value (if he has half a chance to do it) was for Charles Dickens, to the day of his death, the great roads of Kent that go down to Dover ; and the gardens and hopfields and the towers of Rochester Cathedral. In so far as he had any traditions, that was his traditional environment ; just as in so far as he had any culture, it was that of the great comic novelists of England a hundred years before. He was so far traditional by instinct that he never forgot either of the influences ; he named one of his sons after Henry Fielding ; and, when he came to comfort and affluence, he made his home on Gad's Hill, on that great Kentish road where Falstaff had played the glorious fool long ago.

The Common Man

The private life of Dickens, however, is of little importance to the outline of criticism here involved, and is indeed in its own nature somewhat irrelevant and accidental. Its chief tragedy was almost an accident, and its premature close was a sort of defeat brought about by an excess of triumphs. It is well known that in his early youth, while he was still a parliamentary reporter living in London after his boyhood in Chatham, he married the daughter of one of his literary patrons named Hogarth, and that by a long process of disagreement, about which critics can always disagree, he came to be alienated from his wife; though, curiously enough, remaining on terms of perfectly sober and fraternal friendship with one of her sisters. There is no need to pronounce upon a problem which was really kept private, by the not undignified prejudice of the Victorian time; it is enough to say that no very grave charge was ever brought against either party by any of the small group of people who knew the truth. It is more relevant here to remark that at almost the same moment as his marriage occurred his first and perhaps most triumphant entry into literature. His first book, commonly called Pickwick or the Pickwick Papers, is supreme among his works in many ways, but especially in the way here in question: that it is a purely personal creation and owes nothing to any other book. It is all the more amusing to remember that a spiteful attempt was made by some of his enemies to suggest that it owed everything to its original illustrator, an artist named Seymour, who drew spirited sporting sketches of the sort then fashionable. It is a peculiarly false insinuation, in a literary sense. For it is the whole point of Pickwick that its rush of inspiration not only leaves Seymour's first ideas behind, but leaves Dickens' first ideas quite as far behind. We might say that the whole point of Pickwick is that it does not stick to the point; or at least that the point is not Pickwick, in the sense of the

A Tale of Two Cities

President of the Pickwick Club. The best things in *Pickwick* have nothing to do with the principal characters, still less with the preliminary chapters, and least of all with the early illustrations. It is an exceptional case in which the story grows better the more it strays from the story. Dickens did not preserve this limpid and perfect liberty in his later stories. He produced better novels, but never so good a book. Still, we can say of the ensuing series of books that, whatever else they were, they were not bookish. They showed Dickens interested in different things, but never any other authors influencing Dickens. Thus, in his next book, *Oliver Twist*, which he seemed resolved to make as grim and lurid as *Pickwick* had been gay and luminous, he was in fact protesting against many social evils, which had already produced noble protests from great men of that age. The workhouse he hated had been hated as healthily by Cobbett or by Hood, by Cartwright or by Carlyle. But nobody could say that one word of *Oliver Twist* sounds as if it were suggested by the style of Cobbett or by the style of Carlyle. *Nicholas Nickleby* and *Martin Chuzzlewit* show him even more obviously walking down his own street, in some ways even a narrow and Cockney street; the same applies to *The Old Curiosity Shop*; and, though *Barnaby Rudge* is a sort of experiment in the way of a historical novel, it is not much more really historical than the Old Curiosity Shop or its Wardour Street curiosities. *Dombey and Son* has the same now established balance of perfect comedy and rather imperfect melodrama; and though *David Copperfield* strikes far deeper, and releases a much finer spring of inspiration, it is even more personal than the rest. Dickens has found a new source of inspiration, but not by reading anybody else's book; rather by reading his own diary. The same statement applies to that fine book, *Great Expectations*, and a much sharper social criticism, still extorted by contemporary facts rather than contemporary culture, appears in the unconscious or unclassifiable Socialism of *Hard Times*. It mixes his own observations less with mere fancies than did his first protest in *Oliver Twist* ; but it is always his own observations and nobody else's. There is little to vary this verdict in the other two novels of *Bleak House* and *Little Dorrit*. It is only when we come to the book which is here specially in question, *A Tale of Two Cities*, which appeared in 1859, that we have anything like the particular impression of which I speak ; that Dickens has felt the pressure of an imaginative atmosphere outside his own bursting sufficency and energy, that energy from whose centrifugal fury all fancies but his own had been spurned away.

This compact and competent, and some would say conceited, sense of self-expression does in *A Tale of Two Cities*, for the first time, seem to admit something external, something that might be called an echo. Indeed, in one way, it might be called the echo of an echo. It is Carlyle's French Revolution rather than Michelet's French Revolution ; in other words, it is not entirely or exactly the French Revolution of the French Revolutionists. Dickens does tend to neglect, as Carlyle did tend to neglect, the extent to which the revolutionists themselves regarded it not as an explosion of unreason, or even an explosion of passion, but as an inevitable explosion of reason. They themselves might almost have said that the explosion was an explanation ; as is the explosion that occurs during a chemical lecture. Carlyle, who had laboriously studied all the documents and historical literature of the French Revolution, never quite understood this. It is small blame by comparison to Dickens, who had never studied any documents or any history or any literature, or hardly any books except his own, if he did not understand it either. But he had studied one book, and that was Carlyle's book ; and the shadow of that luminous but lurid cloud lies over the whole landscape and scenery of his story. It is very difficult to define or prove these merely atmospheric things. A short if clumsy way of putting it is to compare the general tone of Dickens towards the mere notion of a mob, as it is in *Barnaby Rudge*, with his tone towards such a mob in *A Tale of Two Cities*. The comparison, of course, is not quite fair. Even a man so little in touch with history as he, could tell that the second was more historic than the first; that the second was at least an outbreak of liberty, by comparison with an outbreak of bigotry. But there is more in the contrast than that; we feel that he could never have taken a Gordon Rioter seriously, even if he had liked him, as he did so often seem to like his most ludicrous and indefensible characters; as the reader does really, in a way, like Sim Tappertit. He did not like Madame Defarge, but he did take her seriously. If she had occurred in *Barnaby Rudge*, she would have been a vulgar villainess; as she occurred in *A Tale of Two Cities*, she is a Fate. In other words, there is not only a romantic but a mystical element that has entered the story; and though Dickens was in one sense always a romantic, he was certainly never a mystic. In some sense the comparison involves a paradox. Carlyle, as a reactionary, declared that the mob, being made of most men, was made mostly of fools. But Carlyle also allowed for a mystical suggestion that the folly of men was the wisdom of God. Dickens, as a radical, regarded the mob, in so far as it meant most ordinary men, as being composed of reasonable and responsible citizens, whose votes were all valuable and whose intellects were all capable of benefiting by education and discussion. But, in practice, when Dickens did see a mass of men in any sort of elemental disorder, acting in anger or by some accident lawless or unlettered, he was deeply disgusted in every corner of his compact and sensible intelligence, and hated that very wildness which Carlyle half admired. Dickens felt like this, for instance, towards the sprawling licence and spasmodic ferocity of the more wild and western elements of the American Republic. He would, if subjected to the real experience, have been quite as much horrified by the ferocious pugnacity and spontaneous militarism of the mob of the French Republic. Nevertheless, the Carlyean sense of a sort of savage symbolism in the great struggles of history does make the atmosphere of this book, or perhaps of half this book, different from the whole bulk of his other books.

Perhaps it is really impossible for any good citizen to write a *Tale of Two Cities*. He will always see one from the outside and the other from the inside ; and the line of relative reality and unreality in this case runs fairly clear. Thus the description of the old-fashioned London bank is unmistakably written by the old London Dickens. The story of the sacrifice of Sydney Carton, though genuinely touching and noble, especially as compared with some of the Dickensian melo-dramas, is still in a sense a London melodrama, with the larger background of a Paris tragedy. The hero is being heroic for private reasons ; whereas nobody understands or does justice to the French Revolution, who forgets that half its leaders lost their heads by really being heroic for public reasons. It is easy enough to make fun of their classical rhetoric about Brutus who killed his sons, or Timoleon who killed his brother ; but it is not so easy to deny that, if they had too much of this notion of sacrificing private good to public good, we have far too much of the corruption and cowardice that comes of sacrificing public good to private good. The ideals for which that war was waged were insufficient but largely just ; and it is curious and rather moving to note that the author is so far exalted by the atmosphere that he turns in the end to an older and in truth a larger ideal, which exists before and after and affirms the same justice in public and in private life. I know nothing in all the

A Tale of Two Cities

works of this man of genius which is, in the true sense, so
imaginative as that last strange voice, coming from nowhere,
those great timeless words put into the mouth of no mortal
character, spoken suddenly as by a trumpet out of the empty
sky, between the click of the knitting-needles and the crash
of the guillotine: " I am the Resurrection and the Life . . ."

GOD AND GOODS

IT IS often noted, and generally truly enough, that Bolshevism is necessarily connected with atheism. It is not so much realised, perhaps, that atheism is now under an increasing necessity of connecting itself with Bolshevism. For Bolshevism is at least partly positive, even if it is largely destructive. And the history of the purely negative notion, of an abstract attack on religion, has been in this respect a rather curious history. Taken as a whole, indeed it is at once melancholy and comic. Those who in modern times have tried to destroy popular religion, or a traditional faith, have always felt the necessity of offering something solid as a substitute. The queer part of it is that they have offered about a dozen totally different things ; some of them entirely contradictory things ; that the promises perpetually varied, and only the negative threat remained the same.

Just before the French Revolution, among the first eighteenth-century philosophers, it was generally assumed that Liberty was not merely a good thing, but the one and only origin of all good things. The man living according to Nature, the Natural Man or the Noble Savage, would find himself immediately free and happy so long as he never went to church, and was careful to cut the parish priest in the street. These philosophers soon discovered, what the parish priest could have told them at the start, that it is rather more difficult to be a happy animal, than to be a happy man. Indeed, a man cannot be an animal for the same reason that he cannot be an angel; because he is a man. But for some time the philosophers who did not believe in God, whom they regarded as a myth, managed to believe in Nature without realising that she is a metaphor. And they assured those whom they waved on to the burning down of churches, that after that they would be eternally happy in their fields and gardens.

Then after the political revolution came the industrial revolution ; and with it an enormous new importance attached to science. The amiable atheists went back to the people, smiled at them, coughed slightly, and explained that it was still necessary to burn down churches, but that a slight error had been made about the substitute for churches. The second atheist philosophy was founded, not on the fact that Nature is kind, but on the fact that Nature is cruel ; not that fields are free and beautiful, but that scientific men and industrialists are so energetic, that they will soon cover all the fields with factories and warehouses. Now there was a new substitute for God; which was gas and coal and iron and the privilege of turning wheels in order to work these substances. It was now positively stated that economic liberty, the freedom to buy and sell and hire and exploit, would make people so blissfully happy that they would forget all their dreams of the fields of heaven ; or for that matter of the fields of earth. And somehow that also has been a little disappointing.

Two Earthly Paradises had collapsed. The first was the natural paradise of Rousseau ; the second the economic paradise of Ricardo. Men did not become perfect through being free to live and love ; men did not become perfect through being free to buy and sell. It was obviously time for the atheists to find a third inevitable and immediate ideal. They have found it in Communism. And it does not trouble them that it is quite different from their first ideal and quite contrary to their second. All they want is some supposed betterment of humanity which will be a bribe for depriving humanity of divinity. Read between the lines of half a hundred new books—outlines of popular science and educational publications on history and philosophy—and you will see that the only fundamental feeling in them is the hatred of religion. The only positive thing is negative. But they are forced more and more to idealise Bolshevism, simply because it is the only thing left that is still new enough to be offered as a hope, when every one of the revolutionary hopes they have themselves offered has in its turn become hopeless.

FROM MEREDITH TO RUPERT BROOKE

THE TITLE of the Age of Reason has been given to the eighteenth century, though the typical eighteenth-century man who invented it probably meant it as a prophetic and optimistic description of the nineteenth century or the twentieth century. Certainly if Thomas Paine had foreseen the actual nineteenth century, he would have called it the Age of Romanticism. If he had foreseen the actual twentieth century, he would have called it the Age of Nonsense, the Age of Unreason, especially in the departments originally identified with rationalism, such as the department of science. To him Einstein would have been merely a contradiction in terms and Epstein a disease afflicting bronze and marble. It is therefore not altogether misleading to measure modern developments, for good or evil, as from a sort of datum line of simple or self-evident rationality to be found in the eighteenth century. Whatever else is false, it is false to say that the world has increased in clarity and intelligibility and logical completeness. Whatever else is true, it is true to say that the world has grown more bewildering, especially in the scientific spheres supposed to be ruled by law or explained by reason. The simplification of the older rationalists may have been, and indeed was, an over-simplification. But it did simplify and it did satisfy ; above all, it satisfied them. It would not be altogether unfair to say that it filled them not only with satisfaction but with self-satisfaction. And, as historical divisions are never clean-cut, this rationalistic self-satisfaction descended in part to their children ; in many ways it may be found pervading the nineteenth century, and, in the

The Common Man

case of some rather old-fashioned persons, even our own century.

Nevertheless, the nineteenth century was very different; and the Victorian Age was vividly different. And it was different from the eighteenth century chiefly in this: that the old clarity of rationalism and humanitarianism was more and more coloured and clouded by certain waves of specially modern imagination or hypothesis or taste and fancy. These new notions had been unknown in the Age of Reason and even in the Age of Revolution. These sentiments had never disturbed the generalisations of Jefferson and the Jacobins any more than they had disturbed the doctrines of Johnson and the Jacobites. These sentiments colour everything in the Victorian Age, and they must be understood before attempting any survey of it.

It is generally difficult to illustrate this truth without being involved in a discussion about religion. But there is, as it happens, another outstanding example, which does not directly involve any interest in religion. I mean the enormous interest in race. That would alone be enough to stamp the nineteenth century as something sharply different from the eighteenth century. That would alone be enough to mark off the Victorian from the older Georgian frame of mind. In the eighteenth century, both the reactionaries and the revolutionaries inherited the ancient religious and philosophic habit of legislating for mankind. A man like Johnson thought of men everywhere as under certain religious conditions, though he thought them happier under conditions of subordination. A man like Jefferson thought of men everywhere as under certain moral conditions, though he thought them happiest in a condition of equality. A man like Gibbon might doubt both the moral systems of Johnson and Jefferson. But it never occurred to Gibbon to explain the Decline and Fall of the Roman Empire by exalting the Teuton as such against the Latin as such, or vice versa. Gibbon had religious prejudices, or, if you will, irreligious prejudices. But the notion of having racial prejudices in a quarrel between some brutal Vandal or Visigoth and some petty Byzantine official would have seemed to him as nonsensical as taking sides among Chinese tongs or Zulu tribes. Similarly, the eighteenth-century Tories were traditional but not tribal. Even a man as late as Metternich, while he might be on the watch against French atheism or even Russian orthodoxy disturbing the Austrian Empire, would have troubled his head very little over the fact that the Austrian Empire contained a mixture of Teutons and Slavs. The rise of this romance of race, or, as some would say, of this science of race, was one of the distinct and decisive revolutions of the nineteenth century, and especially of the Victorian Age.

It will be well to mark in what way these colossal clouds of historical imagination or theory actually coloured or discoloured the dead daylight, which an earlier rationalism thought to have dawned upon the world. In the case of Victorian literature, perhaps it is best tested by noting how it affected even the Victorians who might have been expected to escape its effect. Carlyle was not merely affected by it; we might almost say that he was made by it. Anyhow, he was inspired and intoxicated by it; he was at once overwhelmed and made overwhelming. All his history and philosophy was full of this one idea : that all that is good in our civilisation comes, not from the older civilisation, but from a yet older thing that might be called a benevolent barbarism. All light as well as fire, all law as well as liberty, was supposed to be derived from a sort of ethnic energy originally called Germanic, afterwards more prudently called Teutonic ; and now, with almost an excess of caution, called Nordic. The merits of this racial theory, as against the old

The Common Man

Roman theory, of European culture, are difficult to discuss without trenching on controversial themes. Personally I should say that when certain European provinces broke with the Roman tradition, they set up certain Puritan theologies of their own, which could not last, or at any rate have not lasted. Anyhow, it is curious that in each of these provinces the place of both the new and the old religion has really been taken by a stark and rather narrow national pride. The Prussian is more proud of being a Prussian than of being a Protestant, in the sense of a Lutheran. The Orangeman is more proud of being what he calls an Ulsterman than of being a Calvinist, in the sense of studying the strict Calvinist theology. And even in England, where the atmosphere was more mild and the elements more mixed, the same type of intense insular self-consciousness has in some degree developed; and it has been not untruly said that patriotism is the religion of the English. In any case, to take the same test, an Englishman is normally more proud of being an Englishman than of being an Anglican. It was therefore not unnatural that when these lands, that were the extinct volcanoes of the great Puritan fire, sought for a more modern and general bond of association, they should seek it in that sort of pride in the race, which is the extension of the pride in the tribe. It is right to say that there is much in the idea of race that stirs the imagination and lends itself to the production of literature. The ideal of race, like the ideal of religion, has its own symbols, prophecies, oracles and holy places. If it is less mystical, it is equally mysterious. The riddle of heredity, the bond of blood, the doom which in a hundred human legends attends certain houses or families, are things quite sufficiently native to our nature to lend a sincerity to the sense of national or even international kinship. Many may quite honestly have felt that race was as religious as religion. But one thing it certainly was not. It was not as rational as religion. It was not as universal or philosophical as religion. At its best it involved a sort of noble prejudice; and its romanticism clouded the old general judgments upon men as men, whether dogmatic or democratic. Carlyle was the most romantic of all these romantic Victorian writers, and largely owed to this his predominance in the romantic Victorian age. But his popular champions, like Froude and Kingsley, were even more romantic; though in the case of Kingsley the romancing was really honest romancing, while in the case of Froude (I cannot but think) the word romancing is something of a euphemism.

Only, as I have said, the way in which this racial romance penetrated the Victorian culture can best be seen, not in an obvious case like Carlyle, but in much more remote cases like Matthew Arnold or Meredith. To take the latter case first: George Meredith was in one sense an entirely international intellectual; a Liberal humanist; a true child of the French Revolution, which he celebrated in sumptuous odes. But he illustrates the indirect effect of the racial craze, which is that the other side often accepted the distinction. Not only did the Teutonist talk about being a Teuton, but the Celt talked about being a Celt. A great mass of Meredith's social judgment is modified, and, to my taste, a little falsified, by his insistence on setting the Saxon against the Celt, when he has to set the Englishman against the Irishman or the Welshman. He often satirised in the Englishman exactly what the Teutonist praised in the Englishman; and it was often something that the Englishman does not happen to possess. So in the other case: Matthew Arnold made himself specially and supremely the apostle of a cosmopolitan culture; he did a vast amount of real good by insisting on the truism that England is a part of Europe. He was at his best in a contempt for the contempt that was felt for Frenchmen or Irishmen or

The Common Man

Italians. But he could not bring himself to treat them simply as Frenchmen or Irishmen or Italians. He was affected by the universal fashion of ethnology and worried by the racial generalisations. When he talked what was relatively excellent sense about the senseless treatment of Ireland, he thought of such things too much as Celtic Studies and too little as Irish Studies. He also tried to explain the English faults as part of " the German paste in us ", and wasted on anthropology what was meant for the study of mankind. We might take a third example. William Morris was on one side a Communist and almost bound to be an internationalist ; he was on the other side a medievalist, appealing to that ancient beauty that belonged to all Europeans alike. But he was encumbered with a clumsy desire to be Saxon, to treat English as if it were merely the rudimentary language of the Angles ; and moved his admirer, Stevenson, to an intense irritation by writing " whereas " when he only meant " where ".

I have mentioned this particular Victorian fashion, the racial theory of history, as a primary and prominent thing, because it is not generally mentioned at all. We are so accustomed, in reading modern records of recent or ancient things, to gain an impression of an ever-expanding world, called in the only too typical Victorian expression, " the thoughts of men being widened by the process of the suns ", that we often forget the many periods when the world contracted into a new narrowness or exclusiveness, or the thoughts of men visibly shrank and shrivelled under some fresh influence of isolation or distinction. This was certainly true of the tribalism and imperialism that the nineteenth century developed, out of a romance of races, as compared with the first revolutionary generalisations about the human race. The fact is plain, for instance, in the story of the first revolutionary experiment— the American Republic. In the time of Jefferson, many of those who held slaves disapproved of slavery; many of those who approved of slavery did not specially approve of it as negro slavery. The notion of the negro as something peculiarly perilous or pestilent is not an ancient prejudice but a very recent and largely anthropological fashion. It is akin to all that dates from Darwin; and the popularisation by Huxley of an almost pessimistic type of evolution. Modern Southerners are much more hostile to negroes than they were when they owned slaves. As there rose recently in America the anthropological theory that the negro is only an ape, so there rose recently in Europe the anthropological notion that the Pole is only a Slav, or that the Irishman is only a Celt. People were so proud of discovering these larger groups that they failed to notice that they are really looser groups. They belonged to what the eminent Victorian truly called the fairy-tales of science. They had neither the precision that belongs to doctrinal definition nor the practicality that belongs to daily experience. In religion and morals we all really know what we mean by a man, and in the stress of real life we all really know what we mean by an Irishman. It is by no means certain that we all know what we mean by a Celt. Hence something large and imaginative, but formless and partly imaginary, began to spread over popular sentiment with the spread of popular science. It was darker and more dubious than either the humanitarianism of the eighteenth century or the nationalism of the nineteenth. It was not so clean-cut; indeed I will venture to say that it was not so clean. It was mixed with the mud and mist, the chaotic clay and cloud, of primitive and even bestial beginnings; it had only vague visions of barbaric migrations and massacres and enslavements. It started all our recent preference for the prehistoric to the historic. All this must be remembered as an influence overshadowing the second half of the nineteenth century, because it eventually took a more pointed and controversial form which involved not only materialism but pessimism. The earlier rationalists may or may not have been materialists; but they certainly were not pessimists. They were, I admit, rather exaggerated and excessive optimists. It is none the less curious that the general revolutionary tradition, of revolt and criticism of conditions, which began with the philosophy of Rousseau, should have ended with the philosophy of Thomas Hardy.

So much for one side of this later Victorian change. But the mere mention of Hardy and the realistic rebels will remind us that it had another side, which was a very good side. Probably speaking, it consisted in turning the attention from purely political wrongs to fundamental economic wrongs. In this also Carlyle, who belongs to the earlier period, continues to colour and even control the destinies of the later. In the matter of dates Carlyle and Macaulay covered the same period. In the matter of destinies they lived in two different centuries. Macaulay was, for good and evil, entirely a man of the eighteenth century. He was a Whig as Fox had been a Whig; a patriot as Pitt had been a patriot; a Protestant as any Erastian latitudinarian Georgian parson had been a Protestant; a logician as Dr. Johnson was a logician; a historian as Gibbon was a historian. Carlyle, who had brought into history the doubtful romance of blood, also brought into politics the very real tragedy of bread. He stands at the beginning of all the best efforts of the later Victorians to face the problems of labour and hunger that had developed in the depths of the new industrial civilisation. With the great exception of Cobbett, who had stood apart and alone, misunderstood and abused by all parties, it is fair to say that Carlyle started much of the merely social unrest of conscience which has modified the evils of the later nineteenth century. It is needless here to weigh the evil against the good; or to discuss how much of a certain disinterested dignity, in the old Republicans, was lost in his practical and impatient clamour for captains and for kings. It is only necessary to insist on the reality of the contrast and the change. Grattan, a great and typical orator of the eighteenth-century ideal, had said that the Irishman might go in rags, but he must not go in chains. Ruskin and the social reformers reversed the principle, until some of the extreme Socialists, like the Marxian Communists, are now inclined to say that a man must go in chains so that he may not go in rags.

Ruskin was the heir and representative of Carlyle in this later and better Victorian development. It is unnecessary to react against romanticism to such an extent as a recent critic, who summed up Ruskin in a book on the Victorians by saying that at least his economics were all scientifically sound though he could not write for toffee. He certainly could not write in that stately modern style in which toffee figures as the prize of writing. When the critic suggests that he could not write, it merely means that the critic does not like that particular sort of writing, which proves rather the limitations of the critic than the incapacities of the writer. Ruskin certainly wrote poetical prose, which may not for the moment be fashionable in an age of prosaic poetry. But to say that it is not good poetical prose is simply to be ignorant of the varied possibilities of good writing. It is also true that what he did he overdid, which is largely true of the whole of this highly coloured and romantic final development of Victorianism. Even those few who deliberately tried to correct it by understatement managed somehow to overstate their understatement. Matthew Arnold deliberately endeavoured to introduce a French classical balance and critical detachment into English letters. The consequence was that he was called a prig, which was unjust but not unthinkable ; whereas no Frenchman reading Saint-Beuve ever thought of thinking that he was a prig. Walter Pater wished to create an art criticism more detached than that of Ruskin; but he did in fact manage to create the impression of being artificial as well as artistic. It was very difficult to be classic in the later Victorian atmosphere. There was a romantic unrest about it, so that even the umpires were competitive and combative. The loss of a natural repose, in Latin logic or French clarity, was one of the penalties of parting with the spirit of the eighteenth century. Another mark of it was the growth of an intellectual individualism which expressed itself, not only in being *outré*, but actually in being obscure. Browning and Meredith were among the very greatest of Victorians; and over both of them brooded that cloud I have described as coming up to over-shadow the epoch; and though it was coloured gorgeously like a cloud of sunset, it none the less came between many people and the sun.

George Meredith largely stood alone; but he stood as it were representing many others who had also a taste for standing alone. All this last phase is full of men whom it is interesting to remember and yet very easy to forget. It was because of the individualistic isolation of their talents and even their topics. An example is Richard Jefferies, who was "The Gamekeeper At Home"; or T. E. Brown, who made a niche for himself that is somehow at once obscure and popular : or William de Morgan, who with English eccentricity took up literature as a hobby for old age. The danger of all grouping is that we may miss too many of these men who did not fit into groups. Nevertheless, there are two or three groups which may be said to bulk biggest in the period—the period after the triumph of Tennyson and Browning in poetry, or Dickens and Thackeray in fiction. First there appears, primarily through the influence of Ruskin, what was called the

From Meredith to Rupert Brooke

Pre-Raphaelite Group; which began with a Ruskinian version of Christian medievalism and shaded off into later forms of aestheticism, not to say Paganism. The leader, who was also the link, was Rossetti, who accepted with delight the medieval pattern, but blazoned it with bolder and warmer colours than some of the literal Pre-Raphaelites would have approved. With him went his sister Christina, who was medieval in the more orthodox sense; and, in a manner very much his own, William Morris, who made the medieval form the expression of modern discontents and social ideals, instead of Christina Rossetti's religious ideals. The queer transition of the Pre-Raphaelites from a revival of Christianity to a revival of Paganism is complete in the poet Swinburne, who belonged to the set, yet had little in common with the sect. That it had Ruskin at one end and Swinburne at the other illustrates how loose a thing a group is, especially in English literature. Swinburne had three phases; one in which he wrote the best poetry in the worst spirits, or mood or frame of mind for his beautiful boyish singing is not merely in praise of Paganism, but definitely of Pessimism. There is a second period when his spirits are a little better and his poetry a little worse; the period of his political enthusiasm for United Italy and Victor Hugo and the resounding qualities of the word Republic. There is, unfortunately, a third period, in which he imitated himself and did it badly. But the point to seize is that, in his great hour, Swinburne was a spell; he held people like a magic flute, till they forgot that there was any other melody in the world. It is thoroughly typical of such glamours that there has been a violent and very unreasonable reaction against his unreasonable power. With him and Walter Pater the movement ends in its last pagan phase; save perhaps for the queer aestheticism that later became a decadent dandyism in Oscar Wilde.

The Common Man

But already new groups were making this one look old. One was what may be called the Picaresque or Adventurous Group, but may be more recognisable as the group of Stevenson and Henley. Both for good and evil, they reacted into a robust blood-and-thunder literature, which, in the case of Stevenson, who was not only the greater but much the more amiable and balanced of the two, was as blameless as it was bloody. There was, however, a dangerous double use of the very word " blood ". And, quaintly enough, the more dubious element is to be found rather in blood than in bloodshed. The blood that spatters the pages of *Treasure Island* can only promote a respect for the real virtues of courage or loyalty. The blood that is not shed at all, but remains in the human body, was used to encourage a respect for the real vices and weaknesses of pride and racial contempt. For one important point about this group is this : that through them, or some of them, there came into full power and possession that curious religion of Race, which I have described as developing from Teutonic sources a little time before. It is not to be confused with patriotism or the unselfish love of one's country. It is a mere pride in being oneself of a certain real or imaginary race or stock. The Frenchman loves France as if she were a woman; the Nordic Man merely loves himself for being a Nordic Man. This weakness did to some extent spoil the spirited attempt of Henley and his school of masculine critics ; I mean their very just attempt to show that letters should be red-blooded, as against the green-blooded pessimism of the decadents. But whatever their weaknesses, they did fill the age with a new change and stir, and gave to the pessimists something which if not a cure, was at least an antidote and a counter-irritant. The earliest and best work of Mr. Rudyard Kipling came to them like a new breath of prophecy and promise ; Sir Henry Newbolt supported the chorus with two or three of the very

finest modern English lyrics. There was a general fashion of
patriotic poetry, as well as of Jingo journalism—in verse or
otherwise. It was the only point on which that strongest and
most virile of the pessimists, the Shropshire Lad, could be
moved for a moment to a slightly blasphemous cheerfulness.
John Davidson, a dark Scot in a dark and even dim state of
revolt against everything, also was ready to follow the flag
and revolt against everything except the Empire. The point
of all this is not that patriotism revived, for the older poets
and critics took patriotism for granted : but that the special
type of tribal imperialism sprang out of that rather barbaric
root of Race, already noted as a romance of science, which
reacted against the rationalism of the Revolution.

Fortunately, from the same Stevenson and Henley stock of
ideas, came another idea that also filled the age. It came from
Stevenson alone, as distinct from Newbolt, Henley, Kipling
and the rest, and may be called the cult of the child, but
especially of the boy. It would be putting it too harshly, perhaps, to say that Stevenson wanted to go on playing at
robbers ; whereas Henley and the Imperialists wanted to be
robbers. Anyhow, Stevenson saw the fun of what he was
doing when he made the child say that he was the captain of
a tidy little ship ; whereas it is, I believe, the inscrutable
fact that Henley did not see any fun in what he was doing
when he adjured John Bull to " Storm along, John ", and
assured that public character that the whole world would
soon be his own. Through Stevenson's truly magic lantern,
which he described in *The Lantern-Bearers*, there shone a true
reillumination of the mystical melodrama of childhood. And
in that light many followed to the same sort of fairyland;
notably Sir James Barrie, who introduced a sort of irony into
fairyland. He continued what may be called the Stevensonian
stereoscopic view; the looking at the same object in a double

fashion, with the eye of the adult and of the child. But it was mostly through a string of accidental friendships that this fantastic element was connected with the more realistic of the robust school, though of course there were many brilliant individuals who could only be placed with or near that group. Thus Joseph Conrad, though a Pole, was connected with it by his record of hard or violent adventure at sea; and Mr. John Masefield, though he wrote later and longer poems of rural sport or religion, began with rousing sea songs of the buccaneers.

Already, however, a new voice had been heard, and a new influence balanced or rebuked an influence like that of Kipling; and it was a voice from a more remote elfland than the elfland of Peter Pan. Stevenson himself said that he had twice in poetry heard a new note or a unique and arresting voice: once when he read *Love In A Valley* by George Meredith; and once again when he read some verses called *The Lake Island of Innisfree* by William Butler Yeats. Yet it is worth remarking that there still remained this curious persistence of the romance of race, even in what was so naturally hostile to the popular romance of the Anglo-Saxon race. The appearance of a new cultural nucleus in Dublin, while it derived something from the Pre-Raphaelites, and therefore something from the Victorians, was so far Victorian in this special respect, that it managed to get entangled like all the rest with an ethnological term: the term " Celtic ". It did not even substitute the old Irish term " Gaelic ". It is true that Mr. Yeats himself, the founder of the school and one of the first poets of recent times, did not really base his own case on anthropology, but rather on history and (very rightly) even more on legend. But it marks the racial influence already described that the word " Celtic " stuck to the movement, which was really a revival of remote legend and a gentle heathenism of the hills. It also explains

From Meredith to Rupert Brooke

why there was some reaction against it, even in its own home. There are many who came not to care very much about the Celtic Twilight, who have lived to see the Irish Dawn.

About this time, or a little later, in England, there appeared a group formally called Minor Poets; though one of them was certainly a Major Poet. He was classed at the time with John Davidson and Sir William Watson, both of them very genuine poets in their own style; and there is some charming lyricism in their contemporaries, Norman Gale and Richard le Gallienne. Two other writers of fine verse really belong to this period: Ernest Dowson and Lionel Johnson. But I think it fair to say that Francis Thompson, thus classed as one of them, was of another and altogether higher class. He owed something to Coventry Patmore, one of the most really original Victorians, and something to Alice Meynell, a woman who was a poet (not a poetess) of the sort that women were least supposed to be; an intrinsically intellectual poet. But even of these friends he was free; with all the freedom of a creative and supremely productive or fertile genius. His imagery was so imaginative as to be almost crowded; and, in a different sense from the more analytical Victorians, dark with excess of light. Because he was Catholic many would expect him to be Gothic; but there was something in his exuberance that resembled rather the very best of the Baroque.

The necessity of marking the period by moods has led us here to mark it too exclusively by poets, who are the only permanent record of moods. It need not be said that work of another and what some think a more solid sort had been going forward in those last years; some of it very solid indeed, certainly in the best and perhaps also in the more questionable sense. Fiction, for instance, had followed other guides besides romance. The immense influence of Thomas Hardy was there; with his strong sense of the truth of the earth, as

The Common Man

also of the tragedy of the dust. It had set many able men working in a mine of realism. The two ablest and most typical in this tradition were Arnold Bennett and John Galsworthy. If I do not speak here at length of men of genius like H. G. Wells and Bernard Shaw, it is because they are in a sense the opening of another world, and are most vividly lit up by the glare of the Great War and the existing social perils; and these things really mark the close of the period. For an appalling apocalypse came upon all life, and therefore upon all literature; and the most fitting emblems of such splendour and terror, and the arts of peace torn across, and youth going to its death singing, remain with the last few poems of Rupert Brooke.

THE DANGERS OF NECROMANCY

WE OFTEN lament that the world is divided into sects, all with different narrow ideas. The real trouble is that they all have different broad ideas. It is when it comes to being broadminded that they are most narrow, or at any rate most different. It is their generalisations that cut across each other. The Buddhist believes he is broadminded when he says that *all* efforts at personal achievement and finality, east or west, Christian or Buddhist, are equally vain and hopeless. But I think that is a narrow negation, sprung from special spiritual conditions in Upper India. A modern agnostic thinks he is broadminded when he says that *all* religions or revelations, Catholic or Protestant, savage or civilised, are alike mere myths and guesses at what man can never know. But I think *that* is a narrow negation, sprung from special spiritual conditions in Upper Tooting. My idea of broadmindedness is to sympathise with so many of these separate spiritual atmospheres as possible; to respect or love the Buddhists of Tibet or the agnostics of Tooting for their many real virtues and capacities, but to have a philosophy which explains each of them in turn and does not merely generalise from one of them. This I have found in the Catholic philosophy ; but that is not the question here, except in so far as there is, I think, just this difference : that the largeness of the other schemes is an unreal largeness of generalisation, whereas the largeness of our scheme is a real largeness of experience. Anybody can say that all Africans are black, but it is not the same as having a wide experience of Africa.

This difference about the obvious in generalisation struck

me sharply, and with some amusement, in a debate on Spiritualism in the *Daily News*. A well-known secularist said that it is all very well to say that scientific men and intelligent people accept Spiritualism; but (he added, as with a sort of hiss) remember that wise men for ages actually accepted Witchcraft. He returned more than once to this biting and blasting word; and the argument obviously was, "Modern spirit-rapping by men like Lodge may look very plausible and scientific; but a ghastly fate awaits you; you will be the derision of history; you will be compared to the brutal, brainless, bestially ignorant people who believed in *Witchcraft.* Ha, ha, how will you like *that?*"

Now all this makes me smile in a sad but broadminded manner. Because it seems to me to be quite the other way. I am not by any means certain, one way or the other, that there is really such a thing as Spirit-rapping. I am absolutely certain that there is such a thing as Witchcraft. I impute a belief in it to common sense, to experience and the records of experience, and to a broad view of humanity as a whole. I impute disbelief in it to inexperience, to provincial ignorance, to local limitations, and all the vices that balance the virtues of Tooting. Common sense will show that the habit of invoking evil spirits, often because they were evil, has existed in far too vast a variety of different cultures, classes and social conditions to be a chance piece of childish credulity. Experience will show that it is *not* true that it disappears everywhere before the advance of education; on the contrary, some of its most evil ministers have been the most highly educated. Record will show that it is *not* true that it marks barbarism rather than civilisation; there was more devil-worship in the cities of Hannibal and Montezuma than among the Esquimaux or the Australian bushmen. And any real knowledge of modern cities will show that it is going on in London and Paris today.

The Dangers of Necromancy

The truth is that the eighteenth and nineteenth centuries had their little local limitations, which are already breaking down. Wishing to expel the superhuman and exalt the human, they grossly simplified the human. The great Huxley (on whose name be praise) said in the innocence of his heart, " It may be doubted if any man ever really said, ' Evil, be thou my good.' " He could not believe that any scepticism could touch common morality, by which he really meant Christian morality. But such innocence is also ignorance. Nothing is more certain than that certain highly lucid, cultivated and deliberate men have said, " Evil, be thou my good " ; men like Gilles de Rais and the Marquis de Sade. Please God they repented in the end, but the point is that they did pursue evil ; not pleasure, or excess of pleasure, or sex or sensuality, but evil. And it is quite certain that some pursued it beyond the bounds of this world ; and called evil forces from beyond. There is very good evidence that some of them got what they asked for.

Now a Catholic starts with all this realistic experience of humanity and history. A Spiritualist generally starts with the recent nineteenth-century optimism, in which his creed was born, which vaguely assumes that if there is anything spiritual, it is happier, higher, lovelier and loftier than anything we yet know ; and so opens all the doors and windows for the spiritual world to flow in. But we think this is just as simple an ignorance as if an eighteenth-century sentimentalist, reading into Rousseau a notion that savage man is like Adam in Eden, had gone to live in the Cannibal Islands to be surrounded with happiness and virtue. He would be surrounded, perhaps, but in a more bodily and unpleasant sense. One sentimental fashion may assume there are no cannibals ; another optimistic fashion that there are no devil-worshippers—or no devils. But there are. That is the fact of experience that is the key to many mysteries, including the mysterious policy of the Roman Catholic Church.

GIOTTO AND ST. FRANCIS

ST. FRANCIS of Assisi has been for ages a popular saint; in our own age he has for the first time been in some danger of being a fashionable saint. That sort of distinction of the drawing-rooms, which is said to have been a temptation rejected by many saints in their lifetime, which is certainly a peril besetting most popular preachers all their lives, has come at last to this popular preacher six hundred years after his death. It is natural that artists should be interested in the poet who was practically the founder of medieval and therefore of modern art. And it is only too true that, wherever we admit the artist, it is very difficult to exclude the æsthete. This sort of light literary fuss, though often sincere as a sentiment and even valuable as a tribute, is the very opposite of that sort of solid and traditional popularity which St. Francis had among countless generations of peasants. There is something about peasant traditions, and even about peasant legends, which knows how to keep close to the earth. It is a mark of true folklore that even the tale that is evidently wild is eminently sane. We see this in the most extravagant stories of the saints, if we compare them with the extravagant theories of the sophists and the sentimentalists. Take, for instance, that most beautiful attribute for which St. Francis is rightly loved throughout the modern world : his tenderness towards the lower animals. It is illustrated in medieval folklore by fancies but not by fads. It is impossible to imagine any fable more fabulous, in the sense of fantastic and frankly incredible, than the story of St. Francis making a business bargain with a very large and dangerous wolf ; drawing up a legal document with carefully numbered promises and concessions from the party of the first part and the party of the second part; the wild beast solemnly lodging a legal affidavit by the number of times he nodded his head. And yet there is in that fairy-tale a rustic and realistic sagacity that comes from real relations with animals, and is therefore perhaps called by the picturesque name of horse-sense. It was not written by the modern monomaniac animal-worshipper. It is a pleasant story because the saint is considering the peasants as well as the wolf. St. Francis was not the sort of man to agree with the hypothetical Hindoo who would be slowly devoured by a Bengal tiger, and remain in a state of philosophical absent-mindedness, because tigers are quite as cosmic as Hindoos. The Christian common sense of St. Francis, even in this wild fable, seized on the vital fact; that men must be saved from wolves as well as wolves from hunger, or even more so, and that this could only be done by some sort of definite arrangement. And it does put its finger upon the difficulty; in the absence of communication and therefore of contract between men and beasts. It realises that a moral obligation must be a mutual obligation. St. Francis contemplating the mountain wolf, hits on the same point as Job contemplating the monstrous Leviathan : " Will he make a pact with thee ? " That is a sort of solid popular instinct, which was never lost by the really popular saint, in spite of anything which strangers might stare at as his antics or his agonies. Men remembered that he had been a good friend to them as well as to birds and beasts ; and the fact is still apparent in the most remote and extravagant rumours of him. It is in this that he differs from some of the rather un-balanced and unnatural humanitarians of modern times. As a matter of fact, St. Francis does not by any means stand alone among medieval or other saints in this protest and protection of animals against men ; though he probably does stand alone in his poetical and imaginative power of stamping the memory of it in picturesque images on the popular mind. Some of the greatest medieval priests long before St. Francis, St. Anselm, for instance, were famous for demanding kindness to the brute creation; many of them, St. Hugh of Lincoln, for instance, had an even more eccentric taste in pets; for St. Hugh, instead of preaching to the birds, seems to have allowed a large bird to accompany him everywhere like a curate. But what is notable about this medieval theory of mercy is something ultimately mild and reasonable, however freakish was its expression; a comprehension of the common needs of common people, and a humanitarianism that did not exclude humanity. In that sense, it is the modern age that is the age of fanatics.

This fact of St. Francis becoming a modern fashion, after having been for so long a medieval tradition, might well arouse in his real admirers a fear of his cult becoming merely artistic in the sense of merely artificial. And yet, in spite of one or two incongruous interventions, this has not really taken place. It is perhaps the highest tribute to the truth and sincerity of St. Francis that even now he can keep his simplicity in the face of fashionable admiration; as the Franciscan in the story kept the fashionable crowd at a distance by playing antics on a seesaw. And this remarkable escape from the suffocation of sophistication is nowhere better expressed than in what still remains, even to the eye of the traveller—the naked nobility of his native town.

A traveller at all experienced in the ways of travellers, not to say of trippers, will approach the steep city of Assisi with some feelings of doubt and even of fear. He will know that the modern discovery of the medieval saint may yet be followed by disasters, more subtle than those which superstition has traced in the modern disinterment of the Egyptian king. He will know that there are things to which guide-books are not the best guides; which are seen better by solitary pilgrims than by sociable tourists; and, without any sort of superiority let alone misanthropy, he will have had experience already of places which crowds of visitors have made less worth visiting. He will know that quarrels not untouched by quackeries have insulted the great silence of Glastonbury; he will know that there is some truth in the report that a bustle of sight-seeing and a bawling for baksheesh has spoiled for many the spiritual adventure of Jerusalem. Knowing how many aimless æsthetes, how many irresponsible intellectuals, how many mere sheep of show and fashion follow this track through Italy, he may well fear to find obliterated the ancient simplicity of Assisi. But when he sees it, if I may answer for at least one among many such travellers, he will receive what I can only describe as a cool shock of consolation.

The city is founded upon a rock; the city is a rock; and it is too simple for anybody to spoil. It has proved practically impossible to paint or gild or pad or upholster or even to scratch that rock. In the main lines of it an austerity alone remains in the memory; and even the beauty of the milder landscape is itself austere. There may be, indeed there is, the usual accumulation in corners of the popular trinkets or traditional toys of devotion, which some people are so unfortunately fastidious as to resent; but that is not the sort of peril of which I am thinking, even from the point of view of those who would admit it to be in other ways perilous. It is not a question of any abuses among the ignorant or the innocent who look up to the saint; it is a question of the condescending culture that looks down to him; not a matter of importing idolatry into the institution of a patron saint; but a matter of patronising the patron. And though multitudes in this rather snobbish state of mind must have passed through

so established a station of the Italian pilgrimage, they have not
in fact left any trail behind them, as they have in so many
similar places ; the hills have forgotten them and their personalities have passed away with the smell of their petrol. St.
Francis is still left alone with his own friars and mostly with
his own friends ; and especially with that great first friend
who was his interpreter to the expanding civilisation that came
after him ; the friend who could express in images what Francis
himself had always felt as imagery, or what we call imagination;
the painter who translated the poet—Giotto.

The advance of art criticism is a continual retreat ; it would
seem in some strange manner destined to march perpetually
backwards into older and older periods. At the beginning of
the nineteenth century the critics had finally accepted the
normality of the Ancient Greeks. By the end of the nineteenth
century the critics were already inaugurating the novelty of the
Ancient Egyptians. We must all, by this time, be familiar with
expressions of admiration for the art of the Caveman, scrawled
in rock and red ochre with an unmistakable spirit and even
distinction of draughtsmanship ; the cult of the prehistoric
which has given a new meaning to the cult of the Primitives.
It will soon seem perfectly natural to be talking about the
modernised and decadent sophistication of the Second Stone
Age as compared with the rich but well-balanced civilisation of
the First Stone Age. The further we go back to explore, the
more we find that is really worth exploring ; and the nearer we
are to the real primitive man, the further we are from the ape
or even the savage. This being true even of the tremendous
scope of the whole history of the human tribe, it is not to be
wondered at that men have made the same discovery about the
high and complex culture of Christendom. The spotlight of
artistic interest and concentration has been steadily travelling
backwards ever since I was a child. I can remember faintly

that in my first years it was still felt as something of a paradox to maintain that the quaintness of Botticelli could be taken as seriously as the solid finish of Guido Reni ; that Ruskin was still a revolutionist for preferring the dayspring of the Renaissance in the fourteenth century to the dregs of the Renaissance in the eighteenth. Even as late as that, for most people, Giotto was still not so much a Primitive as a primitive man. He was a sort of savage who had done some service by discovering that it was possible to scratch something resembling a rudimentary human figure on the walls of his cave. For most people all serious art still lay between Raphael and Reynolds. As I grew up, the Ruskinian revolution prevailed, and most men came to realise that Giotto was a great painter ; but even those men generally regarded him as the first great painter. But now, in yet more recent times, the artists are yet more like archæologists, in the sense of going back to what is yet more archaic. The change that has passed over the most recent phase of art criticism can be sufficiently suggested by this one case of Giotto. I referred somewhere, in the Ruskinian manner, to Giotto as the figure who stands at the beginning of Christian art. One of the most creative of modern sculptors, whom many would call a medievalist, wrote to assure me that Giotto stands at the end of Christian art ; with something like a broad hint that Giotto brought it to an end.

The spotlight has moved further back, and is now illuminating what even Ruskin and the romantic medievalists would have regarded as a desert of dead and barbaric formalism ; the true Dark Ages. Our progressives are now bound with golden chains to the decline of Byzantium, rather than to the rise of Florence. It is quaint to think how little harm a blundering nickname need do in the long run. All the admirers of Gothic call it Gothic, though it was originally meant to stamp it as barbaric. And all the admirers of Byzantine call it

The Common Man

Byzantine; though the very adjective is already in use as a symbol of stiff degradation and decline. The new theories about rhythm and design have done justice to the old pictures which the romantics regarded merely as diagrams or patterns. The change from Cimabue to Giotto is at least not so certainly an unmixed improvement as it appeared to the Victorian medievalists. There is, as it were, a new school of Pre-Raphaelites, who are not only pre-Raphael, but pre-Giotto. The shining figure of the shepherd no longer stands against a background of black and barbarous darkness; but in a sort of double light, in itself involving some of these subtler problems of balance and recurrence; having on his right hand the wide white daybreak of Rome and Assisi and Paris and all the West, and on his left the long and gorgeous golden sunset of the great city of Constantine.

But in truth this double light may make for a better enlightenment, both about Giotto and his master St. Francis. The two artistic movements, coming one after the other, have between them done some justice to two halves of medieval history, and an earlier and a later period of Christendom, both of which had been underrated and misunderstood. There is a sort of mathematical beauty in the harshness of Byzantine art which is only beginning to be understood; but there is none the less another and livelier kind of beauty in the more humanised art of the later Middle Ages; something suggestive of a moment when a dead design comes to life, or a pattern begins to move, or even to dance. Some humorist wrote a work called "The Loves of the Triangle", and a mystical theologian might find in it a profound significance touching the loves of the Trinity. In other words, the old abstract expression of divine beauty was the expression of a truth, but the other truth of its expression in the concrete was none the less true. Now what is true of the early abstract art and the

Giotto and St. Francis

humanistic revolution of Giotto, is equally true of the abstract theology and the humanistic revolution of Francis. Some modern writers on the first Franciscans talk as if Francis was the first to invent the idea of the Love of God and the God of Love; or at least was the first to go back and find it in the Gospels. The truth is that anybody could find it in any of the creeds and doctrinal definitions of any period between the Gospels and the Franciscan movement. But he would find it in the theological dogmas as he would find it in the Byzantine pictures, drawn out in stark and simple lines like a mathematical diagram, asserted with a sort of dark clarity for those who can appreciate the idea of logical content and balance. In the sermons of St. Francis, as in the pictures of Giotto, it is made popular by pantomime. Men are beginning to act it as in a theatre, instead of representing it as in a picture or a pattern. Thus we find that St. Francis was in many ways the actual founder of the medieval miracle play; and there is all this suggestion of a stiff thing coming to life in the tale of his contact with the Bambino, illustrated in one of Giotto's designs. And thus we find in Giotto himself a quality unique and hardly to be repeated in history. It is a sense, not only of movement, but of the first movement. There is still something in his figures that suggests that they are like the pillars of a church moved by the spiritual earthquake of a divine visitation, but even so moved slowly and with a sort of reluctant grandeur. The figures are still partly architectural while the faces are alive with portraiture. This first moment of motion has much to do with that sense of morning and youth which so many admirers of medievalism have felt, and which I shall continue to feel, with all respect to the medievalist sculptor. Nothing is nearer to the nerve of primal wonder, which is the soul of all the arts, than that strange saying of the blind man in the Gospels, that when he was half awakened to sight, he saw " men as trees walking." There is something about the figures of Giotto that suggests men as trees walking. The Byzantine School will not permit me to say that before his eyes were thus opened, the artist had been wholly blind. But I will still maintain that there was something like a miracle, in the transition from treating trees as tracery and men as trees, to the realisation of the new shock of liberation ; and how, at the word of God, they could arise and walk.

And here again we strike the parallel between the artist and the saint. The followers of St. Francis were, above all things, men who could walk. Many of them even walked with that sort of dazed unfamiliarity and doubtful balance, being suddenly robbed by a whirlwind of all the props of property. But they walked, because a new spirit of walking, and even of wandering, had entered into the static scheme of medieval Christianity ; just as a new spirit of gesture and drama had entered into the static scheme of decorative art. The difference between the Friars and the Monks was, after all, that the Friars now walked like men where the Monks had once stood like statues. I mean nothing but admiration for the Benedictine monks, as for the Byzantine mosaics : or, for that matter, the grand and almost grim rationality of the great abstract dogmas. But there had come upon these flat and spacious things, carved in stone or ordered like statues, a new depth or dimension ; a new quality of drama and motion. The popular propaganda of St. Francis, throwing thousands of wandering friars out into roads of the world, was the beginning of what we call the modern spirit ; the spirit of romance and experiment and earthly adventure. For once a modern phrase which is much misused, may be rightly used. The Benedictines were, in the exact sense, an Order ; as the plan of a cathedral is an Order. The Franciscans were, in the exact sense, a movement. Historically, perhaps, the most interesting

Giotto and St. Francis

of the great pictures by Giotto which are displayed in the Upper Church of Assisi, is that which commemorates the famous dream of the great Pope Innocent the Third; in which he saw the strange beggar, from whom he had almost turned away in the street, upholding the whole toppling load of St. John Lateran, and indeed, in a larger symbolism, the whole load of St. Peter and the Church founded on a rock. More than one historian has suggested that, humanly speaking, it was St. Francis who prevented all Christendom from coming to an end under the double destructive drive and drag of Islam without and the pessimist heresies within. This particular picture is also worth noting, as a perfect example of that solidity which marked the simplicity of the medieval mind. Modern writers have referred often enough to medieval dreams and dark clouds and dim mystical fancies. But in fact the medievals never dealt in these things, even where they would have been justified in dealing in them. There is scarcely any modern of any school, who could deliberately draw a picture of a vision in the watches of the night, especially a vision so very visionary, so transcendental and so tremendously symbolic, as that of an unknown saint upholding a universal church, without bringing into the picture some shadow of unreality, or remoteness, of a lurid halo of the preternatural; at least of mystery and the tints of twilight. But the medieval dream is more solid than the modern reality. The medieval artist has dealt with it with a directness which belongs to the vigorous realism of innocence and of childhood; the sort of actuality which has been wholly untouched by the many sorts of scepticism which masquerade as mysticism. The dream is full of something very extraordinary; something which did indeed, for those who can understand it, shine on the evil and the good throughout the epoch that we call the Dark Ages: broad daylight.

The Common Man

In another sense, however, the spirit illuminating these great medieval designs is not so much generally the spirit of daylight as in a rather curious and peculiar sense, the spirit of daybreak. Of that highly medieval design it is true to say something of what Keats said of the highly classical design of his Grecian Urn. It is a sort of immortal moment of morning, and that which is a mere transition in time fixed as an absolute for eternity. We are so accustomed, in modern times, to think in terms of what we call progress, that we seldom admit, except in a poetical parenthesis, that there is such a thing as a perfect moment which is better than what comes after, as well as better than what went before. Yet it might well be maintained that art in all its history had no better moment, either before or after, than this in which all that was good in the old framework and formalism still remained with the upstanding strength of a great building, but in which there had already entered that rush of life and growth, which had turned it into something like a forest, without having as yet turned it into anything like a jungle. The naturalistic spirit of the nineteenth century, when it first began to understand the genius of Giotto or St. Francis, as interpreted by the talent of Ruskin or of Renan, was bound to fasten especially on the fanciful and charming episode of the Sermon to the Birds. For that generation was less concerned about the preservation of churches and more about the preservation of birds, even if it were in the equivocal sense of the preservation of game. It would be easy to illustrate the whole development, we might even say, the whole ascent and descent, under the emblem or example of the bird. The birds of the primal and symbolic epoch were simplified and somewhat terrible : as in the Eagle of the Apocalypse or the Dove of the Holy Ghost. All other birds in the Byzantine scheme would have been as abstract and typical as the birds of an Egyptian hieroglyphic. The birds

Giotto and St. Francis

of the later realistic epoch, when the painters of the nineteenth century had brought to the last perfection, or the last satiety, the studies of optics or of physics begun in the sixteenth, might well have been a most detailed and even bewildering display of ornithology. But the birds to whom St. Francis preached, in the vision of the thirteenth-century art, were already birds that could fly and sing, but not yet birds that could be shot or stuffed; they had ceased to be merely heraldic without becoming merely scientific. And as, in all studies of St. Francis, we always return to that great comparison which he at once denied with all his humility and desired with all his heart, we may say that they were not wholly unlike those strange birds in the legend, which the Holy Child pinched into shape out of scraps of clay, and then started into life and swiftness with a clap of His little hands.

THE NEW GROOVE

THE POET Tennyson, like a true Victorian, must have written a good many of his poems in the train; travelling by railroad being the chief invention and institution of his age. Indeed he confesses to have written the poem of Lady Godiva while waiting for the train; and to judge by the careful construction of the blank verse the train must have been very late. But there are other Tennysonian lines which Tennyson would seem to have written while he was asleep in the train. They have that peculiar mixture of jumble and jingle familiar to those who go to sleep in trains and only feel the metallic rhythm of the wheels mingling with the most shapeless and senseless dreams. It was at some such moment of profound slumber that Lord Tennyson composed the more progressive and prophetic portions of *Locksley Hall*; and this is clearly proved by the convincing, nay, damning, fact that one of the lines does really and truly run:

Let the great world spin for ever down the ringing grooves of change.

Psychologists will be interested in the curious displacement of words and disorder of ideas, which is characteristic of sentences invented in a dream. To the ordinary waking intelligence the words would appear to have no meaning. Grooves do not change; they do not necessarily ring; they do not even ring the changes. But, just as a sleeper in a railway-carriage will murmur, in the shock of awakening, some sentence betraying a secret he would probably have concealed

The New Groove

if awake; as that he is travelling first-class with a third-class ticket, or that the corpse of a creditor is concealed under the seat—so Tennyson, in this very extraordinary line of verse, did really betray the secret, and even the crime, of his own intellectual world and most of the world that has come after it.

For what is the matter with most of what calls itself the modern mind is simply grooves; and our habit of being content in the grooves, because we are told that they are grooves of change. And it is, as I say, a revealing fact that even when the modern poet wishes to describe change, even when he wishes to glorify change, he does still instinctively describe it as a groove. This is a mark that has been left on very much of the modern world, ever since the beginning of the mechanical and industrial epoch. But it had its first and clearest form in this fixed conception of travelling by rail. It may be specially noted that we speak of the modern mind being in a groove rather than in a rut. A rut was a term commonly used of a cart-track; in the simple times when we did not put the cart before the horse. When a living thing went before us there was something of doubt or adventure or hesitation in the tracks it made for itself, even if they became grooves for others. There were strange curves in his course who hitched his wagon even to a horse, and who had not yet given up horses for horse-power. There were sometimes very wild and fantastic tracks in his, who hitched his wagon to a star. But, apart from all such figures or fancies, the essential pecularity of the groove is that there can be nothing new about it except that it may take us to new places, or possibly take us *past* new places, at an entirely new rate of speed. That is the essential of what I mean by the modern groovings; that its only form of progress is going quicker and quicker along one line in one direction. It has not the curiosity to stop, nor the adventurous courage to go backwards.

The Common Man

Let us take, for the sake of clarity, this familiar case of the railway-train. A history of the locomotive steam-engine has often been presented in all its stages of improvement; the evolution of the modern train from the first clumsy models of Puffing Billy. But the engine did not produce anything but faster and faster engines; and the vital point is that nobody ever expected that it would. Nobody, even in a flight of fancy, wondered whether it would develop in any other direction, except the direction of its own groove. For instance, nobody ever suggested that it might develop its own type of architecture, so that the building of cars or carriages should be like the building of temples or town-halls. Yet there might perfectly well have been four or five schools of architecture for the designing of trains, as there are for the designing of temples. It would be a pleasing fancy if the architectural style of the train varied according to the country it was crossing or visiting. The Pennsylvania Railway Station in New York is a noble and serious piece of architecture; and it is really a sort of salute to the great city of Philadelphia towards which its gates are set. It might quite well have fallen out that what was done for the station could be done for the steam-engine; and the very design and colour of the vehicle vary according to whether it was going to the old French cities or the Red Indian plains; to the snows of Alaska or the orange-groves of Florida. Indeed I think there would have been much poetic symbolism in a hundred forms, probably guarded by rituals and dedicated to gods or patron saints, if it had so happened that the steam-engine was discovered by ancient Greeks or medieval Christians, and not by the Philistines of the Victorian time. But the point is here that nobody ever thought of such things; and certainly nobody thought of testing the progress of the train by such tests. There was only one test of the train and that was the test of the groove; of the smoothness of the groove; of the straightness of the groove; of the swiftness with which it travelled along the groove. There was something, in the tone of the whole thing, that prevented even mere fancy from breaking away in any other direction; or wondering, even vainly, if it could ever carry a castle like an elephant or a figurehead like a ship.

Now, in spite of the wildest claims to independence, the intellectual life of today still strikes me as being mainly symbolised by the train or the track or the groove. There is any amount of fuss and vivacity about certain fixed fashions or directions of thought; just as there is any amount of rapidity along the fixed rails of the railway-track. But if we begin to think about really getting off the track, we shall find that what is true of the train is equally true of the truth. We shall find it is actually harder to get out of the groove, when the train is going fast, than when the train is going slowly. We shall find that rapidity is rigidity; that the very fact of some social or political or artistic movement going quicker and quicker means that fewer people have the courage to move against it. And at last perhaps nobody will make a leap for real intellectual liberty, just as nobody will jump out of a railway-train going at eighty miles an hour. This seems to me the primary mark of what we call progressive thought in the modern world. It is in the most exact sense of the term limited. It is all in one dimension. It is all in one direction. It is limited by its progress. It is limited by its speed.

I have said that it has not the curiosity to stop. If the train-dwellers were really travellers, exploring a strange country to make discoveries, they would always be stopping at little wayside stations. For instance, they would always be stopping to consider the curious nature of their own conventional terms; a thing which they never do, by any chance.

Their catchwords are regarded solely as gadgets or appliances for getting them where they are going to ; they never cast back a thought upon where the catchword comes from. Yet that is exactly what they would do if they were really thinking, in any thorough and all-round sense. Of course it will be understood, touching these intellectual fashions, that great masses, probably the mass of mankind, never travel on the train at all. They remain in their villages and are much, happier and better ; but they are not regarded as the intellectual leaders of the time. What I complain of is that the intellectual leaders can only lead along one narrow track ; otherwise known as " the ringing groove of change ". Take, in this matter of current phrases, the example of the controversy about advanced and futuristic art. I do not mean to consider the art but to consider the controversy ; as illustrating what has been said about the advisability of stopping and the stupidity of the non-stop train.

Now although, of course, the actual masses are quite unconverted to Picasso or Epstein, yet the terms of controversy, the only tags of argument known to the newspapers, the only familiar and almost popular sophistries outside mere popular abuse, are on the side of the new schools. I mean that modern men are not familiar with the rational arguments for tradition ; but they are familiar, and almost wearily familiar, with the rational arguments for change. Whichever side may be really right in the question of art (which obviously depends largely on the particular artists), the whole modern world is verbally prepared to regard the new artist as right and the old artist as wrong. It is prepared to do so by the whole progressive philosophy ; which is often rather a phraseology than a philosophy. The language which comes most readily to everyone's mind is the language of innovation ; but it is a language that is rather exercised than examined. For

The New Groove

instance, it is probable that more people are even now acquainted with the poems of Mr. W. B. Yeats than with the poems of Miss Edith Sitwell. But many, many more people understand what Miss Sitwell means, when she simply says that she is criticised in her day as Keats was criticised in his day, than could possibly understand what Mr. Yeats means, when he says that nothing quite new can be used in poetry ; or that innocence is only born out of ceremony and custom. For the former argument is a familiar argument of all modern progressives and reformers ; the latter sayings are very profound sayings of a man who really thinks for himself. I agree that in many other things, and especially in the best examples of her poetry, Miss Sitwell also can think for herself. I only say that this particular argument (" John the Baptist was laughed at and I am laughed at " ; " Galileo was disbelieved and I am disbelieved ")—this particular argument is part of the regular recognised bag of tricks of reformers and revolutionists ; it is a part of the very old apparatus of the New Movement. Now if we apply this, for instance, to the quarrels about painting or sculpture we shall find the same situation : that, whichever side is right, the whole apparatus of modern talk favours the idea that the new thing is always right. There are a definite selection of phrases used, but not often examined. For instance, should any Philistine faintly protest against Helen of Troy being sculptured with a head of the exact shape of the Great Pyramid, or Titania with a figure following the grand simple lines of the hippopotamus at the zoo, or even perhaps his own favourite daughter presenting herself to the public in the appealing and even touching condition of having her nose and eyelids cut off—whenever such a criticism is heard, whether it be right or wrong, it will be answered with the precision of clockwork, by a phrase to the effect that some people want art to be " pretty-pretty ". Now the first act of any independent mind will be to criticise this criticism; and especially to feel a curiosity about the curious form of it. Why does everybody say, " pretty-pretty "? Why not say that some people do not like what is " ugly-ugly ", or possibly what is " beastly-beastly "? What is the meaning of this weird repetition, like a recurring decimal? If you have the sort of independent curiosity that stops at wayside stations, if (in short) you are not merely in a hurry to get to the fashionable terminus, you may well pause upon a phrase like that, not without profit. You will perceive that the phrase is, in fact, a rather pathetic attempt to reproduce the wondering exclamation of a child. And that would be alone enough to destroy the argument. For a child has a very sound sense of wonder at what is really wonderful; and by no means merely a vulgar and varnished taste in what is conventionally beautiful. The thing that a genuine child might call " pretty-pretty " is not the soapy portrait of a débutante or an upholstered group of a royal family; it is much more likely to be a flash of red fire or the strong colours of a great garden flower or something that really is elemental and essential; something in its way quite as " stark " (as our dear friends would say) as the Great Pyramid or the great pachyderm. Children are not snobs in art any more than in morals. And if they often have also a pleasure in things that are really " pretty ", in the sense of a graceful girl by Greuze or a cloud of pink blossom in spring, it is simply because there is a perfectly legitimate place in art for what is pretty; and it is not in the least disposed of by jabbering the same word twice over and calling it " pretty-pretty ". Anyhow, the more supercilious moderns make a bad blunder in imputing childishness in defence of some things that could only be defended as being in the higher sense childish. It was Cezanne himself who said, " I am trying to recover the direct vision of a child."

The New Groove

It is the same with all the cant phrases already in circulation, for the purpose of defending any eccentricity, even before it exists. Thus everybody is familiar with the phrase that art is not photography, and that only photography is required to be realistic. Everybody is familiar with the phrase, and nobody is familiar with the holes or errors in the phrase. As a matter of fact nothing is less realistic than photography. At the very start it is cut away from all reality exactly as marble sculpture is cut away from reality, by being conventionally colourless ; by divorcing the great optical union of colour and form. But it is not really realistic even about form. The thing it does reproduce more or less realistically is light and shade, and the light often falsifies the form and always falsifies the colour. If we want true form it must be drawn for us more or less abstractedly by a draughtsman ; and when it is so drawn by Leonardo or Michelangelo, it cannot be dismissed as photographic, any more than as " pretty-pretty ". The modern artist may have his own reasons for drawing legs as if they were bolsters or sausages ; but that does not make the strong sweeping lines, of sloping bone or gripping muscle, in a great Florentine drawing, a dull mechanical reproduction, valuable only as the vulgar snapshot of a trivial fact. Those lines are strong and beautiful, as the lines of waterfall and whirlpool are beautiful. In fact, they are exactly like the beautiful abstract forms, which the modern artist would like to invent—if he could.

I have taken only this one type, of the talk about new schools of art, to illustrate what I mean by saying that the world is in such a hurry to be new that it does not even pause upon the truths of the new school, let alone of the old. Of the million men and women who have heard those two phrases, how many have heard any phrases out of the opposite phraseology and philosophy ? I mean any which offer a philosophical defence of the other philosophy ? Of all those who have been told (somewhat needlessly) that Epstein does not profess to be pretty, how many have heard that case for civilisation, in which its very strength is shown in being able to rear and poise and protect prettiness ? The very cyclopean massiveness of the foundations of the city is best proved in the fact that no earthquake can shake the ivory statuette upon the pedestal or the china shepherdess upon the shelf. How many have considered the more ancient argument, of a culture that is sufficiently athletic to be elegant ? Or, to take another example, how many have understood the scientific and psychological arguments for antiquity itself ? Of all those who can recall being told to admire a modern picture, merely because it is even more unlike life than a photograph, or being told to admire modern poetry, for no reason whatever except that it is more prosaic than slang—of all those, how many even remember the sound remark made long ago by Oliver Wendell Holmes ; that the grand Latin poets actually grow grander by being quoted again and again ; that the words actually grow together with time, as do the sections of a seasoned violin ? I am not saying that the truth is all on the side of tradition ; I am only saying that the publicity is all on the side of innovation. Until the recent rise of the Humanist group in America, hardly anybody, even of the educated classes, possessed even the vocabulary for a defence of tradition. The very words in use, the very structure of the sentences, the ordinary tone of the whole public Press, prevented me from using the real and reasonable arguments against mere novelty. England, strangely enough, has even less of a working Humanist vocabulary than America. Here also working journalistic ethics have been too much cut down and simplified to a few crude ideas, of commercial activity or continuous reform. I shall be completely misunderstood if I am supposed to be calling for a return

ticket to Athens or to Eden; because I do not want to go on
by the cheap train to Utopia. I want to go where I like. I
want to stop where I like. I want to know the width as well
as the length of the world; and to wander off the railway-
track in the ancient plains of liberty.

THE REAL DR. JOHNSON

IT IS possible that there are still people in England who do not adore Dr. Johnson. These persons must be removed, if possible, by persuasion. A short and plain attempt to persuade them must take precedence of subtler questions in every discussion of the great man. Now this old and superficial misunderstanding of Johnson (now nearly extinct) expresses itself in two main popular notions—that he was pedantic and that he was rude. He occasionally was rude ; he never was pedantic. He was probably the most unpedantic man that ever lived ; certainly you and I are much more pedantic than Dr. Johnson. For pedantry means the worship of dead words ; and his words, whether long or short, were always alive. He played long words and short words against each other with impromptu but infallible art. I am far from books, and I quote from memory, but I think that a Scotchman, vexed at the ritual jeers of Johnson against his country, said : " Do you remember that God made Scotland ? " Johnson replied promptly : " Sir, you are to remember that he made it for Scotchmen." Then, after a pause, he said in grave meditation : " Comparisons are odious ; but God made hell." Now the vague popular opinion of Johnson would concentrate on long words like " comparisons " and " odious ", and retain the impression that he was pedantic. It would be just as easy to concentrate on words like " hell " and give the impression that he was vulgar. The only true way of testing the matter is to look at the whole sentence and ask oneself if there is a single word, long or short, out of its place. Johnson was the reverse of pedantic, for he used long words only where they would be effective. Generally it came to this, that he spoke pompously when Boswell spoke flippantly and flippantly when Boswell spoke pompously—a very sound rule. When Boswell confronted him with the brute facts of a lonely tower and a baby, he answered, with distant dignity : " Sir, I should not much like my company." But when Boswell justified some morally backsliding bishop or vicar with that elaborate hash of sophistry and charity which is still used to excuse the rich, Johnson answered him with a few short words, so full of Christianity and common sense that I should not be allowed to print them.

The charge of rudeness is much more real ; but about this also an impression still surviving requires a great deal of correction. Taken in conjunction with the charge of pedantry, it has created the image of a bullying schoolmaster, a superior person who thinks himself above good manners. Now Johnson was sometimes insolent, but he was never superior. He was not a despot, but exactly the reverse. It was his sense of the democracy of debate that made him loud and unscrupulous, like a mob. It was exactly because he thought the other men as clever as himself that he sought in desperate cases to bear them down by clamour. Everyone knows the brilliant description of him by one of his best friends : "If his pistol misses fire he knocks you down with the butt of it." But few realise that this is the act of a simple and heroic fellow fighting against a superior force. Johnson was a man of great animal impulsiveness and of irregular temper, but intellectually he was humble. He always went into every conflict with the idea that the other man was as good as he was, and that he might be defeated. His bellowings and bangings of the table were the expressions of a fundamental modesty. We can feel this element, I think, in everything he said, down to those last awful words upon his death-bed, when he spoke of Burke, the one man who had really excited and arrested him, "If I saw him now it would kill me." His fate in these respects has been strange. He has been called the pedant par excellence because he was the one thoroughly unpedantic person of a pedantic age. He has been called a conversational tyrant, because he was the one man of his mental rank who was ready to argue with his inferiors. On the one hand it is often said that he translated English into Johnsonese. But let it be remembered that he was the only man of his time who could translate Johnsonese back into English. Half a hundred critics in that age might have said of a play, "It does not possess sufficient vitality to preserve it from putrefaction", but only Johnson could have said also, "It has not wit enough to keep it sweet." There were numerous great men in the eighteenth century who kept a club or court of dependents, where they had things entirely their own way. I need not prove the point; the greatest satirist of that age has made the image immortal.

> Like Cato gave his little Senate laws,
> And sat attentive to his own applause.

But Johnson was the reverse of attentive to people who were applauding him. Johnson was furiously deaf to people who were contradicting him. So far from being a stately and condescending king like Atticus, Johnson was a kind of Irish member in his own Parliament. All these are but broken and incidental examples; everything about the man rang of reality and honour; he never thought he was right without being ready to give battle; he never thought he was wrong without being ready to ask pardon.

We have all heard enough to fill a book about Dr. Johnson's incivilities. I wish they would compile another book consisting of Dr. Johnson's apologies. There is no better test of a man's ultimate chivalry and integrity than how he behaves when he is wrong; and Johnson behaved very well. He understood (what so many faultlessly polite people do not understand) that a stiff apology is a second insult. He understood that the injured party does not want to be compensated because he has been wronged; he wants to be healed because he has been hurt. Boswell once complained to him in private, explaining that he did not mind asperities while they were alone, but did not like to be torn to pieces in company. He added some idle figure of speech, some simile so trivial that I cannot even remember what it was. " Sir," said Johnson, " that is one of the happiest similes I have ever heard." He did not waste time in formally withdrawing this word with reservations and that word with explanations. Finding that he had given pain, he went out of his way to give pleasure. If he had not known what would irritate Boswell, he knew at least what would soothe him. It is this gigantic realism in Johnson's kindness, the directness of his emotionalism, when he is emotional, that gives him his hold upon generations of living men. There is nothing elaborate about his ethics; he wants to know whether a man, as a fact, is happy or unhappy, is lying or telling the truth. He may seem to be hammering at the brain through long nights of noise and thunder, but he can walk into the heart without knocking.

RABELAISIAN REGRETS

THERE has arisen in our time an extraordinary notion that there is something humane, open-hearted or generous about refusing to define one's creed. Obviously the very opposite is the truth. Refusing to define a creed is not only not generous, it is distinctly mean. It fails in frankness and fraternity towards the enemy. It is fighting without a flag or a declaration of war. It denies to the enemy the decent concessions of battle ; the right to know the policy and to treat with the headquarters. Modern " broadmindedness " has a quality that can only be called sneakish ; it endeavours to win without giving itself away, even after it has won. It desires to be victorious without betraying even the name of the victor. For all sane men have intellectual doctrines and fighting theories ; and if they will not put them on the table, it can only be because they wish to have the advantage of a fighting theory which cannot be fought.

In the things of conviction there is only one other thing besides a dogma, and that is a prejudice. If there is something in your life for which you will hold meetings and agitate and write letters to the newspaper, but for which you will not find the plain terms of a creed, then that thing is properly to be described as a prejudice, however new or noble or advanced it may seem to be. But indeed I think that when these ages are seen in proper perspective, men will say that the chief mark of the end of the nineteenth century and the beginning of the twentieth was the growth of vast and victorious prejudices. I give, in passing, some instances of what I mean. Thus, for instance, it is a brave and logical creed which declares, like

Rabelaisian Regrets

Mahomet and some modern Puritans, that the drinking of fermented liquor is really wrong. But the modern world has not adopted this clear creed and never will. What it has done has been to spread everywhere a strong but vague prejudice against certain forms of drinking, particularly those adopted by the poor. We have not made it wicked to drink ale, but we have made it slightly disreputable to go into a public-house. In other words, we have made it slightly disreputable, if you drink ale, to be poor or to be sociable. What it comes to is this : that any one wishing to sneer at me can get a laugh by saying I am a beer-drinker, but he will not commit himself to the statement that the thing that he has sneered at is wrong. He may hit me, because he is appealing to a prejudice ; but I may not hit him because he is not appealing to a creed. He will not set anything up for me to hit. He wants, somehow or other, to avoid calling liquor wrong and yet to call me wrong for touching liquor. This is not latitudinarianism ; it is ordinary human cowardice.

There are a great many other instances which could be given. For instance, fashionable opinion does not actually declare (as do, I believe, certain Eastern religions) that ablutions and bodily cleanliness are primary things, above even ordinary morals ; but it does create a loose popular impression that it has scored off a personality or a nation more by saying that it is dirty than by saying that it is avaricious or timid or unchaste. No new creed is preached about cleanliness, but a strong sentimental emphasis and partiality is attached to the thing, making it more important than other things. Of course cleanliness is only made so very important at present because it happens to be a thing quite easy for the rich and very difficult for the poor. My only concern here, however, is to point out the method by which it has been made important ; never by explaining or defining its importance, as in a creed ; always by assuming its importance, as in a prejudice. I have no space to go at length into other examples, but the reader can easily put the cases to himself; and he can employ this general test: that in the case of half the most typical movements of the last thirty years, nobody can say how or when they really began. In no barbaric twilight or tangled forest or confusion of the dark ages did huge forces ever come so silently or secretly into the world as they come to-day. No one knows or can name the real beginning of Imperialism or of the popularity of the Royal Family (a thing quite recent yet quite untraceable), or of the taking for granted, in so many minds, of the materialist philosophy or of the practical imposition of teetotalism as a discipline on the Nonconformist public ministry. These things come out of the night and are formless even when they are forming everything else.

But discussions on the subject of the Censor and other theatrical problems have brought before the public a supreme instance of what I mean. We have been asked for the hundredth time to find some solution of that problem of the combination in art of truth with sexual modesty; and the result of considering this has been that we find ourselves face to face with a profound and most important change in public opinion on this subject; a change that has been going on, perhaps, for the last twenty years, perhaps ever since the coming of the Puritans; but a change which is, at any rate, of the utmost import to the wholesomeness of ethics, and a change which has proceeded in the same powerful silence as the growth of a tree. It is this difference between new English and old English ethics in the matter of verbal delicacy of which I wish to speak here. The subject is difficult, it is even emotional and painful; and I think it will do no harm to begin with some of the general human principles of the problem, even if they are as old and obvious as the alphabet.

Rabelaisian Regrets

There is not really much difference of opinion among normal men about the first principles of decency in expression. All healthy men, ancient and modern, Western and Eastern, hold that there is in sex a fury that we cannot afford to inflame ; and that a certain mystery must attach to the instinct if it is to continue delicate and sane. There are people, indeed, who maintain that they would talk of this topic as coldly or openly as of any other ; there are people who maintain that they would walk naked down the street. But these people are not only insane people, they are in the most emphatic sense of the word stupid people. They do not think ; they only point (as children do) and say " Why ? " Even children only do it when they are tired ; but exactly this tired quality is most of what passes in our time not only for thought but for bold and disturbing thought. To ask, " Why cannot we discuss sex coolly and rationally anywhere ? " is a tired and unintelligent question. It is like asking, " Why does not a man walk on his hands as well as on his feet ? " It is silly. If a man walked systematically on his hands, they would not be hands, but feet. And if love or lust were things that we could all discuss without any possible emotion they would not be love or lust, they would be something else—some mechanical function or abstract natural duty which may or may not exist in animals or in angels, but which has nothing at all to do with the sexuality we are talking about. All the ideas of grasp or gesture, which to us make up the meaning of the word " hand ", depend upon the fact that hands are loose extremities used not for walking on but for waving about. And all that we mean when we speak of " sex " is involved in the fact that it is not an unconscious or innocent thing, but a special and violent emotional stimulation at once spiritual and physical. A man who asks us to have no emotion in sex is asking us to have no emotion in emotion. He has forgotten the subject-matter

with which he deals. He has lost the topic of the conversation.
It may be said of him, in the strict meaning of the words, that
he does not know what he is talking about.

And if men have never doubted that there should be a
decorum in such things, neither have they ever doubted that
that decorum might be carried much too far ; that courage and
laughter and wholesome truth might be sacrificed to the
proprieties. So far, I say, humanity is essentially unanimous.
It is in the discussion as to which thing shall be suppressed and
which permitted, in the selection of the more harmless from
the more harmful types of candour, that we begin to find the
difference between different civilisations and different religions
among men. And it is exactly upon the point of such a difference as this that I wish to speak here. Among other societies
and ages our own society and age has made a choice in this
matter. We have said, substantially by a general feeling, that
one kind of expression shall be allowed and another rendered
impossible. We have chosen, and I think we have chosen
wrong.

Before going deeper into this most difficult subject there
is at least one general statement to be made. The evil of
excess in this matter really consists of three quite separate
evils. Verbal impropriety or excess can spring from three
quite different motives, three quite different states of mind,
which have really very little to do with each other. It is
necessary to unpick these three strands before we go any
further. Ordinary popular discussion of the problem always
hopelessly mixes them up. Briefly, they may be stated thus :
impropriety arises either from a really vicious spirit, or from
the love of emphasis, or from the love of analysis.

The first can be dismissed with brevity and with relief.
There is such a thing as pornography ; as a system of deliberate erotic stimulants. That is not a thing to be argued about

with one's intellect, but to be stamped on with one's heel. But the point about it to be noted for our purpose is that this form of excess is separated from the other two by the fact that the motive of it *must* be bad. If a man tries to excite a sex instinct which is too strong already, and that in its meanest form, he *must* be a scoundrel. He is either taking money to degrade his kind or else he is acting on that mystical itch of the evil man to make others evil, which is the strangest secret in hell.

But when we come to the two motives of emphasis and of analysis, it is essential to observe that in both cases the motive may be beautiful, even when the result is most disastrous. The motive for impropriety arising out of emphasis can be best illustrated by a comparison with the habit of swearing. Swearing is, of course, the strongest possible argument for the religious view of life. A man cannot satisfactorily affirm anything about this world except by getting out of this world. The things commonly called fables are so true that they alone can give final ratification even to the things commonly called facts. A man in Balham cannot even call his dog a good dog without summoning to his aid either the angels or the devils. The Balhamite, like the Roman, if he cannot bend the gods will move Acheron ; but he never thinks of trying to move Balham. Religion is his only resort for purposes of real emphasis ; and often, even when he is attacking religion, his instinctive way of attacking it is to say that it is a damned lie. The most natural way of talking is the supernatural way of talking. And indeed this may be considered a good working test for all modern fads and philosophies which pretend to be religions. The new faiths founded on evolution or an impersonal ethic are always claiming that they also can produce holiness ; and no Christian has any right in Christian charity to deny that possibility. But if the question really is whether the things in question are religions in the sense that Christianity or Mohammedanism are religions, then I should suggest a different test. I should not ask whether they can produce holiness, but whether they can produce profanity. Can any one swear by ethics? Can any one blaspheme evolution? Many men now hold that a mere adoration of abstract morality or goodness is the core and sole necessity of religion. I know many of them; I know that their lives are noble, and their intellects just. But (I say it with respect and even hesitation) would not their oaths be a little mild? I do not mean that they ought to swear, or that anybody ought to swear, I mean that if it comes to swearing one can see in such a competition the vast difference in actuality between the new sham religion which talks about the holiness within, and an old practical religion which worshipped a real holiness without. You can see the difference in the weakness of the oaths considered as literature. The man of the Christian Churches said (occasionally), " Oh, my God! " The man of the ethical societies says (presumably), " Oh, my goodness! "

It is generally true, I say, that the whole circle of this physical universe does not contain anything strong enough for the purposes of a man who really means what he says; even about a small dog. Yet there is one exception to this generalisation. There is one thing which belongs to this world, but which is yet so fierce and startling, so full of menace and ecstasy, that it seems at times to partake of the character of miracle. This thing is the thing called sex; and on this also from time to time the man with the small dog in Balham will call in his dire need. Men used to swear by their heads; they still in a manner swear by their bodies. Sex is actual enough to swear by. To take but one coarse democratic test, people scribble about it on walls as they do about religion. Nobody ever scribbled on a wall about ethics. Above all, the language of sex can be used as a kind of violent invocation; a reinforce-

ment of common words by the strongest words. I will not
pause here to ask the reason of this ; whether saying " damn "
and saying other things unprintable have something to do with
the fact that sex is the great business of the body, and salvation the great business of the soul. It is enough to say that any
one can read the thing I mean and any one can hear it. He can
read the thing best perhaps in Aristophanes or in Rabelais. He
can hear the thing best in the street outside.

But though he can find it in the street outside, he cannot
find it in any of the books or newspapers sold in the street.
There is no law against indecent ideas ; but there is a quite
efficient and practical law against indecent words. Slowly
throughout the eighteenth century word after word was
dropped until by the Victorian time it was insisted that no
coarse phrases should be used even in defending coarseness.
I am myself under the limitations of this very local prejudice.
I am compelled to prove my case in many pages because I have
to talk as one talks in a respectable magazine. I could prove
my case in ten minutes if I could talk as two respectable
married men really talk on the top of an omnibus. It is
sufficient, however, to put the matter thus : When a navvy
uses what is called obscene language it is almost always to
express his righteous disgust at obscene conduct. And here
the navvy is at one with all the most really masculine poets or
romancers ; he is at one with Rabelais, with Swift, and even
with Browning. Browning uses a foul metaphor to express
the foulness of those who profess sympathy with human
sorrows merely out of their own morbidity. You can find
the phrase in " At the Mermaid." Browning uses the same
foul metaphor to express the foulness of those who cannot
understand a man's prompt grasp of the presence of a good
woman. You can find the phrase in the speech of Cappon-
sacchi. In short, the emphatic use of sexual language has this

great advantage that it is commonly used purely in the interests of virtue. The virtuous cabman may (and does) call a man a blank, in a state of furious and innocent horror at the idea of any one being a blank. But this is not true in the case of the third impulse to indecorum. The third impulse is that which I have called the analytical; the mere curiosity of the mind about how the relations of the sexes are to be considered and classified. This covers all that we now call the Problem Play, and all that we associate with the realistic and psychological novel, and all the millions of proposals for the rearrangement of marriage. The dialogue in *The Little Eyolf* horrified many people; but it did not contain a single coarse word. Mr. George Moore, Mr. Richard Le Gallienne, and the lady called "Victoria Cross" have in turn been accused of being needlessly daring; but not one of them dare use words straight out of Bunyan or the Bible. The analytic indecency is now more free than it ever was among free men. The emphatic indecency is more stifled than it ever was among free men; more stifled than it ever was among slaves.

I am not concerned here to deny that the modern fashion of analysing sex is in general a good thing. Certainly there is grossly too much hypocrisy about sex; not in the English people, but in the literature and journalism which the English people, for some incomprehensible reason, permit to speak for them. There is no hypocrisy on the top of an English omnibus; but I warmly agree that there is really too much hypocrisy in the front page of an English newspaper, or within the covers of an English book. Let us agree that Ibsen had a right to suggest that marriage is an unpleasant fact as well as a pleasant one; that as well as the more chivalrous side of sex which is exaggerated by the Victorian poets, there is also the realistic and scientific side of sex, which was exaggerated by the old monks. Let me concede altogether and at once the fact

Rabelaisian Regrets

that the modern tendency to dissect sex and to subdivide it, to put it into pigeon-holes, is a just and necessary measure. I will not even say here that the tendency has gone too far. But I will say this : what will you do if it does go too far ? Suppose you wake up some fine morning and find indecencies which are quite ludicrous being taken quite seriously. Suppose you find certain sins put in a pigeon-hole when they ought to be put in a dust-hole. Suppose that after twenty years of scientific study you find that you have all the dirty jokes back again, the only difference being that you must enjoy them without laughing at them. Suppose, in short, that you are confronted with the exasperating spectacle of people chewing sins, instead of spitting them out of their mouths like their fathers ; what will you do then ? How will you express your feelings if you are faced with that horrible fashion of taking sex seriously—of which the true name is Phallic Worship ? I know what you will do : you will call upon the shades of Rabelais and Fielding to deliver you out of that foul idolatry ; and perhaps the English people will answer you and speak. It is common enough to talk of the English people speaking ; but if ever they do speak they will speak as Rabelais spoke, and as English cabmen speak now.

THE HOUND OF HEAVEN

" THE Hound of Heaven ", the greatest religious poem of modern times and one of the greatest of all times, was produced under certain peculiar historical conditions, which accentuate its isolation. To begin with, the religious poem is a religious poem, not only in what we should call the real sense, but in what some would call the limited sense. The word " religion " is used in these days in an expansive or telescopic fashion, sometimes inevitable, sometimes nearly intolerable. It is used of various realms of emotion or spiritual speculation more or less lying on the borders of religion itself; it is applied to other things that have nothing to do with religion ; it is applied to some things that are almost identical with irreligion. But the line between legitimate and illegitimate expansion of a word is so difficult to draw, that there is little to be gained by questioning it except that mere quarrel about a word that is called logomachy. There always are some confusions about a definition or exceptions to a rule. The great principle that Pigs is Pigs does not dispose entirely of the existence of pig-iron, or of cannibals calling a man a long pig. We all know the plain practical man, the sceptic in the crowd, the atheist on the soap-box, who boasts that he calls a spade a spade, and generally calls it a spyde. But even he may have to deal with the learned and sophisticated man, who will prove to him, that even in the case of the ace of spades which he planks down in playing poker, the spade is not really a spade ; being derived from the Spanish *espada*, a sword. If once we begin to quibble and quarrel about what words ought to mean, or can be made to mean, we shall find ourselves in a mere world of words, most wearisome to those who are concerned with thoughts. For the latter it will be enough to realise that there certainly was and is a certain *thing*, to which our fathers found it more practical to attach and limit the name of religion; that they recognised that the thing had many forms, and that there were many religions; but that they were equally certain of what things were not religions, including much that modern moralists call a wider religious life. They recognised a Protestant religion and a Catholic religion, and probably thought one or other of them true; they recognised a Mohammedan religion, even if they thought it false; they recognised a Jewish religion, which had once been true and by a sort of treason had become false; and so on. But they did not recognise a religion of Humanity; or a " religion of the Life Force ": or a religion of creative evolution; or a religion which has the object of ultimately producing a god who does not yet exist. And the distinction is better preserved by noting these examples than by an attempt to fix the elusive evasions of the verbal sophists of today.

What we mean when we say that " The Hound of Heaven " is a real religious poem is simply that it would make no sense if we supposed it to refer to any of these modern abstractions, or to anything but a personal Creator in relation to a personal creature. It may be, and indeed is, a generous and charitable mood to look out on all the multitudes of men with sympathy and social loyalty. But it was not the multitudes of men that were pursuing the hero of this poem " down the nights and down the days ". It may be a good thing for men to look forward to mankind someday producing a superior being, thousands of years hence, who will be like a god compared with the common mass of men. But it was not some superior person born a thousand years hence, who drove the sinner in this story from refuge to refuge. He was not running away

from the Life Force, from a mere summary of all natural
vitality, which would be expressed equally in the pursued or
the pursuer. For it requires quite as much Life Force to run
away from anybody as to run after anybody. He was not
swiftly escaping from a slow adaptive process called evolution,
like a man pursued by a snail. He was not alarmed at a gradual
biological transformation, by which a Hound of Heaven
might be evolved out of a Hound of Hell. He was dealing
with the direct individual relations of God and Man, and the
story would be absolutely senseless to anybody who thought
that the service of Man is a substitute for the service of God.
This is where the practical habit of speech, among our religious
ancestors of all religions, proves its validity and veracity.
Francis Thompson was a Catholic, and a very Catholic
Catholic. In some aspects of art, poetry and pomp, the Catholic
is more akin to the pagan; in some aspects of philosophy and
logic (though this is little understood), he has more sympathy
with the sceptic or the agnostic. But in the solid central fact
of the subject or subject-matter he is still something utterly
separate from sceptics and even from pagans; and all Christians
have their part in him. A perfectly simple and straightforward
member of the Salvation Army knows what " The Hound of
Heaven " is about, even if he knows it better without reading
it, and would recognise its central theology as promptly as
the Pope. But the mere humanist, the mere humanitarian, the
universal aesthete, the patroniser of all religions, he will never
know what it is about, for he has never been near enough to
God to run away from Him.

Now the next point of interest is that this poem of purely
personal religion, so directly devotional, so dogmatically
orthodox, appeared at a time when it might least be expected,
and at the end of an historical process that might have seemed
to make it impossible. The nineteenth century had been, at

least on the surface, one triumphal procession of progress, away from these theological relations, which were accounted narrow, towards ideals of brotherhood or natural living which seemed to be more and more broad. We might say that the poets had led the procession, for even at the beginning of the nineteenth century Shelley and Landor and Byron and Keats had moved in various ways towards a pantheistic paganism; and the tendency was continued by Victor Hugo in Europe and by Walt Whitman in America. There were, of course, continual cross-currents and confusions. Even an appeal to pantheism is something like an appeal to theism, and it was difficult to imitate the pagans without discovering, like St. Paul, that they were very religious. The contradiction came out quaintly in the case of Swinburne, who was always trying to prove that he was an atheist by invoking about ten different gods in a style exactly copied from the Old Testament.

Roughly speaking, however, I myself remember fairly well the curious cultural conditions in which the genius of Francis Thompson arose; for, though I was a boy at the time, a boy can sometimes absorb the atmosphere of a society, with the same subtle subconscious instinct with which a child can absorb the atmosphere of a house. I read all the minor poets; and it was specially an age of minor poets. The curious thing is that Francis Thompson was considered, criticised, appreciated or admired as one of the minor poets. I can remember Mr. Richard Le Gallienne, who is one of the survivors of that epoch, defending himself with spirit, but with a certain air of audacity, against the charge of fulsome exaggeration in saying that there was in the poems of this Mr. Thompson an Elizabethan richness and sometimes almost a Shakespearian splendour. Mr. Le Gallienne was quite right; but the main point is that his defence was a general defence of minor poets, and of this poet as a minor poet. It had hardly occurred to

The Common Man

the world in general that Francis Thompson was a major poet; we might almost say a major prophet. There was in all that world of culture an atmosphere of paganism that had worn rather thin. But hardly anybody thought that the future of poetry could be anything but a future of paganism. It was then, in the slowly deepening silence, as in the poem of Coventry Patmore, that there was first heard, afar off, the baying of a hound.

That is the primary point about the work of Francis Thompson; even before its many-coloured pageant of images and words. The awakening of the *domini canes*, the Dogs of God, meant that the hunt was up once more; the hunt for the souls of men; and that religion of that realistic sort was anything but dead. In Patmore's poem the dog is " an old guard-hound " ; and we may say, without irreverence, that the first impression or lesson was that there is life in the old dog yet. In any case, it was an event of history, as much as an event of literature, when personal religion returned suddenly with something of the power of Dante or the *Dies Irae*, after a century in which such religion had seemed to grow more weak and provincial, and more and more impersonal religions appeared to possess the future. And those who best understand the world know that the world is changed, and that the hunt will continue until the world turns to bay.

THE FRIVOLOUS MAN

BY ONE of those queer associations that nobody can ever understand, a large number of people have come to think that frivolity has some kind of connection with enjoyment. As a matter of fact, nobody can really enjoy himself unless he is serious. Even those whom we commonly regard as belonging to the butterfly classes of society really enjoy themselves most at the crises of their lives which are potentially tragic. Men can only enjoy fundamental things. In order to enjoy the lightest and most flying joke a man must be rooted in some basic sense of the good of things; and the good of things means, of course, the seriousness of things. In order to enjoy even a *pas de quatre* at a subscription dance a man must feel for the moment that the stars are dancing to the same tune. In the old religions of the world, indeed, people did think that the stars were dancing to the tunes of their temples; and they danced as no man has danced since. But thorough enjoyment, enjoyment that has no hesitation, no incidental blight, no *arrière pensée*, is only possible to the serious man. Wine, says the Scripture, maketh glad the heart of man, but only of the man who has a heart. And so also the thing called good spirits is possible only to the spiritual.

The really frivolous man, the frivolous man of society, we all know, and any of us who know him truthfully know that if he has one characteristic more salient than another it is that he is a pessimist. The idea of the gay and thoughtless man of fashion, intoxicated with pagan delights, is a figment invented entirely by religious people who never met any such man in their lives. The man of pleasure is one of the fables of the pious. Puritans have given a great deal too much credit to the power which the world has to satisfy the soul; in admitting that the sinner is gay and careless they have given away the strongest part of their case. As a matter of fact, Puritanism commonly falls into the error of accusing the frivolous man of all the wrong vices. For instance, it says (and it is a favourite phrase) that the frivolous man is "careless". In truth the frivolous man is very careful. Not only does he spend hours over dressing and similar technical matters, but a great part of his life is passed in criticising and discussing similar technical matters. At any odd hour of the day we may find him talking about whether one man has the right kind of coat or another man the wrong kind of dinner-service; and about these matters he is far more solemn than a Pope or a General Council. His general air about them might be described as rather sad than serious, as rather hopeless than severe. Religion might approximately be defined as the power which makes us joyful about the things that matter. Fashionable frivolity might, with a parallel propriety, be defined as the power which makes us sad about the things that do not matter.

Frivolity has nothing to do with happiness. It plays upon the surface of things, and the surface is almost always rough and uneven. The frivolous person is the person who cannot fully appreciate the weight and value of anything. In practice he does not appreciate even the weight and value of the things commonly counted frivolous. He does not enjoy his cigars as the gutter boy enjoys his cigarette; he does not enjoy his ballet as the child enjoys "Punch and Judy". But, in fairness to him, it must be admitted that he is not alone in being frivolous: other classes of men share the reproach. Thus, for instance, bishops are generally frivolous, moral teachers are generally frivolous, statesmen are generally frivolous, conscientious objectors are generally frivolous. Philosophers and poets are often frivolous; politicians are always frivolous. For if frivolity signifies this lack of grasp of the fullness and the value of things, it must have a great many forms besides that of mere levity and pleasure-seeking. A great many people have a fixed idea that irreverence, for instance, consists chiefly in making jokes. But it is quite possible to be irreverent with a diction devoid of the slightest touch of indecorum, and with a soul unpolluted by a tinge of humour. The splendid and everlasting definition of real irreverence is to be found in that misunderstood and neglected commandment which declares that the Lord will not hold him guiltless that taketh His name in vain. This again is supposed vaguely to have some connection with buffoonery and jocularity and play upon words. But surely that is not the plain meaning of the phrase. To say a thing with a touch of humour is not to say it in vain. To say a thing with a touch of satire or individual criticism is not to say it in vain. To say a thing even fantastically, like some fragment from the scriptures of Elfland, is not to say it in vain. But to say a thing with a pompous and unmeaning gravity; to say a thing so that it shall be at once bigoted and vague; to say a thing so that it shall be indistinct at the same moment that it is literal; to say a thing so that the most decorous listener shall not at the end of it really know why in the name of all things you should have said it or he should have listened to it—this is veritably and in the weighty sense of those ancient Mosaic words to take that thing in vain. The Name is taken in vain many times more often by preachers than it is by secularists. The blasphemer is, indeed, fundamentally natural and prosaic, for he speaks in a commonplace manner about that which he believes to be commonplace. But the ordinary preacher and religious orator speaks in a commonplace manner about that which he believes to be divine.

The Common Man

This is the breach of one of the Commandments; it is the sin against the name. Take, if you will, the name wildly, take it jestingly, take it brutally and angrily, take it childishly, take it wrongly; but do not take it in vain. Use a sanctity for some strange or new purpose and justify that use; use a sanctity for some doubtful and experimental purpose and stake your act on your success; use a sanctity for some base and hateful purpose and abide the end. But do not use a sanctity for no purpose at all; do not talk about Christ when you might as well talk about Mr. Perks; do not use patriotism and honour and the Communion of Saints as stopgaps in a halting speech. This is the sin of frivolity, and it is the chief characteristic of the great majority of the conventionally religious class.

Thus we come back to the conclusion that real seriousness is at a discount alike among the irreligious and the religious, alike in the worldly and in the unworldly world.

TWO STUBBORN PIECES OF IRON

IN DISCUSSING such a proposal as that of the co-education of the sexes it is very desirable first of all to realise clearly what it is that we want the thing to do. The thing might be upheld for quite opposite reasons. It might be supposed to increase delicacy or to decrease it. It might be valued because it was a sphere for sentiment or because it was a damper for sentiment. My sympathies would move me in a discussion entirely according to what difference its upholders thought it would make. For myself, I doubt whether it would make much difference at all. Everyone must agree with co-education for very young children ; and I cannot believe that even for elder children it would do any great harm. But that is because I think the school is not so important as people think it nowadays. The home is the really important thing, and always will be. People talk about the poor neglecting their children ; but a little boy in the street has more traces of having been brought up by his mother than of having been taught ethics and geography by a pupil teacher. And if we take this true parallel of the home we can see, I think, exactly what co-education can do and what it cannot do. The school will never make boys and girls ordinary comrades. The home does not make them that. The sexes can work together in a school-room just as they can breakfast together in a breakfast-room ; but neither makes any difference to the fact that the boys go off to a boyish companionship which the girls would think disgusting, while the girls go off to a girl companionship which the boys would think literally insane. Co-educate as much as you like, there will always be a wall between the sexes until love or lust breaks it down. Your co-educative playground for pupils in their teens will not be a place of sexless camaraderie. It will be a place where boys go about in fives sulkily growling at the girls, and where the girls go about in twos turning up their noses at the boys.

Now if you accept this state of things and are content with it as the result of your co-education, I am with you; I accept it as one of the mystical first facts of Nature. I accept it somewhat in the spirit of Carlyle when somebody told him that Harriet Martineau had " accepted the Universe ", and he said, " By God, she'd better." But if you have any idea that co-education would do more than parade the sexes in front of each other twice a day, if you think it would destroy their deep ignorance of each other or start them on a basis of rational understanding, then I say first that this will never happen, and second that I (for one) should be horribly annoyed if it did.

I can reach my meaning best by another route. Very few people ever state properly the strong argument in favour of marrying for love or against marrying for money. The argument is not that all lovers are heroes and heroines, nor is it that all dukes are profligates or all millionaires cads. The argument is this, that the differences between a man and a woman are at the best so obstinate and exasperating that they practically cannot be got over unless there is an atmosphere of exaggerated tenderness and mutual interest. To put the matter in one metaphor, the sexes are two stubborn pieces of iron; if they are to be welded together, it must be while they are red-hot. Every woman has to find out that her husband is a selfish beast, because every man is a selfish beast by the standard of a woman. But let her find out the beast while they are both still in the story of " Beauty and the Beast ". Every man has to find out that his wife is cross—

Two Stubborn Pieces of Iron

that is to say, sensitive to the point of madness : for every woman is mad by the masculine standard. But let him find out that she is mad while her madness is more worth considering than anyone else's sanity.

This is not a digression. The whole value of the normal relations of man and woman lies in the fact that they first begin really to criticise each other when they first begin really to admire each other. And a good thing, too. I say, with a full sense of the responsibility of the statement, that it is better that the sexes should misunderstand each other until they marry. It is better that they should not have the knowledge until they have the reverence and the charity. We want no premature and puppyish " knowing all about girls ". We do not want the highest mysteries of a Divine distinction to be understood before they are desired, and handled before they are understood. That which Mr. Shaw calls the·Life Force, but for which Christianity has more philosophical terms, has created this early division of tastes and habits for that romantic purpose, which is also the most practical of all purposes. Those whom God has sundered, shall no man join.

It is, therefore, a question of what are really the co-educators' aims. If they have small aims, some convenience in organisation, some slight improvement in manners, they know more about such things than I. But if they have large aims, I am against them.

HENRY JAMES

AN ARTIST who is at once individual and complete attracts a type of praise which is a sort of disparagement; and even those who overrate him underrate him. For the tendency is always to insist on his art; and by art is often meant merely arrangement. Because a very few colours can be harmoniously arranged in a picture, it is implied that he has not many colours on his palette. And as a study by Henry James was often in its tones something of a nocturne in grey and silver, even his eulogists managed to imply something slight or even thin about his work. Before attempting to touch upon what was really peculiar in the tone of it, it is necessary to correct, and even to contradict, this tenuous impression by the reminder of what he had in common with other great writers. For Henry James must be considered as a great man of letters; and the greatness itself is something which existed in geniuses utterly unlike him. It might seem startling and even comic to compare him to Dickens or even to Shakespeare; but what makes him great is what makes them great, and what alone can make a literary man in the ultimate sense great. It is ideas; the power of generating and making vivid an incessant output of ideas. It is untrue to say that what matters is quality and not quantity. Most men have made one good joke in their lives; but to make jokes as Dickens made them is to be a great man. Many forgotten poets have let fall a lyric with one really perfect image; but when we open any play of Shakespeare, good or bad, at any page, important or unimportant, with the practical certainty of finding some imagery that at least arrests the eye and probably enriches the memory, we are putting our trust in a great man. We are taking at random from a whole store of what are truly to be called great inventions when we think of Mrs. Todgers' wooden leg, or Mr. Fledgby's nose, or Mr. Pecksniff's pinions, or Mr. Swiveller's double-bedded room.

And wide as the distance may seem, it is true, in exactly the same sense, that we are taking at random from a treasury of unique inventions when we think of any two or three of the numberless new ideas of Henry James; of the two people who grew afraid of the mystical coincidence of never meeting; of the man who ceased to exist when he was left alone; of the mysterious unity that ran through all a writer's books like "the figure in the carpet"; of the pearls that were counted false for purposes of respectability and real for purposes of sale; of the sudden supernatural calm created like a garden in the skies by the breakdown of the brain at its busiest; of the wife who would not justify herself to her husband because his whole life was in his chivalry; and so on through a thousand more. Such an idea, though it may be as delicate as an atmosphere, is nevertheless as precise as a pun. It cannot be a coincidence; it is always a creation. He has been attacked for making a great deal of small things; but most of those who attacked him were making a great deal of large nothings. The point that is important about him is not whether the things with which he dealt were as small as some think them, or as large as he could make them; whether it was a fine shade in vulgarity or an occult tenacity of vice; whether it was the restless ten minutes of a visitor coming too early, or the restless ten years of a lover moved too late. The point is that the things were things; that we should have lost them if he had not given them; that no mere perfections of prose would have been a substitute for them; in short, that he never wrote about nothing. Each small notion had the serious thing called value—like a jewel, or, like what is both smaller and more valuable than a jewel, a seed.

His greatness is the greatest thing about him, therefore, and it is of a kind with that of other creative men. But when this large and rather neglected aspect has first been allowed for, it is possible to consider him as a peculiar and fastidious writer. Certainly his work is of a sort to which it is difficult to do justice amid the pulsation of the direct public energies with which most of us who are at all public-spirited feel ourselves concerned today. We should need to be at leisure in those large and vague spaces of gardens and great neglected houses which are the background of so many of his spiritual dramas, to grow fond of the fine shades of a whole science of shadows ; and slowly appreciate the multitudinous colours of what seems at first monochrome. Some of his finest stories were ghost stories ; and one must be alone to meet a ghost. And yet even the phrase I use indicates its own limitations, for no one seized more swiftly than Henry James the greatness of this awful time, in which we have to think even of ghosts in crowds. He had always been in his innermost being a mystic, and the dead were near to him ; and he rose more magnificently, perhaps, than any other to that hour in which the dead were so living and so near to us all. A unique purity and disinterestedness had always attended his pen, and he had the reward of it in realising moral proportion. He had never failed to see small things ; nor did he fall into the more modern and enlightened error of failing to see big ones. He had no difficulty in adjusting his subtlety to the stupendous simplicity of a war for justice ; his brain, like a Nasmyth hammer, had not unlearnt in a long course of tapping how to fall and shatter.

That he should feel the prodigy of the Prussian insult to mankind will only surprise those who have read him superficially ; or perhaps only read his more superficial sketches.

Henry James

He by no means exhibits manners as more than morals; though he may exhibit manners as more than many would think them. In a story like *The Turn of the Screw* he has rather the character of a divine detective. The woman who probes the stagnant secret of the depraved boy and girl is resolved to forgive and, therefore, unable to forget. She is a kind of inquisitor; and her morality is altogether of the old thorough and theological sort. It is a summons to repent and die, rather than a vague capacity to die and repent. And when at the last the deliverance of the boy's soul seems to be delayed by the appearance at the window of his evil genius, " the white face of the damned ", it is perhaps the one place in all modern literature where that monosyllable is not a joke. And it is strongly significant that men of any belief and no belief have universally fallen back on such phraseology to find terms for the sneering savagery of the present enemy of Christendom. Honest grey-haired atheists are found judging the Prussian upon the paradoxical principle that there may be heaven, there must be hell. And the nations can find nothing but the language of demonology to describe a certain poison of pride, which is none the less a tyranny because it is also a temptation.

Henry James always stood, if ever a man did, for civilisation; for that ordered life in which it is possible to tolerate and to understand. His whole world is made out of sympathy; out of a whole network of sympathies. It is a world of wireless telegraphy for the soul; of a psychological brotherhood of men of which the communications could not be cut. Some-times this sympathy is almost more terrible than antipathy; and his very delicacies produce a sort of promiscuity of minds. Silence becomes a rending revelation. Short spaces or short speeches become overweighted with the awful worth of human life. Minute unto minute uttereth speech, and instant unto instant showeth knowledge. It is only when we have realised how perfect is the poise of such great human art that we can also realise its peril, and know that any outer thing which cannot make it must of necessity destroy it.

It has been customary to talk of Henry James's American origin as something almost antagonistic to the grace and rarity of his art. I am far from sure that this is not to miss a fine and serious strain in it. There is an element of idealism in the American tradition, which is very well typified in the sincere and sometimes exaggerated external deference to women. This particular sort of purity in the perceptions, very marked in him, he had originally owed, I think, to something other than the more mellow and matured European life in which he came afterwards to take his deepest pleasures. The older civilisation gave him the wonderful things he wanted; but the wonder was his own. His attitude in private life remains for anyone who has seen it as something infinitely higher than politeness; an attitude towards things, and something that can only be called an impersonal reverence. Despite all their modernism, some of his love stories have a dignity that might be dressed in the clothes of an antique time. They should have moved upon high-terraced lawns among great and gentle ladies, and their squires who were something more than gentlemen. As Mr. Yeats says somewhere:

> There have been lovers whose thought love should be
> So much compounded of high courtesy,
> That they would sigh and quote with learned looks
> Precedents out of beautiful old books.

The books of Henry James will always be beautiful; and I believe they are young enough to be old.

THE STRANGE TALK OF TWO VICTORIANS

THE FAITH always returns in a counter-attack; and it is generally not only a successful attack but almost always a surprise attack.

Here more than anywhere it is the unexpected that happens; the religion supposed to be rotting away slowly in unlettered peasantries was found present in pressing numbers in the new industrial towns; the creed compassionately tolerated in a few old sentimentalists is today making converts among the young almost entirely of the hard-headed logicians.

But this tendency to a reconciliation with intellectuals, once regarded as a reconciliation with irreconcilables, has produced, among other queer points in the position, this fact; that the newest group consists rather too much of those who are in a position to teach, while there is not yet a sufficient crowd, or larger public, of those who are in a position to learn. There is, for instance, a huge mass of material in Catholic history for very good novels or plays; and there are a considerable proportion of Catholics capable of writing them; but there is not yet a sufficient number of ordinary readers capable of reading them, in the sense of understanding them. This is especially true of the high historic quality of irony.

An Englishman realising the real religious history of his country constantly comes upon small social and political episodes, of which the irony is as grand as Greek tragedy; and then he remembers most of the other Englishmen, and has to own that it would be Greek to them. The very ironic

point which gives him grim gratification would be quite
pointless, because the public at large would probably take
the suggestion quite seriously and never even see the joke.

So, till very lately at least, the public hardly saw the joke
of talking about the Virgin Queen or the Glorious Revolution. You cannot have drama without a public; you cannot
have irony without an instructed public.

I was wondering the other day whether anybody had
thought of a play, or rather a scene, which could be a very
fine scene written by anybody well read in eighteenth-century
England. It might be called "Five Irishmen."

Seated round a table in a coffeehouse (but conspicuously
not drinking coffee) would be Goldsmith, an old Tory almost
a Jacobite; Sheridan, a younger Whig almost a Jacobin;
Burke, a Whig more alarmist than any Tory about disturbing
the balance of the British Constitution (which he had largely
made up out of his own highly imaginative head); Grattan,
a Whig orator also, but native to the Irish Parliament;
and (if he could be dragged in somehow) somebody more
dangerous, like Lord Edward of Tone, foreshadowing the
Irish Rebellion. All these men were Protestants. All, either
in their own persons or through their families, could be
traced back in some way to the time when it seemed that
the heart of Ireland was broken; and for a man who did
not abandon the Faith there was no normal hope on
earth.

I think somebody could make a fine study, in several
stages, of how layer after layer began to crack and that
awful forbidden ancestral Thing rose slowly to overshadow
them like a ghost. They would begin decorously, of course,
probably discussing Catholic Emancipation with cold pagan
liberality; and the wine and the words and the Irish
passion for personal recrimination, and especially for family

reminiscence, would bring strange things spouting from the depths; and through a wild scene I actually seemed suddenly to hear the high voice of Sheridan, shrill with intoxication, crying out some taunt: "Have ye forgotten that, O'Bourke?" And then I remembered that an audience in a London theatre would probably make nothing of the notion of that great eternal Thing terribly returning; because any number of them do not know that it is eternal and hardly that it is great.

In Edith Sitwell's very graceful sketch of Queen Victoria, I came on another quaint little drama, which in this case would be a duologue. Also, in this case, the thing really happened. It is there described briefly and impartially; but anyone knowing persons and period can easily understand and expand it; and to me it is enormously amusing; amusing and also enormous. It has exactly that grim Greek irony of the contrast between great things known and the greater thing that is not known. It was a discussion, and even a dispute between two very eminent Victorians. It was concerned with the news of the proclamation of the dogma of the Immaculate Conception.

They were both good men; they were both men of the first prominence in the public eye. Both had the finest culture of the Protestant; both had a faint streak of the prig; but both had a warmth of generous conviction for their own favourite causes; neither certainly was a fool; neither was a No-Popery man in the narrow and vulgar sense; both believed themselves flooded with the full daylight of the age of enlightenment and liberty; and, at the same time, both had hobbies and intelligent interests that might soften them toward older religious traditions.

One was a great reader of the Fathers and the first devotional literature; the other had a genuine taste in what was still often regarded as the childish cheap jewellery of medieval painting. One was a High Churchman of the Oxford Movement; the other was a liberal Lutheran. One was the great Gladstone; the other was Albert, the Prince Consort.

The two men talked and disagreed. They sharply disagreed. The point on which they disagreed was extraordinary. But it was not a hundredth part as extraordinary as the part on which they agreed.

Mr. Gladstone was greatly grieved because he had found the Prince Consort in a state of indecent hilarity, he thought, over the news about the Immaculate Conception. Indecent hilarity is not a vice conspicuously staining Prince Albert's name, any more than Gladstone's; two more solemn disputants would be hard to find. But Prince Albert was the more cheerful, because (he said in effect) it is always a good thing when an evil system tottering to its fall, does some one wildly insane and frantic act of arrogance; which will quite certainly bring it to a final crash. Rome had staggered along somehow till now; but, obviously, Rome would never have a leg to stand on after this.

But Mr. Gladstone (of the Oxford Movement) could not join in this simple German triumph over the disaster and disgrace that had at last destroyed the Eternal City. In those deep tones of reproach he could command so well, he rebuked the Prince for his insensibility to this blasting and blackening of a name that had meant so much in history; no Christian, he felt, could be insensible to the utter downfall of so large a section of the Christian world. He meant it. He was tremendously upset about it. He returned to the subject afterwards; repeatedly imploring Prince Albert to drop at least one tear upon the ruins of St. Peter's, now lying as desolate as Stonehenge.

But the Prince also was firm; and remained in his somewhat rare state of high spirits over the news that the unduly protracted business was finished; and the Pope had done himself in at last.

And all this was because—of what? Because one more crown had been added to that tower of crowns that crowd after crowd, city after city, nation after nation, age after age, have reared higher and higher on the image which is of all others most strongly based and founded and built, as regards this earth, in the affection of the universal people. And Prince Albert, with his unselfish labours for the education of the working classes, and Gladstone, with his confident appeal to the great heart of the people, understood so little of what that crown and image really meant to millions of ordinary poor people, in all the countrysides and cities of half the world, that they actually expected that it would be dethroned like a tyranny, for this last toppling insolence in the demands of a tyrant.

The one extraordinary thing on which these extraordinary men agreed, it seems, was that the decision would be *unpopular*. ... One of Belloc's Ballades had a refrain chiefly remembered by the Envoi, which ran:

> Prince, is it true that when you met the Czar
> You said that *English people* think it low
> To coax to life a half-extinct cigar?
> Good Lord, how little wealthy people know!

Anyhow, the one assumption shared by these admirable public men seems to have been wrong somewhere. Applewomen did not rush madly out of church; seamstresses in garrets did not dash their little images of Mary to the ground, on learning that she was named Immaculate.

The Common Man

Four years after these potentates had their regrettable difference, while the Bishop still frowned and the parish priest feared to believe, little knots of poor peasants began to gather round a strange starved child before a crack in the rocks, from whence was to spring a strange stream and almost a new city; the rocks she had heard resound with a voice crying, "I am the Immaculate Conception. . . ."

"Good Lord, how little wealthy people know!"

LAUGHTER

IF WE in any sense propose for discussion the subject of Laughter, we shall normally notice that our neighbours receive it in one of two ways. Either they laugh, which is perhaps the best thing they could do with a proposal for the analysis of laughter; since practice is better than precept; and anyone sitting down, as I do here, to write a whole article on this subject is a very proper object for the derision of mankind. But if they have sense enough to laugh, they will also probably have sense enough to go away; the colloquy will be cut short and exhibit only the kind of wit which is identified with brevity.

If, on the other hand, we mention Laughter to them and they do not laugh, what they always do is this; to twist their silly faces into expressions of ferocious gravity and gloom and begin to talk about Primitive Psychology, and the automatic reflexes of Pithecanthropus; and after a month or two of this cheery little chat, they practically always bring out the result (which is an unmistakable sign and a symptom of their dying minds) that " laughter is, after all, founded on some form of the instinct of cruelty ". The whole being a neat and polished exposition of the great modern habit of being as unscientific as possible in the use of scientific words. They have not yet proved that there is any instinct of cruelty, any more than there is an instinct of chewing glass. Some lunatics do chew glass; even some eminent men have done it; I think the famous Sir Richard Grenville had the habit. Some men have a perversion called cruelty; but if primitive men develop a talent for humour from a perversion of cruelty, it is quite as difficult to explain how they developed the perversion as how they developed the talent. We might as well explain the beginning of poetry by saying that Pithecanthropus was addicted to cocaine. The whole thing is one of those impudent insinuations of popular science, quite unsupported by serious science, but having a very strong moral or anti-moral motive ; to suggest by innumerable irresponsible hints that human beings owe everything to semi-human beings called primitive men ; and that these were utterly degraded creatures, dwelling in a darkness of hatred and fear.

On the face of it, all this theory of laughter is laughable. Anybody can make a child laugh by some simple inversion or incongruity ; such as putting spectacles on the teddy bear. Are we asked to believe that a dark troglodyte stirs in the cave of the infant's skull, and takes pleasure in torturing the teddy bear with unfamiliar optical conditions ; or fiendishly rejoices in the agony of an aged uncle when temporarily deprived of his goggles ? The sort of literature at which children really laugh is the simplest sort of nonsense like " the cow jumped over the moon ". Are we to suppose children lie awake and laugh to think of the long and chilly journey of the lost quadruped, in the cold altitudes wholly unsuited to warm-blooded mammals ? It is obvious that the mind is amused with incongruity, when there is no direct or indirect idea of discomfort. Why it is amused with incongruity is indeed a very deep question, and we shall get no further with such questions until we adopt a totally different attitude to the whole story of man ; until we have the patience to respect a great many of the mysteries as mysteries, and wait for an explanation which really explains ; instead of jumping at any explanation that merely explains away. But I suspect it will be found connected with the idea of human dignity rather than indignity ; and rather related to the strangeness of man on this strange earth, than to the mere dull brutalities connecting him with the dull mud.

It is not surprising that an age exhibiting this monstrous spectacle, of men being sombre and pessimistic about the origin of Laughter, should also exhibit some loss of the simpler sort of laughter in its literature and art. And I fancy even those who might claim that we produce more humour would admit that we produce less laughter. But the poison of the anti-human heresy I have mentioned works back in a curious fashion into the practice of those who have heard the theory; and the ideas of cause and effect act and react on each other. It may be that only in a dry age could pedants be found to trace back all mirth to malignity; it may be that the atmospheric suggestion of that origin has made the mirth less mirthful, and more dry if not more malignant. But certainly, at the best, the tendency of recent culture has been to tolerate the smile but discourage the laugh. There are three differences involved here. First, that the smile can unobtrusively turn into the sneer; second, that the smile is always individual and even secretive (especially if it is a little mad), while the laugh can be social and gregarious, and is perhaps the one genuine surviving form of the General Will; and third, that laughing lays itself open to criticism, is innocent and unguarded, has the sort of humanity which has always something of humility. The recent stage of culture and criticism might very well be summed up as the men who smile criticising the men who laugh. We may read in any current novel, " Grigsby stroked his chin and smiled a rather superior smile." We seldom read, even in a novel, " Grigsby flung back his head and howled at the ceiling with a slightly superior laugh." The moment Grigsby abandons himself so far as to laugh he has lost something of that perfect superiority of the Grigsbys, for which they are famous in fashionable circles, and for which so many of their fellow-creatures would love to kick them, as old Weller kicked Mr. Stiggins. For it is a complete mistake to suppose that there is less cruelty since we abandoned the good old custom of kicking Mr. Stiggins. The only difference is that it is Mr. Grigsby who is allowed to be cruel; because of the lack of simpler and humbler men to enjoy the innocent pleasure of kicking him. In the mind of Mr. Grigsby, at that exquisite moment when he smiles, there is infinitely more cruelty, in the sense of mere malice, than there was in the mind of Weller when he applied the boot, or Dickens when he wrote the book. The chief mark of the most modern change in the world is that milder social manners do *not* go with warmer social feelings. The chief fact we have to face today is the absence of even that amount of democratic comradeship which was involved in coarse laughter or merely conventional ridicule. The men of the older fellowship may have sometimes unjustly disliked a scapegoat or an alien, but they liked each other much more than a good many literary men now like each other. It is obvious in a thousand ways that there was more communal sentiment, or if you will sentimentality, in the camps where Bret Harte's ruffians brandished bowie-knives and revolvers, or in the public-house cellar where Mr. Bardell was knocked on the head with a quart pot, than in many a modern intellectual circle in which the soul is at last finally isolated, like the heads in hell held apart in their rings of ice. Therefore, in this modern conflict between the Smile and the Laugh, I am all in favour of laughing. Laughter has something in it in common with the ancient winds of faith and inspiration; it unfreezes pride and unwinds secrecy; it makes men forget themselves in the presence of something greater than themselves; something (as the common phrase goes about a joke) that they cannot resist. The saint is he who enjoys good things and refuses them. The prig is he who despises good things and enjoys them. But when he hears a really good thing, which he really enjoys, then he can no longer despise it. On that awful and apocalyptic occasion, he does not smile; he laughs.

TALES FROM TOLSTOI

IN ONE sense there is a real and actual law of progress by which we grow simpler as we grow more civilised, for the more we scan and study the phenomena around us the more they tend to unify themselves with the power behind them, and the whole of existence thus seen for the first time seems something of an entirely new shape and colour, a fresh and surprising thing. And all the great writers of our time represent in one form or another this attempt to re-establish communication with the elemental or, as it is sometimes more roughly and fallaciously expressed, to return to nature. Some think that the return to nature consists in drinking no wine; some think that it consists in drinking a great deal more than is good for them. Some think that the return to nature is achieved by beating swords into ploughshares; some think it is achieved by turning ploughshares into very ineffectual British War Office bayonets.

It is natural, according to the Jingo, for a man to kill other people with gunpowder and himself with gin. It is natural, according to the humanitarian revolutionists, to kill other people with dynamite and himself with vegetarianism. It would be too obviously Philistine a sentiment, perhaps, to suggest that the claim of either of these persons to be obeying the voice of nature is interesting when we consider that they require huge volumes of paradoxical argument to persuade themselves or anyone else of the truth of their conclusions. But the giants of our time are undoubtedly alike in that they approach by very different roads this conception of the return to simplicity. Ibsen returns to nature by the angular exterior of fact, Maeterlinck by the eternal tendencies of fable. Whitman returns to nature by seeing how much he can accept, Tolstoi by seeing how much he can reject.

Now, this heroic desire to return to nature is, of course, in some respects, rather like the heroic desire of a kitten to return to its own tail. A tail is a simple and beautiful object, rhythmic in curve and soothing in texture ; but it is certainly one of the minor but characteristic qualities of a tail that it should hang behind. It is impossible to deny that it would in some degree lose its character if attached to any other part of the anatomy. Now, nature is like a tail in the sense that it is vitally important if it is to discharge its real duty that it should be always behind. To imagine that we can see nature, especially our own nature, face to face is a folly ; it is even a blasphemy. It is like the conduct of a cat in some mad fairy tale who should set out on his travels with the firm conviction that he would find his tail growing like a tree in the meadow at the end of the world. And the actual effect of the travels of the philosopher in search of nature when seen from the outside looks very like the gyrations of the tail-pursuing kitten, exhibiting much enthusiasm but little dignity, much cry and very little tail. The grandeur of nature is that she is omnipotent and unseen, that she is perhaps ruling us most when we think that she is heeding us least. "Thou art a God that hidest Thyself," said the Hebrew poets. It may be said with all reverence that it is behind a man's back that the spirit of nature hides.

It is this consideration that lends a certain air of futility even to all the inspired simplicities and thunderous veracities of Tolstoi. We feel that a man cannot make himself simple merely by warring on complexity ; we feel, indeed, in our saner moments that a man cannot make himself simple at all. A self-conscious simplicity may well be far more intrinsically ornate than luxury itself. Indeed, a great deal of the pomp and sumptuousness of the world's history was simple in the truest sense. It was born of an almost babyish receptiveness ; it was the work of men who had eyes to wonder and men who had ears to hear.

> King Solomon brought merchant men
> Because of his desire
> With peacocks, apes and ivory,
> From Tarshish unto Tyre.

But this proceeding was not a part of the wisdom of Solomon ; it was a part of his folly—I had almost said of his innocence. Tolstoi, we feel, would not be content with hurling satire and denunciation at " Solomon in all his glory ". With fierce and unimpeachable logic he would go a step further. He would spend days and nights in the meadows stripping the shameless crimson coronals off the lilies of the field.

Any collection of Tales from Tolstoi is calculated to draw particular attention to this ethical and ascetic side of Tolstoi's work. In one sense, and that the deepest sense, the work of Tolstoi is, of course, a genuine and noble appeal to simplicity. The narrow notion that an artist may not teach is pretty well exploded by now. But the truth of the matter is that an artist teaches far more by his mere background and properties, his landscape, his costume, his idiom and technique—all the part of his work, in short, of which he is probably entirely unconscious, than by the elaborate and pompous moral dicta which he fondly imagines to be his opinions. The real distinction between the ethics of high art and the ethics of manufactured and didactic art lies in the simple fact that the bad fable has a moral, while the good fable is a moral. And the real moral of Tolstoi comes out constantly in his stories, the great moral which lies at the heart of all his work, of which he is probably unconscious, and of which it is quite likely that he would vehemently disapprove. The curious cold white light of morning that shines over all the tales, the folklore simplicity with which " a man or a woman " are spoken of without further identification, the love—one might almost say the lust—for the qualities of brute materials, the hardness of wood, and the softness of mud, the ingrained belief in a certain ancient kindliness sitting beside the very cradle of the race of man—these influences are truly moral. When we put beside them the trumpeting and tearing nonsense of the didactic Tolstoi, screaming for an obscene purity, shouting for an inhuman peace, hacking up human life into small sins with a chopper, sneering at men, women, and children out of respect to humanity, combining in one chaos of contradictions an unmanly Puritan and an uncivilised prig, then, indeed, we scarcely know whither Tolstoi has vanished. We know not what to do with this small and noisy moralist who is inhabiting one corner of a great and good man.

It is difficult in every case to reconcile Tolstoi the great artist with Tolstoi the almost venomous reformer. It is difficult to believe that a man who draws in such noble out-lines the dignity of the daily life of humanity regards as evil that divine act of procreation by which that dignity is re-newed from age to age. It is difficult to believe that a man who has painted with so frightful an honesty the heartrending emptiness of the life of the poor can really grudge them every one of their pitiful pleasures from courtship to tobacco. It is difficult to believe that a poet in prose who has so powerfully exhibited the earth-born air of man, the essential kinship of a human being with the landscape in which he lives, can deny so elemental a virtue as that which attaches a man to his own ancestors and his own land. It is difficult to believe that the man who feels so poignantly the detestable insolence of oppression would not actually, if he had the chance, lay the oppressor flat with his fist. All, however, arises from the search after a false simplicity, the aim of being, if I may so express it, more natural than it is natural to be. It would not only be more human, it would be more humble of us to be content to be complex. The truest kinship with humanity would lie in doing as humanity has always done, accepting with a sportsmanlike relish the estate to which we are called, the star of our happiness, and the fortunes of the land of our birth.

THE NEW CASE FOR CATHOLIC SCHOOLS

ANY AMOUNT of nonsense has been talked about the need of novelty, and in that sense there is nothing particularly meritorious about being modern. A man who seriously describes his creed as Modernism might just as well invent a creed called Mondayism, meaning that he puts special faith in the fancies that occurred to him on Monday ; or a creed called Morningism, meaning that he believed in the thoughts that occurred to him in the morning but not in the afternoon.

Modernity is only the moment of time in which we happen to find ourselves, and nobody who thinks will suppose that it is bound to be superior, either to the time that comes after it or to the time that went before. But in a relative and rational sense we may congratulate ourselves on knowing the news of the moment, and having realised recent facts or discoveries that some people still ignore.

And it is in that sense that we may truly call the fundamental concept of Catholic Education a scientific fact, and especially a psychological fact. Our demand for a complete culture, based on its own philosophy and religion, is a demand that is really unanswerable, in the light of the most vital and even the most modern psychology. For that matter, for those who care for such things, there could hardly be a *word* more modern than *atmosphere*.

Now, so long as they are engaged in doing anything whatever except arguing with us, our modern and scientific friends are never tired of telling us that education must be treated as a whole ; that all parts of the mind affect each other ; that

nothing is too trivial to be significant and even symbolic ;
that all thoughts can be coloured by conscious or unconscious
emotions ; that knowledge can never be in watertight com-
partments ; that what may seem a senseless detail may be
the symbol of a deep desire ; that nothing is negative, nothing
is naked, nothing stands separate and alone.

They use these arguments for all sorts of purposes, some
of them sensible enough, some of them almost insanely silly ;
but this is, broadly speaking, how they argue. And the one
thing they do not know is that they are arguing in favour
of Catholic education, and especially in favour of Catholic
atmosphere in Catholic schools. Perhaps if they did know
they would leave off.

As a matter of fact, those who refuse to understand that
Catholic children must have an entirely Catholic school are
back in the bad old days, as they would express it, when
nobody wanted education but only instruction. They are
relics of the dead time when it was thought enough to drill
pupils in two or three dull and detached lessons that were
supposed to be quite mechanical. They descend from the
original Philistine who first talked about " The Three R.s " ;
and the joke about him is very symbolic of his type or time.
For he was the sort of man who insists very literally on
literacy, and, even in doing so, shows himself illiterate.

They were very uneducated rich men who loudly demanded education. And among the marks of their ignorance
and stupidity was the particular mark that they regarded
letters and figures as dead things, quite separate from each
other and from a general view of life. They thought of a
boy learning his letters as something quite cut off, for instance,
from what is meant by a man of letters. They thought a
calculating boy could be made like a calculating machine.

When somebody said to them, therefore, " These things

must be taught in a spiritual atmosphere ", they thought it was nonsense; they had a vague idea that it meant that a child could only do a simple addition sum when surrounded with the smell of incense. But they thought simple addition much more simple than it is. When the Catholic controversialist said to them, " Even the alphabet can be learnt in a Catholic way ", they thought he was a raving bigot, they thought he meant that nobody must ever read anything but a Latin missal.

But he meant what he said, and what he said is thoroughly sound pyschology. There is a Catholic view of learning the alphabet; for instance, it prevents you from thinking that the only thing that matters is learning the alphabet; or from despising better people than yourself, if they do not happen to have learnt the alphabet.

The old unpsychological school of instructors used to say: " What possible sense can there be in mixing up arithmetic with religion ? " But arithmetic is mixed up with religion, or at the worst with philosophy. It does make a great deal of difference whether the instructor implies that truth is real, or relative, or changeable, or an illusion. The man who said, " Two and two may make five in the fixed stars ", was teaching arithmetic in an anti-rational way, and, therefore, in an anti-Catholic way. The Catholic is much more certain about the fixed truths than about the fixed stars.

But I am not now arguing which philosophy is the better; I am only pointing out that every education teaches a philosophy; if not by dogma then by suggestion, by implication, by atmosphere. Every part of that education has a connection with every other part. If it does not all combine to convey some general view of life, it is not education at all. And the modern educationists, the modern psychologists, the modern men of science, all agree in asserting and re-asserting this—until they begin to quarrel with Catholics over Catholic schools.

In short, if there is a psychological truth discoverable by human reason, it is this; that Catholics must either go without Catholic teaching or possess and govern Catholic schools. There is a case for refusing to allow Catholic families to grow up Catholic, by any machinery worth calling education in the existing sense. There is a case for refusing to make any concessions to Catholics at all, and ignoring their idiosyncrasy as if it were an insanity. There is a case for that, because there is and always has been a case for persecution; for the State acting on the principle that certain philosophies are false and dangerous and must be crushed even if they are sincerely held; indeed that they must be crushed, especially if they are sincerely held.

But if Catholics are to teach Catholicism all the time, they cannot merely teach Catholic theology for part of the time. It is our opponents, and not we, who give a really outrageous and superstitious position to dogmatic theology. It is they who suppose that the special " subject " called theology can be put into people by an experiment lasting half an hour; and that this magical inoculation will last them through a week in a world that is soaked through and through with a contrary conception of life.

Theology is only articulate religion; but, strange as it seems to the true Christians who criticise us, it is necessary to have religion as well as theology. And religion, as they are often obliging enough to remind us when this particular problem is not involved, is a thing for every day of the week and not merely for Sunday or Church services.

The truth is that the modern world has committed itself to two totally different and inconsistent conceptions about education. It is always trying to expand the scope of education; and always trying to exclude from it all religion and philosophy. But this is sheer nonsense. You can have an education that teaches atheism because atheism is true, and it can be, from its own point of view, a complete education. But you cannot have an education claiming to teach all truth, and then refusing to discuss whether atheism is true.

Since the coming of the more ambitious psychological education, our schools have claimed to develop all sides of human nature; that is, to produce a complete human being. You cannot do this and totally ignore a great living tradition, which teaches that a complete human being must be a Christian or Catholic human being. You must either persecute it out of existence or allow it to make its own education complete.

When schooling was supposed to consist of spelling, of counting and making pothooks and hangers, you might make out some kind of case for saying that it could be taught indifferently by a Baptist or Buddhist. But what in the world is the sense of having an education which includes lessons in " citizenship ", for instance; and then pretending not to include anything like a moral theory, and ignoring all those who happen to hold that a moral theory depends on a moral theology.

Our schoolmasters profess to bring out every side of the pupil; the æsthetic side; the athletic side; the political side, and so on; and yet they still talk the stale cant of the nineteenth century about public instruction having nothing to do with the religious side. The truth is that, in this matter, it is our enemies who are stick-in-the mud, and still remain in the stuffy atmosphere of undeveloped and unscientific education; while we are, in this at any rate, on the side of all modern psychologists and serious educationists in recognising the idea of atmosphere. They sometimes like to call it environment.

VULGARITY

VULGARITY is one of the great new modern inventions; like the telephone or the wireless set. It may be plausibly maintained that the telephone is less of an instrument of torture than the thumbscrew or the rack, and in the same way that other ages had other vices that were worse than this new or modern vice. As we may find fanciful sketches of aeroplanes in the sketchbooks of Leonardo da Vinci, or speculations very near to modern physics in the philosophers of ancient Greece, so we may find here and there in history a hint or foreshadowing of the great and golden vision of vulgarity that was later to burst on the world. We may find it in the smell of Punic plutocracy that stank in the nostrils of Greeks and Romans, or in a certain touch of bad taste in an æsthete like Nero.

Nevertheless, the thing is so new that the new world has not yet really found a name for it, but has had to borrow a rather misleading name, which is really the Latin word for something else. So we have to go on using the Greek name of amber as the only name of electricity because we have no notion what is the real name or nature of electricity. And so we have to go on using the Latin word *vulgus*, which only meant the common people, to describe something that is not particularly common among the common people.

Indeed, through long stretches of human history, and over wide spaces of the habitable globe, it is very uncommon among the common people. Farmers living by long agricultural traditions, peasants in normal villages, even savages in savage tribes, are hardly ever vulgar. Even when they massacre and enslave, even when they offer human sacrifice or eat human

Vulgarity

flesh, they are hardly ever vulgar. All travellers attest to the natural dignity of their carriage and the ceremonial gravity of their customs. Even in the more complex modern cities and civilisations the poor as such are not particularly vulgar.

No; there is a new thing, which really needs a new name, and still more, a new definition. I do not say I can define vulgarity; but, having just been reading a modern book about love, I feel inclined to throw out a few suggestions.

In so far as I can get near to its essence, it consists largely of two elements, which I should describe as facility and familiarity. The first means that a man does really, as the phrase goes, " gush "; that is, his self-expression flows without effort, selection or control. It does not come from him like picked and pointed words, passing through an articulate organ; it simply streams from him like perspiration. He need never stop explaining himself, for he understands neither himself nor the limits of explanation. He is the sort of man who understands women; he is the man who can always get on with the boys; he finds it easy to talk, easy to write, easy to speak in public, for his own self-satisfaction carries with it a sort of huge cloud and illusion of applause.

And the second element is familiarity, which, if understood, would be called profanity. Horace spoke of the " profane vulgar ", and it is true that this familiarity is the loss of holy fear and a sin against the mystical side of man. In practice it means handling things confidently and contemptuously, without the sense that all things in their way are sacred things. Its most recent mode is the readiness to write torrents of tosh on either side of any serious subject, for you hardly ever get *real* vulgarity on a frivolous subject.

The point is that the fool is so subjective that it never occurs to him to be afraid of the subject. For instance, he can be a Pagan fool, as well as a Puritan fool, in the debate on modern

The Common Man

morals; but in the first case there will be torrents of tosh about love and passion and the right to live and in the other, exactly similar torrents of tosh about Christian manhood and healthy boyhood and noble motherhood and the rest. The trouble is that they are so infernally familiar with these things.

Never do you find that note in a real lover writing of the woman he loves or in a real saint writing of the sin he hates. Both say the right thing, because they would rather say nothing at all.

THE REVIVAL OF PHILOSOPHY—WHY·?

THE BEST reason for a revival of philosophy is that unless a man has a philosophy certain horrible things will happen to him. He will be practical; he will be progressive; he will cultivate efficiency; he will trust in evolution; he will do the work that lies nearest; he will devote himself to deeds, not words. Thus struck down by blow after blow of blind stupidity and random fate, he will stagger on to a miserable death with no comfort but a series of catchwords; such as those which I have catalogued above. Those things are simply substitutes for thoughts. In some cases they are the tags and tail-ends of somebody else's thinking. That means that a man who refuses to have his own philosophy will not even have the advantages of a brute beast, and be left to his own instincts. He will only have the used-up scraps of somebody else's philosophy; which the beasts do not have to inherit; hence their happiness. Men have always one of two things: either a complete and conscious philosophy or the unconscious acceptance of the broken bits of some incomplete and shattered and often discredited philosophy. Such broken bits are the phrases I have quoted: efficiency and evolution and the rest. The idea of being " practical ", standing all by itself, is all that remains of a Pragmatism that cannot stand at all. It is impossible to be practical without a Pragma. And what would happen if you went up to the next practical man you met and said to the poor dear old duffer, "Where is your Pragma?" Doing the work that is nearest is obvious nonsense; yet it has been repeated in many albums. In nine cases out of ten it would mean doing the work that we are least fitted to do, such as cleaning the windows or clouting the policeman over the head. " Deeds, not words " is itself an excellent example of " Words, not thoughts ". It is a deed to throw a pebble into a pond and a word that sends a prisoner to the gallows. But there are certainly very futile words ; and this sort of journalistic philosophy and popular science almost entirely consists of them.

Some people fear that philosophy will bore or bewilder them ; because they think it is not only a string of long words, but a tangle of complicated notions. These people miss the whole point of the modern situation. These are exactly the evils that exist already ; mostly for want of a philosophy. The politicians and the papers are always using long words. It is not a complete consolation that they use them wrong. The political and social relations are already hopelessly complicated. They are far more complicated than any page of medieval metaphysics ; the only difference is that the medievalist could trace out the tangle and follow the complications ; and the moderns cannot. The chief practical things of today, like finance and political corruption, are frightfully complicated. We are content to tolerate them because we are content to misunderstand them, not to understand them. The business world needs metaphysics—to simplify it.

I know these words will be received with scorn, and with gruff reassertion that this is no time for nonsense and paradox ; and that what is really wanted is a practical man to go in and clear up the mess. And a practical man will doubtless appear, one of the unending succession of practical men ; and he will doubtless go in, and perhaps clear up a few millions for himself and leave the mess more bewildering than before ; as each of the other practical men has done. The reason is perfectly simple. This sort of rather crude and unconscious person always adds to the confusion ; because he himself has two or three different motives at the same moment, and does not distinguish between them. A man has, already entangled hopelessly in his own mind, (1) a hearty and human desire for money, (2) a somewhat priggish and superficial desire to be progressing, or going the way the world is going, (3) a dislike to being thought too old to keep up with the young people, (4) a certain amount of vague but genuine patriotism or public spirit, (5) a misunderstanding of a mistake made by Mr. H. G. Wells, in the form of a book on Evolution. When a man has all these things in his head, and does not even attempt to sort them out, he is called by common consent and acclamation a practical man. But the practical man cannot be expected to improve the impracticable muddle ; for he cannot clear up the muddle in his own mind, let alone in his own highly complex community and civilisation. For some strange reason, it is the custom to say of this sort of practical man that " he knows his own mind ". Of course this is exactly what he does not know. He may in a few fortunate cases know what he wants, as does a dog or a baby of two years old ; but even then he does not know why he wants it. And it is the why and the how that have to be considered when we are tracing out the way in which some culture or tradition has got into a tangle. What we need, as the ancients understood, is not a politican who is a business man, but a king who is a philosopher.

I apologise for the word " king ", which is not strictly necessary to the sense ; but I suggest that it would be one of the functions of the philosopher to pause upon such words, and determine their importance and unimportance. The Roman Republic and all its citizens had to the last a horror of the word " king ". It was in consequence of this that they invented and imposed on us the word " Emperor ". The great Republicans who founded America also had a horror of the word " king " ; which has therefore reappeared with the special qualification of a Steel King, an Oil King, a Pork King, or other similar monarchs made of similar materials. The business of the philosopher is not necessarily to condemn the innovation or to deny the distinction. But it is his duty to ask himself exactly what it is that he or others dislike in the word " king ". If what he dislikes is a man wearing the spotted fur of a small animal called the ermine, or a man having once had a metal ring placed on the top of his head by a clergyman, he will decide one way. If what he dislikes is a man having vast or irresponsible powers over other men, he may decide another. If what he dislikes is such fur or such power being handed on from father to son, he will enquire whether this ever occurs under commercial conditions today. But, anyhow, he will have the habit of testing the thing by the thought; by the idea which he likes or dislikes; and not merely by the sound of a syllable or the look of four letters beginning with a " R ".

Philosophy is merely thought that has been thought out. It is often a great bore. But man has no alternative, except between being influenced by thought that has been thought out and being influenced by thought that has not been thought out. The latter is what we commonly call culture and enlightenment today. But man is always influenced by thought of some kind, his own or somebody else's; that of somebody he trusts or that of somebody he never heard of, thought at first, second or third hand; thought from exploded legends or unverified rumours; but always something with the shadow of a system of values and a reason for preference. A man does test everything by something. The question here is whether he has ever tested the test.

I will take one example out of a thousand that might be taken. What is the attitude of an ordinary man on being told of an extraordinary event : a miracle ? I mean the sort of thing that is loosely called supernatural, but should more properly be called preternatural. For the word supernatural applies only to what is higher than man; and a good many modern miracles look as if they came from what is considerably lower. Anyhow, what do modern men say when apparently confronted with something that cannot, in the cant phrase, be naturally explained? Well, most modern men immediately talk nonsense. When such a thing is currently mentioned, in novels or newspapers or magazine stories, the first comment is always something like, " But my dear fellow, this is the twentieth century!" It is worth having a little training in philosophy if only to avoid looking so ghastly a fool as that. It has on the whole rather less sense or meaning than saying, " But my dear fellow, this is Tuesday afternoon." If miracles cannot happen, they cannot happen in the twentieth century or in the twelfth. If they can happen, nobody can prove that there is a time when they cannot happen. The best that can be said for the sceptic is that he cannot say what he means, and therefore, whatever else he means, he cannot mean what he says. But if he only means that miracles can be *believed* in the twelfth century, but cannot be believed in the twentieth, then he is wrong again, both in theory and in fact. He is wrong in theory, because an intelligent recognition of possibilities does not depend on a date but on a philosophy. An atheist could disbelieve in the first century and a mystic could continue to believe in the twenty-first century. And he is wrong, in fact, because there is every sign of there being a great deal of mysticism and miracle in the twenty-first century; and there is quite certainly an increasing mass of it in the twentieth.

But I have only taken that first superficial repartee because there is a significance in the mere fact that it comes first; and its very superficiality reveals something of the subconsciousness. It is almost an automatic repartee; and automatic words are of some importance in psychology. Let us not be too severe on the worthy gentleman who informs his dear fellow that it is the twentieth century. In the mysterious depths of his being even that enormous ass does actually mean something. The point is that he cannot really explain what he means; and *that* is the argument for a better education in philosophy. What he really means is something like this, "There is a theory of this mysterious universe to which more and more people were in fact inclined during the second half of the eighteenth and the first half of the nineteenth centuries; and up to that point at least, this theory did grow with the growing inventions and discoveries of science to which we owe our present social organisation—or disorganisation. That theory maintains that cause and effect have from the first operated in an uninterrupted sequence like a fixed fate; and that there is no will behind or within that fate; so that it must work itself out in the absence of such a will, as a machine must run down in the absence of a man. There were more people in the nineteenth century than in the ninth who happened to hold this particular theory of the universe. I myself happened to hold it; and therefore I obviously cannot believe in miracles." That is perfectly good sense; but so is the counter-statement; "I do not happen to hold it; and therefore I obviously can believe in miracles."

The advantage of an elementary philosophic habit is that it permits a man, for instance, to understand a statement like this, "Whether there can or can not be exceptions to a process depends on the nature of that process." The disadvantage of not having it is that a man will turn impatiently even from so simple a truism; and call it metaphysical gibberish. He will then go off and say: "One can't have such things in the twentieth century"; which really is gibberish. Yet the former statement could surely be explained to him in sufficiently simple terms. If a man sees a river run downhill day after day and year after year, he is justified in reckoning, we might say in betting, that it will do so till he dies. But he is not justified in saying that it cannot run uphill, until he really knows why it runs downhill. To say it does so by gravitation answers the physical but not the philosophical question. It only repeats that there is a repetition; it does not touch the deeper question of whether that repetition could be altered by anything outside it. And that depends on whether there *is* anything outside it. For instance, suppose that a man had only seen the river in a dream. He might have seen it in a hundred dreams, always repeating itself and always running downhill. But that would not prevent the hundredth dream being different and the river climbing the mountain; because the dream is a dream, and there *is* something outside it. Mere repetition does not prove reality or inevitability. We must know the nature of the thing and the cause of the repetition. If the nature of the thing is a Creation, and the cause of the thing a Creator, in other words if the repetition itself is only the repetition of something willed by a person, then it is *not* impossible for the same person to will a different thing. If a man is a fool for believing in a Creator, then he is a fool for believing in a miracle; but not otherwise. Otherwise, he is simply a philosopher who is consistent in his philosophy.

A modern man is quite free to choose either philosophy. But what is actually the matter with the modern man is that he does not know even his own philosophy; but only his own phraseology. He can only answer the next spiritual message produced by a spiritualist, or the next cure attested by doctors at Lourdes, by repeating what are generally nothing but phrases; or are, at their best, prejudices.

Thus, when so brilliant a man as Mr. H. G. Wells says that such supernatural ideas have become impossible "for intelligent people", he is (for that instant) not talking like an intelligent person. In other words, he is not talking like a philosopher;

because he is not even saying what he means. What he means is, not " impossible for intelligent men ", but, " impossible for intelligent monists ", or, " impossible for intelligent determinists ". But it is not a negation of *intelligence* to hold any coherent and logical conception of so mysterious a world. It is not a negation of intelligence to think that all experience is a dream. It is not unintelligent to think it a delusion, as some Buddhists do ; let alone to think it a product of creative will, as Christians do. We are always being told that men must no longer be so sharply divided into their different religions. As an immediate step in progress, it is much more urgent that they should be more clearly and more sharply divided into their different philosophies.

VANDALISM

VANDALISM is of two kinds, the negative and the positive; as in the Vandals of the ancient world, who destroyed buildings, and the Vandals of the modern world, who erect them. A long procession of those typically modern thinkers, who are too tired to think, has already left behind a trail or tradition of language; by which it is vaguely suggested that whatever is constructive is good and only what is destructive is bad. Anyone wishing to lose himself in mazes of such logic, or rather illogicality, may put to himself some particular proposition; as that it is good to construct a stake, with faggots, for burning a man alive, and yet bad to destroy a growing plantation or cut down trees, which is the only possible way of doing it. But in the particular case of Vandalism, it is very specially necessary to remember that the real argument is all the other way. Of two bad things, it is better to be the barbarian who destroys something, which for some reason he dislikes or does not understand, and who may yet sincerely like other things that he does understand, rather than to be the vulgarian who erects something exactly expressive of what he likes; and in that act rears a colossal image of the smallness of his soul. Destructive Vandalism, though a very great evil at the present time, and indeed through all history, has not been in all history so bad as it is now; and certainly not so bad as many more constructive things that exist now.

It is important to remember that there are two kinds of mere destructiveness; neither on the noblest level of human culture, but neither on the most ignoble. First, of course, the

The Common Man

Vandal may be the Iconoclast. He may destroy certain artistic creations because they are really opposed to his moral convictions. Thus a Puritan fanatic from America might conceivably think himself commanded by the Lord to dynamite Westminster Abbey, because it is full of idols; that is of images with a religious character. Curiously enough, he would be half right. It is full of idols; but they are not images of a religious character. Anybody can see at a glance that medieval figures of saints and angels are not worshipped; for the perfectly simple reason that they are themselves represented in the act of worshipping. But the eighteenth-century statues of statesmen and generals really are idols. They are manifestly set up, not to the glory of God, but to the glory of the men there represented; who are to be directly worshipped for their own sake; as the Pagans worshipped demigods and heroes. Lord Polkerton and Admiral Bangs are not themselves represented in the act of worshipping; but in the act of being worshipped. For the eighteenth century, which has been called the Age of Reason, was the real Age of Idolatry. This, however, is a parenthesis. The point is that the American fanatic would be a much finer fellow than the American chain-store man who finds half London in the chains of his cheap and tawdry stores. If the dynamite of the Iconoclast caved in the whole front of Westminster Abbey, I should be far less horrified than I am at a project of a Yankee shopkeeper for building a tower with bells, taller than Westminster Cathedral. It is curious to reflect on the few stray nerves of criticism and sensibility that still remain. I fancy that if an American erected immediately opposite Windsor Castle, on the other side of the river, another castle of exactly the same castellated form and plan, only a little bigger (being made of cheap and rotten material) and then flew the flag of his own ancient family in direct defiance of the personal flag of the King, there would be

Vandalism

a good many people in society who would tell the American, however rich he was, that this was going a bit too far. Which shows how much safer it is to insult religion than to insult royalty.

Secondly, in the great moral philosophy of being fair to Vandals, we must remember that there is a certain element in life which has even a right to its place in life, though that place may not always be easy to find, without displacing better things. We talk of positive and negative, of creation and destruction; but in a sense the association is incorrect. Destruction is not negation; at least it is not always and of necessity negation. There is a positive pleasure in destruction, which can be harmless and is certainly real. It is innocent, for it is felt strongly by children when they first tear up paper or break sticks. But I trust that few of us have so entirely lost our innocence, as to be unable to drink deep joy from smashing up the happy home. Breathes there a man with soul so dead that he has never, when standing in a respectable parlour, felt a wild desire to seize a pot and plant and send it crashing through the bow windows into the front-garden or the street? These things are not entirely to be sterilised; these things also are from God. It is all explained in a ballade which my friends and I composed years ago, after I had shattered a great tumbler all over the carpet. It has the refrain: " I like the noise of breaking glass." And though I should not like the glass of Chartres Cathedral to be broken merely to gratify this taste, I can imagine two types of human beings who might break it and remain human. A lunatic might do it because he thought it unChristian to make pictures of the life of Christ; and a boy might do it because he liked the noise of breaking glass. So much for the defence of the more dignified Vandal—the Destroyer.

But the new sort of Vandal is much more indefensible. The crude creative Vandal is much more of a pestilence and a peril. There is more to be said for the conqueror, who makes a solitude and calls it peace, than for the other who makes a pandemonium and calls it progress. For he brands upon the eye in memory the positive and vivid picture of his own meanness and stupidity. The barbarians who laid waste the world may have prevailed in so far that some good things were forgotten, but they did not insist that their own base and barbarous things should be remembered. But that is exactly what the "constructive" vulgarian does. That is exactly what the Modern Vandal does. It is a gloomy pleasure to think that if a dissolving civilisation brings in forces more like those of the Ancient Vandals, if vagabond tribes from Asia or Eastern Europe drift in with the old-world, animal, almost automatic destructiveness of the Huns or the Bashi-Bazouks, they at least will wreck and ruin all the new Civilisation without any pretence of reconstructing it; and that towering and glaring flats, or long leagues of flashy glass shop-windows, will lie in rubbish-heaps side by side with better things.

ELIZABETH BARRETT BROWNING

MRS. BROWNING was a great poet, and not, as is idly and vulgarly supposed, only a great poetess. The word poetess is bad English, and it conveys a particularly bad compliment. Nothing is more remarkable about Mrs. Browning's work than the absence of that trite and namby-pamby elegance which the last two centuries demanded from lady writers. Wherever her verse is bad, it is bad from some extravagance of imagery, some violence of comparison, some kind of debauch of cleverness. Her nonsense never arises from weakness, but from a confusion of powers. If the phrase explain itself, she is far more a great poet than she is a good one.

Mrs. Browning often appears more luscious and sentimental than many other literary women, but this was because she was stronger. It requires a certain amount of internal force to break down. A complete self-humiliation requires enormous strength, more strength than most of us possess. When she was writing the poetry of self-abandonment she really abandoned herself with the valour and decision of an anchorite abandoning the world. Such a couplet as—

> Our Euripides, the human,
> With his dropping of warm tears.

gives to most of us a sickly and nauseous sensation. Nothing can be well conceived more ridiculous than Euripides going about dropping tears with a loud splash, and Mrs. Browning coming after him with a thermometer. But the one emphatic point about this idiotic couplet is that Mrs. Hemans would never have written it. She would have written something perfectly dignified, perfectly harmless, perfectly inconsiderable. Mrs. Browning was in a great and serious difficulty. She really meant something. She aimed at a vivid and curious image, and she missed it. She had that catastrophic and public failure which is as much as a medal or a testimonial, the badge of the brave.

In spite of the tiresome half-truth that art is unmoral, the arts require a certain considerable number of moral qualities, and more especially all the arts require courage. The art of drawing, for example, requires even a kind of physical courage. Any one who has tried to draw a straight line and failed knows that he fails chiefly in nerve, as he might fail to jump off a cliff. And similarly all great literary art involves the element of risk, and the greatest literary artists have commonly been those who have run the greatest risk of talking nonsense. Almost all great poets rant, from Shakespeare downwards. Mrs. Browning was Elizabethan in her luxuriance and her audacity, and the gigantic scale of her wit. We often feel with her as we feel with Shakespeare, that she would have done better with half as much talent. The great curse of the Elizabethans is upon her, that she cannot leave anything alone, she cannot write a single line without a conceit :

> And the eyes of the peacock fans
> Winked at the alien glory,

she said of the Papal fans in the presence of the Italian tricolour.

> And a royal blood sends glances up her princely eye to
> trouble.
> And the shadow of a monarch's crown is softened in
> her hair,

is her description of a beautiful and aristocratic lady. The notion of peacock feathers winking like so many London urchins is perhaps one of her rather aggressive and outrageous figures of speech. The image of a woman's hair as the softened shadow of a crown is a singularly vivid and perfect one. But both have the same quality of intellectual fancy and intellectual concentration. They are both instances of a sort of ethereal epigram. This is the great and dominant characteristic of Mrs. Browning, that she was significant alike in failure and success. Just as every marriage in the world, good or bad, is a marriage, dramatic, irrevocable, and big with coming events, so every one of her wild weddings between alien ideas is an accomplished fact which produces a certain effect on the imagination, which has for good or evil become part and parcel of our mental vision for ever. She gives the reader the impression that she never declined a fancy, just as some gentlemen of the eighteenth century never declined a duel. When she fell it was always because she missed the foothold, never because she funked the leap.

" Casa Guidi Windows " is, in one aspect, a poem very typical of its author. Mrs. Browning may fairly be called the peculiar poet of Liberalism, of that great movement of the first half of the nineteenth century towards the emancipation of men from ancient institutions which had gradually changed their nature, from the houses of refuge which had turned into dungeons, and the mystic jewels which remained only as fetters. It was not what we ordinarily understand by revolt. It had no hatred in its heart for ancient and essentially human institutions. It had that deeply conservative belief in the most ancient of institutions, the average man, which goes by the name of democracy. Their ideal, like the ideal of all sensible people, was a chaotic and confused notion of goodness made up of English primroses and Greek statues, birds singing in

April, and regiments being cut to pieces for a flag. They were neither Radicals nor Socialists, but Liberals, and a liberal is a noble and indispensable lunatic who tries to make a cosmos of his own head.

Mrs. Browning and her husband were more liberal than most Liberals. Theirs was the hospitality of the intellect and the hospitality of the heart, which is the best definition of the term. They never fell into the habit of the idle revolutionists of supposing that the past was bad because the future was good, which amounted to asserting that because humanity had never made anything but mistakes it was now quite certain to be right. Browning possessed in a greater degree than any other man the power of realising that all conventions were only victorious revolutions. He could follow the medieval logicians in all their sowing of the wind and reaping of the whirlwind with all that generous ardour which is due to abstract ideas. He could study the ancients with the young eyes of the Renaissance and read a Greek grammar like a book of love lyrics. This immense and almost confounding Liberalism of Browning doubtless had some effect upon his wife. In her vision of New Italy she went back to the image of Ancient Italy like an honest and true revolutionist; for all true revolutions are reversions to the natural and the normal. A revolutionist who breaks with the past is a notion fit for an idiot. For how could a man even wish for something which he had never heard of? Mrs. Browning's inexhaustible sympathy with all the ancient and essential passions of humanity was nowhere more in evidence than in her conception of patriotism. For some dark reason, which it is difficult indeed to fathom, belief in patriotism in our day is held to mean principally a belief in every other nation abandoning its patriotic feelings. In the case of no other passion does this weird contradiction exist. Men whose lives are mainly based upon friendship sympathise with the friendships of others. The interest of engaged couples in each other is a proverb, and like many other proverbs sometimes a nuisance. In patriotism alone it is considered correct just now to assume that the sentiment does not exist in other people. It was not so with the great Liberals of Mrs. Browning's time. The Brownings had, so to speak, a disembodied talent for patriotism. They loved England and they loved Italy; yet they were the very reverse of cosmopolitans. They loved the two countries as countries, not as arbitrary divisions of the globe. They had hold of the root and essence of patriotism. They knew how certain flowers and birds and rivers pass into the mills of the brain and come out as wars and discoveries, and how some triumphant adventure or some staggering crime wrought in a remote continent may bear about it the colour of an Italian city or the soul of a silent village of Surrey.

THE ERASTIAN ON THE ESTABLISHMENT

DEAN INGE is so obviously the most acute, the most cultivated and the most individual of the sceptical school which he represents, that there is sometimes inevitably an appearance of singling him out, when the singularity is only due to his own distinction. It is due, if we must put it more roughly, to there being so very few intellectuals of that school who are worth answering. I have often myself, perhaps, put it more roughly than I intended; but the double duty involved presents a problem not easily solved. The trouble is that he is really in such a false position that the true statement of it sounds itself like a taunt. Yet it may not be meant for a taunt, but only for a truth. His own position certainly does not seem as false to him as it does to us; but to excuse it requires a long explanation which is impossible in so short an expression. For instance, he wrote the other day a severe condemnation of those of the Anglican clergy who favour the Disestablishment of the Church of England. It may seem curt to retort, as I should be first inclined to do, that the Dean naturally hesitates to sever the one very slender strip of red tape that still connects him with Christianity. Yet it is quite true; and it is not necessarily merely hostile.

To understand the curious case of Dean Inge, in a spirit of Christian charity, we must leave for the moment all questions of creed and definition and call up another image before the mind. It is the image that was in the mind of Matthew Arnold when he openly said that, being almost an agnostic himself, he yet wished to preserve the institutions of religion, and especially the literature of religion; that he found these best preserved

The Erastian on the Establishment

in the Church of England and advised nobody to leave it. We must call up the image of a historic hierarchy of priests who are also professors, and whose main business is scholarship and the study of letters; it was not for nothing that both Arnold and Inge had connections with Oxford. Most of such men would probably be Christian in hereditary sentiment and subject-matter; but their Christianity would not, so to speak, be the point. We can even imagine the institution better if we think of it as a Confucian rather than a Christian foundation. The idea of it is a classical culture that is undisturbed. But it has this further essential point; that if its traditions and rites must be undisturbed, so also must its doubts and negations be undisturbed. It must be so traditional that a sceptic is safe there.

Something like this may really have existed in Chinese and other pagan parallels. Something like it probably did exist among the last pagan priests of antiquity. A jolly old heathen Flamen or Pontifex Maximus did not want to be disturbed in explaining away the gods to his friends; and certainly did not want to make himself responsible for drawing the exact line between truth and fable in the metamorphoses of Ovid or the genealogies of Jupiter. And something of the same sort did exist in the Academic Anglicanism of the Erastian age in England, when scholarly Whigs and rather worldly bishops quoted indifferently Horace and Augustine and Gibbon over the nuts and wine. That is the Establishment which Dean Inge really likes to see established; that is the civilised institution which he does really and sincerely believe to be a good thing; a traditional home of learning and liberal education, though mainly for the few; a thing that to the outer world shall be as authoritative as the medieval abbots, but in its inner life be as casual as the Greek philosophers; a thing that need not exclude the heretical, but does exclude the ignorant; a thing that can admit all questions so long as it is never questioned itself.

Now a cultural tradition of that kind can have many marks of dignity and national value; and a man may without absurdity or falsity wish to preserve it as a national thing. But there are a number of conditions to be remembered, which Dean Inge now seems continually to forget. For one thing, the nation must continue in the same mood of respect towards the college of professors, or whatever it is to be called. The modern mood is changing very rapidly; and I think it would be an exaggeration to say that all England is now filled with an affection and veneration for Dons. Another difficulty is that whatever this sort of Chinese synod can do, it cannot exist side by side with a real and passionate religion. It was defeated by the Christians at the end of the Roman era. It was defeated even by the Methodists at the end of the eighteenth century. It is often quoted of poor Charles II that he said that Puritanism was no religion for a gentleman. It is not so often added that he also said that Anglicanism was no religion for a Christian.

This, I fancy, is what the Dean really means; and it explains why he is at once such a conservative and such an iconoclast; such a sceptic and such a Tory. It is not, of course, in so many words what he says. When driven to defend his bunch of bigwigs, with their libraries and endowments, he characteristically takes an old book out of those dusty shelves, and quotes from Burke the thesis that the Church was only the State seen in one light and the State was only the Church seen in another light. Burke always struck me as, of all men, the man with the most imaginative and the most utterly unreal mind. Even as he uttered such a phrase, he must have known that the Church was packed with people who did not believe in it, and that the leaders of the State had almost ceased to pretend to do so. All the time, it is worth remarking, Burke was gravely discussing the admission to the Church of Dissenters whose whole enthusiasm was admittedly concerned with making their Calvinist God if possible more of a devil than he was before. He knew the world around him was crowded with such fanatics and with such blasphemers; and yet he could bring himself to imagine that the actual secular condition of all England was the Church of Christ, if one only slightly shifted one's point of view. But it was rather odd to maintain this even in Burke's time; it is perfectly crazy to maintain it in our time. Dean Inge admits, that two great calamities might really ruin his plan, and make the position of the Church of England impossible. But he thinks that neither is likely enough to be worth considering. One is—what would happen if a large body of England really abandoned Christianity? The other is—what would happen if England went over to Rome? The answer to both these impossibilities is very simple. It is that the second might happen any day, and the first has happened already.

Of course it is possible to play an endless game with the word " Christian " and perpetually extend its epoch by perpetually diminishing its meaning. By the time that everybody has agreed that being a Christian only means thinking that Christ was a good man, it will indeed be true that few persons outside lunatic asylums can be denied the name of Christian. But it is really a mere alteration in the meaning of a word that prevents us saying frankly that a great mass, probably a majority, of our modern people are Pagans. Many of them make a mock of standards of family piety or public dignity that were generally accepted by the Pagans. But most of them, if they have any religion at all, have a religion of pantheism or pure ethics which most of the great Christian characters of history, Catholic or Protestant, would have instantly stamped as pagan. If you had asked Wesley, or Swedenborg, or Dr. Johnson, or Baxter, or Luther, they would have called the modern mood heathen more promptly, if possible, than would Bossuet or Bellarmine. If it is true that the Church is simply the religion of the State, we have got precious near to saying that it is simply the irreligion of the State.

There was a bitter and cynical man (also, I am sure, an Oxford man) who said, " The Church of England is our last bulwark against Christianity ". This is quite unjust as a description of the Church of England. But it is not altogether unjust as a description of Dean Inge. What is really at the back of his mind is this image of a great academic and cultural tradition, established as a national need but not specially as a spiritual need. It is to have religious texts—to criticise ; religious ceremonial—to reform slightly and rather pompously from time to time ; a sort of assumption on religion, in the sense that it could not tolerate the horrors of anything like the Russian denial of religion. But all through, it will be subject to one unmistakable test. It can coexist with Doubt ; but it cannot coexist with Faith.

At the end of his article, Dean Inge tries to toss aside as impertinent the term Erastianism ; the term is too obviously true not to irritate. But in any case he absurdly underrates its meaning at the moment. It is not a question of whether those who form a nation by being Englishmen could in the abstract form a religion by being Anglicans. It is a question of whether a Church which does at least exist, with some who belong to it and some who do not belong to it, should be ruled by those who do not belong to it. Erastianism exists today in the perfectly practical sense that any Jew, Holy Roller or Hyde Park atheist may dictate what that Christian Church shall do on any matter whatever, however intimate and sacred. Bradlaugh was a Member of Parliament; he might well have become a Cabinet Minister and appointed Bishops. Mr. Saklatvala was a Socialist leader and might quite well be a Labour Minister, with a majority in the House and might by Act of Parliament make the Prayer Book anything he chose. That is State Establishment, as now universally understood; that is what Dean Inge desires and presumably defends; or must set about the delicate task of defending.

THE END OF THE MODERNS

ALL SCHOOLS of thought, moderate or revolutionary or reactionary, are agreed that the future is full of new possibilities or perils, that the various forms of revolt in art or thought are the beginning of big changes, and especially that certain geniuses, creative or destructive, have opened the gates of a new world. The Communist may think they are the gates of heaven, or the Conservative that they are the gates of hell. But both substantially agree that they mark not only the end of the world, but the beginning of another world. The modern writers who have been hailed alternatively as dynamic or demoniac are, for good or evil, but the forerunners of others yet more dynamic or more demoniac. Both sides are heartily agreed about this; and I have the misfortune to disagree with both of them.

I think the first fact about what may roughly be called Futurism is that it has no future. It has still a very lively and interesting present. Indeed, it has already a picturesque and romantic past. The life of D. H. Lawrence, for instance, has already become a mere legend, which might be of any antiquity; and the romantic and rather sentimental glamour that has already gathered about him is now quite as distant and diffused as that which gathered round Byron or Burns. As for the present, no period could be entirely dull when Mr. Aldous Huxley was writing in it; but it is significant to notice what he writes. In *Brave New World* he shows that however grimly he may enjoy the present, he already definitely hates the future. And I only differ from him in not believing that there is any such future to hate.

The End of the Moderns

I take these two names as typical of what has been called in the last decade modernity or revolt; but the thesis I would seriously suggest covers something larger and perhaps simpler. The revolutionary elements in our epoch do not mark the beginning, but the end, of an epoch of revolution. I should hesitate to describe a number of distinguished and often honest literary gentlemen as Dregs; or I would have given that short and convenient title to this article. I prefer to put the same meaning, or even the same metaphor, into the words of a revolutionary poet (whose present unpopularity is enough to show how insecure is the future of revolutionary poetry) and while I drink to the memory of Lawrence or the health of Huxley, murmur the words:

> All thine the last wine that I pour is
> The last in the chalice I drain.

That will suggest the same idea in less offensive language. In short, it is doubtless true, in the words of Mr. Jefferson Brick (that pioneer of revolt), that the Libation of Freedom must sometimes be quaffed in Blood; but whether it be in blood or wine, that cup is very nearly dry.

My reason for thinking this has nothing to do with likes or dislikes or the wish being father to the thought; it is the sort of logic that is more like mathematics or chess. To almost all the modern moral and metaphysical systems, as stated by the moderns themselves, I should be content to add the comment, " Mate in three moves." That is, these thinkers have landed themselves in positions which are already doomed by the laws of thought; or, to change the mathematical to the military figure, their positions are outflanked, their communications cut and their ammunition very obviously running short. In many cases, their form of revolt is one that *can* only be a sort of temporary formation.

The Common Man

Merely to explain what I mean, I will take an extremely crude and even clumsy example first. It does not touch the more distinguished types I have mentioned ; but it does show in a very clear and plain shape the sense in which such things are intrinsically fugitive. I mean what may be called the literary use of blasphemy. Earlier, when the spirit of revolt was younger, it was used by some men of genius ; by Swinburne, in whose work it seems now to have entirely lost its sting. Recently a modern writer, actually appointed to make a special study of Swinburne, asked wearily how anybody could get excited about the verses which said that the Galilean also would go down to the dead. It also disturbed the fine literature and very confused cosmic philosophy of Thomas Hardy, who tried to say (at the same time) that God did not exist, and that He ought to be ashamed of existing ; or possibly that He ought to be ashamed of not existing.

This irritable profanity, which is already rather stale among cultivated people, is apparently still quite fresh to the Communists ; but that is because Bolshevist Russia is the most backward State in Europe. It is even said that attempts were made to print atheistic assertions on match-boxes and sell them in England as propaganda. If it is true, they must have a very queer idea of England, to suppose that its somewhat too inert populace could be roused to universal civil war by bad language printed on a match-box. But the only point here is that this sort of bad language, like all bad language, necessarily weakens itself by use. The literature of atheism is bound to fail, exactly in proportion as it succeeds. The Bolshevists have not merely tried to abolish God, which some think a trick needing some ingenuity. They have tried to make an institution of the abolition of God ; and when the God is abolished, the abolition is abolished. There can never be any *future* for the literature of blasphemy ; for if it fails, it fails ; and if it

The End of the Moderns

succeeds, it becomes a literature of respectability. In short, all *that* sort of effect can only be an instantaneous effect; like smashing a valuable vase that cannot be smashed again. The heaven-defying gesture can only be impressive as a last gesture. Blasphemy is by definition the end of everything, including the blasphemer. The wife of Job saw the common sense of this, when she instinctively said, " Curse God and die." The modern poet, by some thoughtless oversight, so often neglects to die.

This is a very crude and popular instance; but it exactly defines what I mean when I say that all these death-dealing dynamic motions carry the seeds of their own death. And when we turn to the more subtle and suggestive writers, such as those I have named, we shall find that this is exactly their own condition. They are not opening the gates either of heaven or hell; they are in a blind-alley, at the end of which there is no door. They are always philosophising and they have no philosophy. They have not reached that reality, that reason of things, or even that fully realised unreason of things, for which they are obviously and indeed avowedly seeking. But, what is here more to the point, they do not (like the old revolutionists) even know the direction in which they are to seek it. They have failed to discover, not only any purpose in the world, but even any purpose in the will. They are witty, brilliant and fashionable bankrupts. They have come to an end; and they have not come to an End. The earlier rebels were happy in being pioneers of the actual forward movements of their time; as Walt Whitman, axe in hand, walked before the actual march of industrial democracy. But Mr. Aldous Huxley can hardly be roused by the word Democracy. D. H. Lawrence, on the other hand, could be roused by the word Industrialism.

So far as that is concerned, the case is simple enough.

The Common Man

Lawrence, whom so many moderns have made a sort of test of modernity, was in fact in violent revolt against anything and everything that can be called modern. He did not merely hate industrial machinery and the servile society it has produced. He hated practically all the effects of science and public education and even political progress. All that is very right and proper; but he also hated intellectualism along with industrialism; though why anybody should think industrialism particularly intellectual, I cannot imagine. But he was perfectly right in his revolt against these things; only they are all in their very nature modern or very recent things. He himself was in favour of very ancient things, and notably of one of the most ancient things on the earth, the worship of the earth itself; the Great Mother: Demeter. But he could not, by his own admission, even do this, without almost literally cutting off his own head. It may be regarded, in a thinker, as at least equivalent to cutting his own throat. He confessed himself, in effect, that he could only worship Demeter from the neck downwards. He could only do it by setting the subconsciousness against the consciousness, or in other words, the dreams against the daylight. It is surely a remarkable gospel for an age of realism. In a famous passage he wrote, "In my dark heart gods are," but added that in his "white mind" they were not, having been washed or whitewashed out by elementary education. But the modern educated mind is not white; it is only pale.

The point is that from every point of view, ancient or modern, his solution is not a solution. A man cannot leave his head at home and send his body dancing through the world and doing as it likes; and there is no earthly reason for supposing that it will do what it ought, from a modern or any other point of view. For instance, if it fancies food, it will steal, and it will steal quite as readily from Communist Stores as from private houses. This is not the beginning of a new life; a gorgeous jungle opening before man as a sort of Mowgli. It is the end of an utterly impossible argument, which cannot be carried any further. A man wallowing in the earth with the animals would not be an animal. He would only be a lunatic; which is the exact opposite of an animal. There was no way out of the intellectual or anti-intellectual *impasse* into which Lawrence had got himself; except the third road which he never thought of . . . possibly because it leads to Rome. If mere rationalism is insufficient, we must get above the reason and not below it. The direct appeal to Nature is utterly unnatural. I admit it was weakly conceded by the Pantheists of the first revolutionary phase; now very remote; and many who would pass for pious accepted it. Professor Babbitt has pointed out some of the dangerous concessions in Wordsworth. Another even more orthodox writer expressed the error of that period. He said that we must rise through Nature up to Nature's God. He was wrong. We must descend from God down to God's Nature. Nature is only right when seen in the light of the highest right; whether it be, as some Humanists would say, in the mind of Man, or as Christians would say, in the mind of God. But they really believe in their God; and Lawrence did not really believe in his Goddess. He passionately disbelieved in everything, except something in which he could not really believe.

Mr. Aldous Huxley, whom I have taken as the other outstanding talent of that time, sees this impossibility and avoids it. But he can only avoid it by cutting down his own standard to something so thin that it can hardly stand. In one of his novels a character sums up much of the general teaching of the author, by saying that Man must not hope to be either an animal or an angel. He adds, significantly, that it is a tight-rope sort of business. Now walking on a tight-rope is both difficult and dangerous; and the author makes the good life really more difficult than it is for an ascetic. He has not only to avoid being an animal, but he must guard against any unlucky accident that might turn him into an angel. That is, he is forbidden to have the enthusiasms and spiritual ambitions that have sustained the saints, and yet he has got to become in cold blood something much more exceptional than a saint. Nobody asks such a realist as Mr. Huxley to idealise the real. But such a realist must surely know that human nature cannot show, at every instant, the valour and vigilance of a spiritual tight-rope walker, cannot suffer more for this ideal than all the heroes, and yet be forbidden even to idealise its own ideal. The plan of life is simply obviously unworkable; where the plans of the wildest mystics and martyrs have proved workable.

I say that I do not abhor these men as the first figures of an advancing anarchist army. On the contrary, I admire these men as the last figures of a defeated anarchist army. I take these two original and forcible writers as types of many others; but the point is that they are not, like the anarchists of history, at the head of an army marching in a determined direction. That is exactly what they are not. Lawrence rushed out against almost everything; Huxley, being more sensitive, recoils from almost everything. But, however valuable be the vivid description of the one or the sharp criticism of the other, they are not valuable as guides; and certainly not as guides to a revolution. They had not the simplification given either by religion or irreligion. There was something grand about D. H. Lawrence groping blindly in the dark; but he really was in the dark, not only about the Will of God, but about the will of D. H. Lawrence. He was ready to go anywhere; but he did not really know where to go next. Aldous Huxley is ideally witty; but he is at his wit's end.

The End of the Moderns

Now of course there are numberless copyists and followers calling themselves revolutionary, who would say that they knew where to go ; simply because they are content with some conventional word like Communism. For Communism is almost the same word as convention ; it means people getting " together ", and nothing else. But that very fact illustrates what I say, when I say that the army is short of ammunition and the end is near. When the great democratic movement began, it was supported by real democratic emotions. Only Comradeship can be the soul of Communism ; for otherwise it has no soul. But the more we note the actual temper of the new rebels, the more we shall note that all that is gone. The men who call themselves Communists are not Comrades. Their tone is bitterly individualistic, and bitterly critical. When Walt Whitman looked at a crowd, it is really true to say that he loved the crowd. When a modern poet, imitating the free verse of Whitman (which was the least free thing about him), describes a crowd, it is always to describe his disgust with the crowd. They have none of the natural sentiments that would correspond with their unnatural dogmas. In other words, the army is short of powder, short of passion, short of the primary impulses that make such an army act. For they are not a vanguard advancing, they are the end of a revolutionary adventure, both for good and evil, which began more than a hundred years ago ; and they are fighting the rearguard action of a retreat. Liberty, Equality and Fraternity really meant something to the emotions of those who first used the phrase. But Fraternity is the last emotion anyone is likely to find in an acrid article or poem by a modern rebel ; Liberty is lost in both systems, old and new ; and Equality only remains in the form of a dull attempt at uniformity, copied from that very mechanical capitalism which the rebels would reject.

The Common Man

Along with those who accept the thing as a label, or hope fallaciously that they may accept it as a fashion, there are some who accept it in a more noble but very negative way; for the very reasons I have urged in this article. I mean that they accept it desperately, as the only way out of an intellectual *impasse*. It is not too much to say that Mr. Middleton Murry accepts Soviets with the gestures of a great heathen accepting suicide. He seems to exult in the thought of it being the end of everything, or at least the end of nearly everything he likes. That is yet another example of the psychology I have attempted to describe; the psychology of men who have come to the end. I do not want to confuse this distinct impression with jaded journalistic talk about pessimism. People will call Mr. Aldous Huxley a pessimist; in the sense of one who makes the worst of it. To me he is that far more gloomy character; the man who makes the best of it. He gives the best advice he can; in conditions of converging impossibility. I do not write here in a hostile spirit about any of these recent realistic or revolutionary writers; on the contrary, I sincerely sympathise with them, because, unlike the earlier revolutionists, they know they are in an intellectual hole. Doubtless, there are thousands of gay and buoyant innovators, who are not intelligent enough to know it. But the same plan of defeat is spread over the whole situation. It can be seen, for instance, in the thousands of thoughtless "sexual" novels, the writers of which are evidently unconscious that they have got into a logical contradiction about the whole position of sex. They inherit the notion that sex is a serious crux and crisis; for indeed this is necessary to the very nature of a novel. In this they are living on the last legacy of Romanticism; which, in its turn, was living on the last legacy of religion. But their new and simple philosophy teaches them that sex is only the sort of necessity that is also a triviality; that sex is no more crucial than smoking. So that the modern novelist, torn between two ideas, has to attempt to write a story about a man who smokes twenty cigarettes and tries to think that each of them is a crisis. In all these things there is an intellectual tangle ; the sort of thing that eventually tightens and throttles. Of this sort of philosopher it is exactly and literally true to say that, if you give him rope enough, he will hang himself. It is consoling to reflect that suicide holds a sublime place in his philosophy.

WALTER DE LA MARE

IT HAS not always been sufficiently understood that a critic of poetry should be a poetical critic. Literary history is littered with the disasters of good critics who become bad critics, merely by colliding with good poets. But·one of the first facts which a good poetical critic will realise, is one which the poet of necessity realises : the limitation of language, and especially the poverty and clumsiness of the language of praise. There is hardly any praise of poets that does not sound as if they were all the same sort of poets, and this is true even when the praise is intended to say precisely the opposite. Thus the habit of calling somebody " unique " has become universal, and we may insist that a man is original, and still leave the impression that originality is about as rare as original sin.

But this difficulty applies in a special way to Mr. Walter de la Mare and his poetry, because the common poetical terms of praise for that poetry are also applied to a totally different sort of poetry. He stands very close, in time and place and appearance, to a group of writers, most of them good writers and some of them great writers, from whom he is really quite free and distinct. Only the epithets applied to him are also applied to them. When we say that he is a dreamy and fantastic poet, an interpreter of elfland, a singer of strange rhymes that have a witchery and wild charm for children, and the rest, we are driven to use a number of terms that have now become a little trite, perhaps, as applied to other talented persons who are utterly different. The fountains, the foundations, the primary principles of imagination and the view of life, are really quite different in a man like Mr. de la Mare from all that they are, let us say, in a man like Sir James Barrie or a man like Mr. A. A. Milne. This, I need hardly say, has nothing to do with depreciating these authors, but only with appreciating each author for his own sake. Yet there is a sort of tangle of tradition, and a recognised traffic in certain subjects, which may well confuse a modern reader about all this sort of literature of fancy. For instance ; we might start by saying that the tradition of *Treasure Island* and its pirates was continued in *Peter Pan* and its pirates. We might say that the elvish children of *Peter Pan* were continued in the elvish children of *When We Were Very Young*. And then we might imagine vaguely that all this sort of thing, the bottle of rum and the crocodile's dinner and the king's breakfast, were all somehow stuffed or stirred up together in a hotch-potch called *Peacock Pie*. But this is to miss the whole point about the poet, and especially where he is rather more than a poet. It would be easy to link him up with the tradition of Treasure Island ; for he has himself written a very fascinating fantasia about Desert Islands. But the association would be an error, for he has not really laid up for himself treasure in the same sort of treasure islands. There is really a sort of dynasty, a Scottish dynasty, of Stevenson and Barrie. But it descended on the infantile side to Scots like Kenneth Graham and on the manly, or at least boyish side to Scots like John Buchan. It has nothing to do with Walter de la Mare ; because his philosophy is different. One way of putting it would be to say that, poetic as are the fairy-tales of the Scots, they are the fairy-tales of the Sceptics. The fairy-tales of de la Mare are not those of the Sceptic but of the Mystic. Take the primary idea with which all the best work for imaginative infancy, as supplied by Stevenson and Barrie, really began. It began with an idea which is called " make-believe ". That is, strictly speaking, it is written by men who do not believe ;

and even written for children who do not believe; children who quite logically and legitimately make believe. But de la Mare's world is not merely a world of illusion; it is in quite another sense a world of imagination. It is a real world of which the reality can only be represented to us by images. De la Mare does not, in the material sense, believe that there is an ogre who crawls round houses and is turned back by the influence of the Holy Child; any more than Barrie believes that there is an immortal little boy who plays physically in Kensington Gardens. But de la Mare does believe that there is a devouring evil that is always warring with innocence and happiness; and Barrie does not believe that innocence and happiness go on having an uninterrupted legal occupation of Kensington Gardens. Stories of the school of *Peter Pan* are radiant and refreshing dreams; but they are dreams. They are the dreams of somebody taking refuge from real life in an inner life of the imagination; but not necessarily of somebody believing that there is also a larger universal life corresponding to that imagination. The first is a fabulist but the second is a symbolist; as if we were to compare the talking animals of La Fontaine with the typical animals of Blake. Blake (though certainly mad in a quiet way) probably did not believe that golden lions and tigers walked about on the hills of Albion; and La Fontaine did not believe that garrulous lions engaged in chatty conversation with foxes. But Blake did believe that certain tremendous truths, only to be shown under the types of golden lions, were really true; and, what is most important of all, were not only within him, but beyond him. So the conversation of Mr. Milne's funny little pigs and bears is as delightful as La Fontaine, and only deceptive in the same sense as La Fontaine. That is to say, it is not false, because it is fictitious; or what was called fabulous. But the rhymes of the Mad Prince, though they would be called fantastic, are

Walter de la Mare

not merely fabulous. The Mad Prince, like the Mad Poet, in the person of poor Blake, is, after all, something essentially different from The Mad Hatter. There are hollow undertones in his queer questions, about green grass for graves, which do really re-echo from things deep and secret as the grave.

Many who remember the apparently nonsensical nursery rhymes which figure among Walter de la Mare's verses for children may imagine that I am drawing a fine distinction; but it is not a distinction of degree but of direction. The parrot and the monkey who attended the dwarfs on the Isle of Lone, may seem quite as disconnected from normal natural history as the owl and the pussy-cat who went to sea. But there remains a real distinction, outside all natural history, between unnatural history and supernatural history. Mr. de la Mare's parrots and monkeys are as symbolical as the strange beasts in the Book of Apocalypse. Only they are symbolical in a sense that means something better than the allegorical. Symbolism is superior to allegory, in so far that the symbol exactly fits; and there is therefore no superfluous explanation that needs to pass through ordinary language, or need be, or indeed can be, translated into other words. If a parrot only means speech, or a monkey only means mischief (as he generally does) then nothing beyond pictorial elegance is gained by not dealing directly with mischief, or speaking plainly about speech. And the mere allegory never gets beyond a pictorial elegance, adorning what might well be unadorned. But the great mystic can sometimes present to us a purple parrot or a sea-green monkey, in exactly such a manner as to suggest submerged or mysterious ideas, and even truths, that could not possibly be conveyed by any other creature of any other colour. The meaning fits the symbol and the symbol the meaning; and we cannot separate them from each other, as we can in the analysis of allegory. And there is a side of spiritual life, so to speak, which might well be represented by sea-green monkeys, whose colouring is not merely arbitrary colouring like that of the mysterious monsters in that admirable but purely nonsensical rhyme about the Jumblies, whose heads were green and whose hands were blue. The colour scheme here is pleasing, but it is no disrespect to the great Mr. Lear of the *Nonsense Rhymes*, to say that his cosmic philosophy would not have been convulsed even if their hands had been green and their heads had been blue. Walter de la Mare's nonsense is never nonsensical in that sense. If his monkey is sea-green, it is for some reason as deep and significant as the sea ; even though he cannot express it in any other way except by patient and uncomplaining greenness. And he would never mention even a green weed, a dock or nettle in a ditch, without meaning it to bear the same witness in the same way.

It is the first paradox about him that we can find the evidence of his faith in his consciousness of evil. It is the second paradox that we can find the spiritual springs of much of his poetry in his prose. If we turn, for instance, to that very powerful and even terrible short story called *Seaton's Aunt*, we find we are dealing directly with the diabolic. It does so in a sense quite impossible in all the merely romantic or merely ironic masters of that nonsense that is admittedly illusion. There was no nonsense about Seaton's Aunt. There was no illusion about her concentrated and paralysing malignity ; but it was a malignity that had an extension beyond this world. She was a witch ; and the realisation that witches can occasionally exist is a part of Realism, and a test for anyone claiming a sense of Reality. For we do not especially want them to exist ; but they do. Now the wonderland of the other charmers of childhood consists entirely of things that we want to exist, or they want to exist. Whether they are of the older

Walter de la Mare

English or Victorian school of Lewis Carroll and Lear, or of the later Scottish school of Stevenson and Barrie, their whole aim is to create a sort of cosmos within the cosmos, which shall be free from evil; a crystal sphere in which there shall be no cracks or flaws or clouds of evil. *Peter Pan* is a wonderful evocation of the happy daydreams of childhood. There is plenty of fighting and ferocity; because fighting and ferocity are among the very happiest dreams of a really innocent and Christian childhood. But Captain Hook the Pirate is not really wicked; he is only ferocious; which, after all, it is his simple duty as an honest and industrious pirate to be. But there are rhymes, even nursery rhymes, of Walter de la Mare in which the shiver is a real shiver, not only of the spine but of the spirit. They have an atmosphere which is not merely thrilling, but also chilling. They lay a finger that is not of the flesh on a nerve that is not of the body; in their special way of suggesting the chill of change or death or antiquity. To do this was against the whole purpose and origin of the fairyland of the later Victorians. Like all literature, it cannot really be understood without reference to history; and, like all history, it cannot really be understood without reference to religion. As scepticism gradually dried up the conventional religion of the English, and even of the Scotch, poetic and humane spirits turned more and more to the construction of an inner world of fancy, that should be both a refuge and a substitute. William Morris, one of the most large and humane of these later Victorians, admitted it in acknowledging the purely decorative vision in his own work:

> So with this earthly Paradise it is,
>   If you will read aright and pardon me
> Who strive to build a shadowy isle of bliss
>   Midmost the beating of the steely sea.

The Common Man

. And it is the irony of the case that these men, who were
rationalists and realists about the real world, were for that very
reason resolved to be radiant optimists when once they were
inside the city of dreams which was their city of refuge. The
pessimists insisted on having happy dreams; the sceptics
insisted on having omnipotent drugs. But the mystic does not
deal in dreams but in visions; that is, in things seen and not
seeming. The mystic does not desire drugs but the drinking
of that wine that wakes the dead; different in nature from any
opiate that soothes the living.

In short, we may say that the early twentieth century presented two movements towards the fanciful or fantastical, and
away from the merely rational or material: a centripetal
movement and a centrifugal movement. The one spiritual
spiral worked inwards, towards the secret subjective dreams of
man; the other worked outwards towards the spiritual powers
or truths that seemed beyond the reach of man. The new
world made by the first was the great, glowing, iridescent
bubble of the Barrie daydream; the world revealed by the
second was that world of strange skies, at the ends of the earth
and the corners of the sea, that appears in the far-off flashes of
the de la Mare imagination. We might say shortly that Stevenson and Barrie could produce grisly buccaneers dripping with
gore without frightening the children; whereas de la Mare
could produce pollarded willows or whitewashed barns with an
imminent risk of frightening the children, and even the grown-
up people. But it is only fair to say that there is a subtlety only
possible to the first method, as well as a subtlety possible to the
second. It is, as has been already suggested, the subtlety
of an irony which at once accepts and discounts illusion.
It is the whole point of the best work of Barrie, for instance,
that somebody is deceiving himself, but also that somebody
is looking on at somebody who is deceiving himself; and

if they are both deceiving themselves, so much the better for the third person who is looking on from a third angle. Much of this sort of work is like a world of mirrors reflected in mirrors; the reduplication of reflection; the shadow of a shade. To name but one instance: a fairy-tale palace is itself only a fancy; but the court scene in *A Kiss for Cinderella* is not merely the fairy-tale fancy, but a child's fancy about the fancy. This sort of intensive imaginative delicacy is in theory a thing of infinite possibilities; and this does belong to the merely subjective school of symbolism. But what I have called the truly symbolic school of symbolism does still belong altogether to another and, I cannot but think, a larger world. It is all that world of the powers and mysteries beyond mankind which even the sceptic would consent to cover with the celebrated label: " Important, If True ". Perhaps as good an example as can be found is in that truly extraordinary sketch by de la Mare called " The Tree ". I can imagine multitudes of quite intelligent people totally unable to make head or tail of it. It is concerned with a fruit merchant and his brother, who was an artist, and with a Tree, which is talked of in a manner utterly indescribable; as if it were not only more important than anything, but were outside the world. Now Barrie might have dealt admirably with a theme like that; and probably made the human comedy clearer. But the difference is precisely this. Even the reader who cannot understand anything else about de la Mare's story does definitely understand this: that somehow the fruit merchant was wrong, and the artist was right; and, above all, the Tree was right. Now if Barrie had told the tale, he would have taken a gentle pride in leaving us in doubt on that very point; of suggesting that the sceptic might be the sane man, and the Tree might be a delusion. But the Tree is not a delusion.

THE MEANING OF METRE

DID Bret Harte imitate Swinburne? Or (more pleasing thought) did Swinburne imitate Bret Harte? Did Swinburne wrestle in spirit with the admirable poem called "The Heathen Chinee", and then start up from his reading inspired and inflamed to write the great Greek tragedy of "Atalanta in Calydon"? To some academic and pedantic minds, I know that this will not appear an exact literary comparison; though it covers a small point that may be called a curiosity of literature. To them it will sound as if I suggested that John Ruskin was merely a plagiarist of Josh Billings. Anyhow, it is a rather curious coincidence that there is one particular poetical metre, consisting of a quatrain and one long line at the end, which is found nowhere else in all literature, so far as I know, except in the finest and most tragic chorus of Swinburne's Atalanta and in the poem of the Heathen Chinee. It would be possible to get quite a pleasing poetical effect by interleaving the verses of the one with the verses of the other and thus producing a complete and continuous poem, all to the same beautiful tune and combining (as only the greatest masterpieces can do) the qualities of the humanist and the humorist; the elements of the grave and gay. There is no space here to weave the whole of the two narratives together; but a verse or two will show that they move with the same melody in the same metre.

> O would that with feet
> Unsandaled, unshod,
> Over-bold, over-fleet,

214

The Meaning of Metre

I had swum not nor trod
From Arcadia to Calydon northward a blast of the envy
   of God.

Which expressions are strong,
Yet would feebly imply
Some account of a wrong
Not to call it a lie
That was worked upon William my pardner, and the same
   being W. Nye.

It may be urged maliciously, by the unmelodious, that the
entity is a mere accident of arrangement on the page; since
the long line could be divided or the short lines linked up. But
this is not true. That last long rolling line is really unique,
like a wave sweeping away all that went before. And the
moral is that metre is not artificial but elemental; it is smooth
like Niagara. That long rushing line does express the sea-
worship of Swinburne; that long meandering line does express
the detached lucidity of Truthful James. Since then, writers
have broken writing to bits to make it explosive. The other
Truthful James—I allude to Henry James—began it with a
shower of commas; the more modern poets are quite capable
of keeping the commas and leaving out the words. Others
would make an explosion, or at least a noise, by some line
like, "Burst. Blast. Burst-Blast back-blasted. Bang!" But it
is not really even so noisy as a line like, "Where the thunder-
ing Bosphorus answers the thunder of Pontic seas"; because
it somehow suggests, not a natural noise that cannot be
stopped, but an artificial noise that actually is stopped, if only
by full stops. Metre is more natural than free verse; because
it has more of the movement of nature, and the curves of wind
and wave.

CONCERNING A STRANGE CITY

EVERYONE has his own private and almost secret selection among the examples of the mysterious power of words, the power which a certain verbal combination has over the emotions and even over the soul. It is a commonplace that literature sometimes has a charm, not merely in the sense of the charm of a woman, but of the charm of a witch. Historical scholars question how the ignorant imagination of the Dark Ages distorted the poet Virgil into a magician; and one answer to the question, possibly, is that he was one. Theologians and philosophers debate about the inspiration of scripture; but perhaps the most philosophical argument, for certain scriptural sayings being inspired, is simply that they sound like it. The great lines of the poets are like landscapes or visions; but the same strange light can be found not only in the high places of poetry but in quite obscure corners of prose. And, in my own personal case, there are no words in literature that more directly produce this indescribable effect than a few that appear, almost accidentally, in one episode of Malory's romance of Arthur. They occur in one of the visions of Sir Galahad; or it may be Sir Percivale, for the rest of the scene has rather faded from my memory, save for the constellation of words that shines in the midst of it. But I think that St. Joseph of Arimathea shows the knight a vision of a veiled object; presumably the Holy Grail. And he adds the sentence: "But you shall see it unveiled in the city of Sarras, in the spiritual place."

The soul of this, of course, escapes analysis; but for all that, an attempt at analysis has certain aspects of interest.

Concerning a Strange City

I can only express what I mean by saying that it is the finite part of the image that really suggests infinity. Most worthy and serious people, instead of saying the spiritual place, would say the spiritual world. Some dismal and disgusting people, instead of saying the spiritual place, would say the spiritual plane. And the immediate chill and disenchantment of these changes is due to a vague but vivid sense that the spiritual thing has become less real. A world sounds like an astronomical diagram, and a plane sounds like a geometrical diagram; and both these are abstractions. But a place is not an abstraction, but an actuality. And the writer not only says definitely that it is a place, but he gives it a definite name like the name of a place. Sarras is not an abstraction; it is not even an allegory. It is not even as if he had said the City of Heaven or the City of Paradise. These, though not unreal, are at least universal. But the name given has *identity*, which is something much more intense than universality. Sarras only means Sarras, as Sarum only means Sarum, or (for that matter) as Surbiton only means Surbiton. But the very fact that we have never heard of it before, and that it is never mentioned again, that it is referred to in passing and without explanation, gives a curious intensity to the hint of something at once distant and definite. The spiritual thrill is all in the idea that the place is a place, however spiritual; that it is some strange spot where the sky touches the earth, or where eternity contrives to live on the borderland of time and space.

I wish there were a real philosophy of comparative religion, and one that was not full of inhuman nonsense. I wish it did not tend to one particular trick of unreason, as for instance when Mr. Wells says that the Christian sacrament of bread and wine was a break-back to primitive blood sacrifices. Or sometimes a man will say that the feeling about a Madonna is only the revival of the worship of Isis, or that the idea of St.

The Common Man

Michael smiting Satan is the same as that about Mithras who slew a bull. Now there are many other more historical objections to this sort of thing, but my primary objection to it is that it not only puts the cart before the horse, but gives me directions for finding my own horse in my own stable, by looking for a primitive Mycenean chariot of which no traces remain. Instead of explaining x by saying it is equal to 5, it undertakes to explain 5 by saying it is equal to x. It is as if a man said, " You may not be aware that your feelings about your wife are best described as those of the Missing Link at the sight of an oyster shell." I know what a Christian feels about the idea that Michael smote a rebel angel. I do not in the least know what a Mithraist felt about the idea that Mithras killed a bull. It may really have been something like the Christian feeling, for all I know ; it may also have been the worst sort of heathen feeling, for all I know. But to have the thing that I do know explained to me by the thing that I don't know, is like nonsense out of *Alice in Wonderland*. It is offering something inexplicable to explain something that needs no explanation. I cannot tell whether anybody really felt anything about Isis comparable to what men feel about Mary ; if anybody did, I am sure I congratulate him. But I decline to have my own feelings revealed to myself, in the light of some remote alleged feelings that no man alive has ever felt. But though there is this abyss of agnosticism between dead faiths and living ones, and between religions that are experienced and religions that are only explored, it might be possible to establish some human connection if the people who did it were more human. If they took the simple things that really are similar, instead of merely trying to assimilate the civilised things to the barbaric things, they might really bridge some of those abysses in the name of the brotherhood of men. If they were not so anxious to say that the sacrament and the sacrifice were both cannibal orgies (which is nonsense) they might say that they were both sacrifices, and had something to do with the philosophy of sacrifice, which is sense. And then, instead of having less respect for the Christians, we might have more respect for the cannibals. If they were not so anxious to compare the Virgin to a heathen goddess, they might possibly compare them both to a human mother, and at least get near to something human, if not to something divine. And in the same way, if they were not so eager to compare a shrine or a sacred soil to fetishism and taboo, they might get some sort of glimpse of what all men mean by making a deity local, or talking of a spiritual place.

At least in the mind of man, if not in the nature of things, there seems to be some connection between concentration and reality. When we want to ask, in natural language, whether a thing really exists or not, we ask if it is really " there " or not. We say " there ", even if we do not clearly understand where. A man cannot enter a house by five doors at once; he might do it if he were an atmosphere; but he does not want to be an atmosphere. He has a stubborn sub-conscious belief that an animal is greater than an atmosphere. In proportion as a thing rises in the scale of things, it tends to localise and even narrow its natural functions. A man cannot absorb his sustenance through all his pores like a sponge or some low sea-organism; he cannot take in an atmosphere of beef or an abstract essence of buns. Any buns thrown at him, as at the bear at the zoo, must be projected with such skill as to hit a particular hole in his head. In nature, in a sense, there is choice even before there is will; the plant or bulb narrows itself and pierces at one place rather than another; and all growth is a pattern of such green wedges. But however it be with these lower things, there has always been this spearlike selection and concentration in man's conception of higher things. And compared with that there is something not only vague but vulgar in most of the talk about infinity. The pantheist is right up to a certain point, but so is the sponge.

Both vitally and verbally, this infinity is the enemy of all that is fine. Such philological points are sometimes more than mere pedantries or mere puns. And it is more than a pedantic pun to say that most things that are fine are finite. We testify to it when we talk of a beautiful thing having refinement or having finish. It is brought to an end like the blade of a beautiful sword; not only to its end in the sense of its cessation but to its end in the sense of its aim. All fine things are in this sense finished, even when they are eternal. Poetry is committed to this concentration fully as much as religion; for fairyland has always been as local, one might say as parochial, as Heaven. And if religion in the recognised sense were removed tomorrow, the poets would only begin to act as the pagans acted. They would begin to say, " Lo, here ", and " Lo, there ", from the incurable itch of the idea that the something must be somewhere, and not merely anywhere. Even if it were in some sense found to be in everything, it would still be in everything and not merely in all. And if men did indeed seek the secret in primitive sacrifices, it was a secret and not a superficiality like fetish-worship. If they did indeed look for it behind the veil of Isis, it was a secret and not a platitude like nature-worship. And if indeed it is better sought in another fashion, it will be a secret, and therefore a real revelation, for those who see it unveiled in the city of Sarras, in the spiritual place.

THE EPITAPH OF PIERPONT MORGAN

IT IS obvious enough that whitewashing a man is quite the opposite of washing him white. The curious thing is that people often try to whitewash a man, and fail, when it might be possible to wash him, and to some limited extent, succeed. The real story, if the culprit only had the courage to tell it, would often be much more human and pardonable than the stiff suspicious fiction that he tells instead. Many a public man, I fancy, has tried to conceal the crime and only succeeded in concealing the excuse. Many a man has sought to bury the sin and only buried the temptation. Suppose that Nelson had covered his relations with Lady Hamilton so discreetly that he left about his movements only a vague suspicion that he had a wife in every port. We should think him a far worse man than we think him, knowing the whole truth. Suppose Parnell had kept his secret so well that his disappearances were put down to an unmarried man's most vulgar and purchased type of vice, instead of an unmarried man's comparatively pardonable fault of infatuation. That great man would seem far less great to us than he does now. In our craven commercial public life there are not many of the Parnell or Nelson sort: but even among our lords and millionaires there are men, I dare say, who are less despicable than they look. If we had the key of their souls we might come upon virtues quite unexpected—or at least upon vices more generous. In many a complex human scandal, I fancy, the first real slander is the acquittal.

But there is another form of this dehumanising defence: and that is the defence of the dead. The idea of observing restraint, if not respect, in speaking of the recently departed rests on a human instinct altogether deep and free: but in modern practice it is turned exactly the wrong way. A dead man should be sacred because he is a man—perhaps a man for the first time. A baby says he is a man; a boy often thinks he is a man; a man takes for granted he is a man, and oftens finds out his mistake. Perhaps one never knows what being a man means until the instant of death. Perhaps in a very manly and even military sense all life is a learning to die. If I were asked to say something by the grave of a man like Pierpont Morgan, I would say: "I will not remember his name. He has fought the great unequal fight; and is of more value than he was."

Now turn to the modern newspaper method; the method of weak whitewash. The *Christian Commonwealth* is a paper with a perfectly genuine, though hazy and patronising, concern for social improvement. Its intentions are certainly not servile, though I think its upshot would be. But it feels as we all do, that the day after poor Morgan's death is not the time for kicking his corpse about: so, being modern, it contrives to speak well of him in the following extraordinary fashion. "It is easy to denounce the methods by which such men amass their vast fortunes, but, making every allowance for the injury done to individuals by the often ruthless methods such men adopt to gain their ends, the great fact stands out, that they are the human agents working out certain economic movements. ... These men are helping to prepare industry for a new form of control and ownership. In the transition stage they amass huge fortunes for themselves, and ruin many who are too weak to withstand them, but it is doubtful if the sum of their harmful inflictions is as great as the evils in the same period caused by the great number of small competing capitalists."

I shall have much to say of this as a social doctrine in a moment. At the start I am only concerned with it as an epitaph.

The Epitaph of Pierpont Morgan

In the mere matter of respect for the dead, I say this. I am ready to pass the grave of Morgan in a decent silence, as a Christian grave. The *Christian Commonwealth* can only think of sacrificing a thousand slaves upon it, as if it were a pagan and prehistoric grave. For to justify or palliate the capitalist today is to sacrifice a thousand slaves. My epitaph on Morgan need not even contain his name; I would write over his grave what I would over my own, " Have mercy upon us, miserable sinners." But just think how the *Christian Commonwealth* epitaph reads, merely as an epitaph ! " Sacred to the Memory of J. Pierpont Morgan : Who, By Methods Peculiarly Easy to Denounce, Amassed a Large Fortune. Having a Preference for Ruthless Methods For the Gaining of His Ends, He Selected for Ruin Such Persons as Were Too Weak To Withstand Him. He Thus Became The Human Instrument of An Economic and Inhuman Movement. He Also Formed Trusts. For of Such is the Kingdom of Heaven." That is the amount of tenderness for the terrible dead that can be reached in the modernist manner. The sacred death is forgotten, but the profane life is excused.

And now for the excuse. In order to write a polite paragraph about a poor old man whose only superiority over any of us is that he has passed what we all must fear, this paper digs up the dusty and discredited rubbish of Bellamy : and maintains the proposition that millionaires bring us nearer to Socialism. The obvious deduction for a Socialist is that he ought to be, in every hour and instant, on the side of the millionaires. No man's wage must be increased by a penny, no man's working day must be shortened by an hour ; for this might delay the swift, sweet process by which the whole earth will soon be owned by its six most unscrupulous inhabitants. Then we shall get Socialism. I don't see why. I never did. But it is self-evident that, if this is the case, every capitalist must be exalted and every workman brought low. The whole argument means nothing unless it means that the rich had better smash us all as soon as possible. There are some who doubt this concept. I am one of them. We say it would not have been Napoleon's best policy to wait till the Allies had conquered him utterly, so that he might only have to write one letter, asking them to give him back the whole of Europe. We say, in our simple way, that it would not have been wise in Montenegro to wait till all the Moslems in Asia were marching upon them ; so as to abolish Islam in one well-expressed proclamation. We entertain similar doubts about the sanity of making capitalists stronger than any of the past emperors of this earth, and then asking them to hand over the only thing for which they have lost their souls.

The final fact is that anyone who subscribes to this epitaph must league himself with the forces of evil until something like the Last Judgment. He must not merely give up Socialism, which is a doctrine. He must also give up Social Reform—which is a dissipation. He must not only abandon the duty of helping the poor ; he must even tear from his heart the pleasure of tormenting them. I see that one paper (the name of which I forget) has even addressed an open letter to me on this matter, asking whether any of my words (which, I sadly confess, have been many) have born any fruit in practice—by which, of course, it means Westminster. Well, I am afraid I must confess that my efforts have been barren, that I have brought forth no fruit fit for the field of social reform. In all the most powerful modern movements I have been impotent. I have never segregated anybody, or tortured anybody, or unsexed anybody, or buried anybody alive—to my knowledge. I am not a philanthropist. I do not think any words of mine have led to one single man being kept in prison beyond his lawful term. I doubt if I have succeeded in adding a single lash to the torture at the triangles. I question whether I have succeeded in deducting so much as a penny from the tiny fortunes of grooms and housemaids. I have cropped no hair off the heads of other people's daughters. I have drawn no blood from poorer men's backs. My claim to be a Progressive is gone for ever; and I know it well. But I am not quite so bitterly opposed to all possible Social Reform as the *Christian Commonwealth* is. I agree that men like Morgan should be pardoned. I even agree that, for purposes of debate, men like Morgan should be excused. But I shall deny till death and damnation that men like Morgan should be encouraged. And if that epitaph does not mean that men like Morgan should be encouraged, it means nothing whatever.

THE NEW BIGOTRY

I NOTICE with some amusement, both in America and English literature, the rise of a new kind of bigotry. Bigotry does not consist in a man being convinced he is right; that is not bigotry, but sanity. Bigotry consists in a man being convinced that another man must be wrong in everything, because he is wrong in a particular belief; that he must be wrong, even in thinking that he honestly believes he is right. The last occasion is one applied mostly to literature and the ability of literary men. And it is all the more like the old bigotry because it is in opposition to it.

We all know what used to happen sometimes in the Puritan period; or the more critical classicism of the eighteenth century. A young idealistic poet would write a copy of verses; mostly verses somewhat in this style :

> O'er rushing waterfall and verdant grove
> The languid moonlight throws a light of love.

The poet was considered quite respectable; perhaps the poem was even a prize poem. Then it was discovered that the poet, when slightly drunk, had expressed doubts about the exact date of the Book of Habakkuk. There was a terrible scandal; the youth was hurled from his college as an atheist; and then the learned critics went back and looked at his poem with a new darkling and suspicious eye. The " rushing waterfall ", after all, had a very revolutionary sound and hinted at pantheistic anarchy. The phrase " languid moonlight " was an'appeal to all the most profligate passions. " Light of love " was a term notoriously of loose significance.

The New Bigotry

Today it is just the opposite ; only equally bigoted. A young idealistic poet, full of the new visions of beauty, writes verses appropriate to such vision ; as, for instance :

Bug-house underbogies belch daybreak back-firing.
Daylight's a void-vomit ; steadying legs to stump.

And all the young critics know he is all right ; he has got cosmic rhythm ; he is a regular guy.

And then a horrid whisper goes round that he was seen outside an Episcopal Church near Vermont. The whole horrid truth is soon known. He has admitted to a newspaper man that he believes in God. Then the young critics go back gloomily and stare at his poetry ; and, strangely enough, see for the first time that there was something awfully old-fashioned in saying " daylight " when Binx might have said " sky-blank " ; and, after all, bogies are just the sort of thing Episcopalians are forced by their bishops to believe in.

This, though some of the worst examples have occurred in England, is a strictly correct biography of a man of genius who has come to us from America—Mr. T. S. Eliot. It would be an exaggeration to say that Mr. Eliot was expelled from Harvard for being a High Churchman, as Shelley was expelled from Oxford for being an atheist. Mr. Eliot's character was not blasted by a religion until later in life, and after he had said all that can be said for modern scepticism and despair.

But this makes it all the funnier. An English critic actually accused him of asking us " to believe the unbelievable ". Whatever is the sense of calling a thing unbelievable when a man like Eliot already believes it. The author of *The Waste Land* knows all there is to know about scepticism and pessimism ; why not admit that his beliefs are beliefs, and go back to a proper criticism of his literature ?

BOOKS FOR BOYS

A RECENT correspondence upon what is called pernicious literature has given rise to several declarations to the effect that the popular literature which is sold to boys in our day is greatly inferior to that of two or three decades ago. At first sight a reflective person might be inclined to suggest that perhaps there were more psychological elements involved in that far-off boyish enjoyment, and in that, as in many other instances of our youthful pleasures, we were not so much enjoying the stories as enjoying ourselves. It is at least possible that the *laudator temporis acti* of whom we are speaking would regard the actual task of reading through those lost romances very much in the same way that he would regard the action of a waiter in a restaurant who brought him fourteen penny buns and a plate of bull's-eyes.

The mental digestion of boys is as strong as their physical digestion. They do not heed the cookery of art any more than the art of cookery. They can eat the apples of the tree of knowledge, and they can eat them raw. It is a great mistake to suppose that boys only read boyish books. Not only do they privately revel in their sisters' most sentimental novels, but they absorb cartloads of useless information. One boy in particular, with whose career from an early age we have the best reasons for being familiar, used to read whole volumes of *Chamber's Encyclopaedia*, and of a very musty and unreliable History of English Trade. The thing was a mere brute pleasure of reading, a pleasure in leisurely and mechanical receptiveness. It was the sort of pleasure that a cow must have in grazing all day long.

Books for Boys

But when all allowance has been made for the omnivorousness of youth, we incline to think that there is probably a considerable amount of truth in the idea that boys' books have to some extent degenerated. They have degenerated probably for the reason that all forms of art degenerate, because they are despised. Probably they were less despised in the days when they still had upon them, as it were, the glamour of the great masters of historical romance. The spirit of Scott and Ainsworth and Fenimore Cooper remained in them even if it was only the reflection of a hundred reflections and each in a distorting mirror.

No one will ever understand the spirit at the back of popular and juvenile literature until he realises one fact, that a large amount of it is the result of that enthusiasm of the young reader which makes him wish to hear more and more about certain heroes, and read more and more of certain types of books. He dowers the creatures of fiction with a kind of boyish immortality. He is not surprised if Dick Deadshot or Jack Harkaway renews his youth through a series of volumes which reaches further than the length of the *Encyclopaedia Britannica*. These books have the vital philosophy of youth, a philosophy in which death does not exist, except, indeed, as an external and picturesque incident which happens to villains.

The serious student of this class of books and papers will go on to observe that a very large mass of such works has arisen directly out of the interest taken in some of the creations of great masters. An irresponsible writer for boys early in the century continued the adventures of Pickwick. An interminable book of Oriental adventure which we read in our boyhood was avowedly a supplement to the *Arabian Nights*, and mingled Aladdin, Sinbad, and Ali Baba in one inexhaustible tale. To take a more vulgar example, it is said that

The Common Man

" Ally Sloper " is simply an infinitely degraded version of Mr. Micawber ; the literary zoologist will trace the same rudimentary organs, the hat, the tie, and the bald head. All this amounts to one of the great laws of the question, the fact that the youthful mind takes hold of certain figures, insists upon them, tears them, as if were, out of the covers of the story, and could follow their adventures in any number of day dreams. Hence one of the essential qualities of this cheap literature—its astonishing voluminousness. A library keeping a record of it would need a dome vaster than the Bodleian.

From this, as we have said, it may be inferred that there is likely enough to have been some decadence of late years, since we are becoming further and further removed from the great historical novelists, who left a kind of glow upon all historic fiction. New literary fashions have arisen, but they are scarcely likely to be imitated in the literature of boys. No publisher has yet brought out with gaudy-coloured illustrations "The Further Adventures of Jude the Obscure". No penny dreadfuls have been devoted to what eventually happened to Pelleas and Melisande. And in this manner we reach once more the inevitable conclusion about debased forms of art; that they are debased because they are not respected. Everything in the world, from a child to a form of fiction, will be bad until we consent to treat it as good. And of all forms of literature in the world, the one most grossly neglected, from an artistic point of view, is the boys' book of adventure.

It is a very peculiar fact, that while the educated middle-class at the present day expends infinite money and trouble upon surrounding the child with the noblest works of art and literature, the boy is in this matter treated as if he were a half-witted and inconsiderable savage. The wretched infant of four years old is expected to drink in the verses of Stevenson and the decorative curves of Walter Crane. But when he has imbibed this atmosphere, when his aesthetic hunger has by hypothesis been aroused, when his mind has developed with the rapid development of boyhood, he is suddenly put off with books and papers which are not literature at all. A child's love for what is pretty is sedulously cultivated as the dawn of an aesthetic sense, but no one seems to realise that a boy's love of adventure is another aesthetic sense quite equally noble and appropriate. A child's love of colour is treated as a spiritual thing, a sort of hint of heaven, but a boy's love of adventure is spoken of as if it were a mere brute appetite, excusable in a growing lad. If a child says, " I like the pretty flowers ", he is applauded for his poetic instinct, but if a boy says, " I like a story about pirates ", he is treated as if he had asked for another slice of pork.

As long as this view continues there can be no worthy school of adventurous fiction. It must be realised that both the child's love of the pretty and the boy's love of the bold are sound and admirable artistic instincts. Neither of them shows that the individual is a cherub who cannot be long for this world, but both of them show that he is a well-equipped and healthy human soul. The child in the fairy-tale is canonised for running after a butterfly. The boy in the penny dreadful is denounced for running away to sea. But the sea is more beautiful than any butterflies.

If, then, we are agreed that the first need of the problem is to understand once and for all that the love of adventure is not a temporary savagery to be satisfied, but an essential artistic tendency to be crowned and brought to consummation, it cannot but seriously affect our view of boys' literature as a whole. We want to realise that the instinct of day dream and adventure is a high spiritual and moral instinct, that it requires neither dilution nor excuse, that it has been the mother of all great travellers and missionaries and knights errant and the patroness of all the brave. The one essential of a writer for boys is that he should not write down to them. He should rather write up, arduously and reverently, as well he may, to the mysterious spirit of youth.

THE OUTLINE OF LIBERTY

THERE is a quality needed today for the spread of all truth, and especially religious truth, which is very simple and vivid, but which I find it very difficult to fit with a word. So many words have become catchwords.

I suppose that our critics, in their learned way, would have recourse to the little-known Greek word *paradox*, if I were simply to say that they are not quite broad-minded enough to be Catholics. In their own jargon, being broad-minded so often means being blankminded.

If I were to say that they suffer from a lack of imagination, they might suppose (heaven help them) that I meant that what we believe is all imaginary. Nor indeed do either of these two terms define the definite thing I intend. It would be nearer the mark if I said that they cannot see all round a subject; or that they cannot see anything against the background of everything else.

The learned man, of what I may call the Cambridge type, is like a man who should spend years in making a minute ordnance map of the country between Cork and Dublin, and never discover that Ireland is an island. It is not a question of understanding something difficult. It is rather a question of opening the mind wide enough to understand something easy. It is not to be attained by years of labour; it is more likely to be attained in a moment of laziness; when the map-maker who has long been poring over the map with his nose close to Cork, may lean back for a moment and suddenly see Ireland. It is much more difficult to get such men to lean back for a moment and see Christendom.

The Common Man

The Catholic Church is always being defined in terms of the particular quarrel that she happens to have with particular people in a particular place. Because the Protestant sects in Northern Europe, for one or two centuries, disapproved of rosaries and incense and candles and confessional boxes, there was a widespread impression that Roman Catholics were simply people who liked confessional boxes and candles and incense and rosaries. But that is not what a Manichee or a Moslem or a Hindoo or an ancient Greek philosopher would say about Roman Catholics.

Buddhists have incense; Moslems have something very like rosaries; and hardly any healthy heathen human being on earth could conceive why anybody should have any particular hatred of candles. Buddhists would say that Catholics were people who insisted on a personal God and personal immortality. Moslems would say that Catholics were people who believed that God had a Son who assumed human form, and who did not think it idolatrous that He should afterwards assume pictorial or sculptural form. Every group in the world would have its own angle or aspect; and the Protestant would hardly recognise the same object which he had only considered in his own aspect.

Nevertheless, each of these, taken in itself, is in a sense narrow; and to dwell upon it narrows the issue. What we want is to have some general impression of the whole background of humanity, especially of heathen humanity, against which we can see the outline of the object, as, in the map of Ireland, the island is seen against the sea.

Now the real background of all that human heathenry is rather a grey background. There are particular patches, which happen to be close to us in place and time, which have been freshly painted in various ways. So freshly painted that nobody knows yet how long the colours will last. As

The Outline of Liberty

the Imperialists wanted to paint the map red, so the Internationalists and Idealists now want to paint the map pink. But none of them has painted half so much of the map anything as they, in their optimism, have sometimes supposed. And even in the areas where a sort of official optimism prevails, as in parts of America, there is a great deal more of the old ordinary melancholy of men than anyone could gather from newspaper headlines or political programmes. And I believe that the most general philosophy of men left to themselves, and perhaps the most practical illustration of the Fall of Man, is a vague impression of Fate.

If a man will really talk to the poor, in almost any country, I think he will generally find that they are either Christians or fatalists. This fatalism is more or less varied or complicated, of course, in various places by various mythologies or philosophies. It will generally be found that the mythology is a sort of poetry, embodying a worship of the wild forces of nature ; a nature-worship which, when broken up, ·is called polytheism, and, when united, is called pantheism. But there is sometimes very little left of theism in pantheism.

Then there are whole districts where there is true theism, which is, nevertheless, permeated with a mood of fatalism. That, I suppose, is true at least of large areas of Islam. Then there are what may be called the philosophies of resignation, which probably cover equally large areas of the ancient civilisation of Asia.

We need not insist here on any controversial points against or even about these things. But I take it as certain that all those notes of recurrence and cosmic rhythm, and a cycle beginning and ending with itself, which repeat themselves so frequently in connection with Buddhism and Brahminism and Theosophy, are in a general sense allied to an almost impersonal submission to an ultimately impersonal law. That is the tone of the whole thing; and, as I have said, the tone or tint of it strikes us as rather grey; or at least, neutral and negative.

It is the same with almost all we know of the pagan myths and metaphysics of antiquity. It is a modern slander on pagans to represent paganism as almost identical with pleasure. But anyhow, nobody acquainted with the great Greek and Latin literature, even in the smallest degree, will ever dream of identifying paganism with optimism. It would at least be a great deal nearer the truth to say that there, as everywhere else, the fundamental character of paganism is pessimism. But in any case, it can quite fairly be said that it is fatalism.

Upon this grey background there is one splash or star of silver or gold; a thing like a flame. It is quite exceptional and extraordinary. Of its many extraordinary characters, this is perhaps the chief; that it proclaims Liberty. Or, as the only true meaning of that term, it proclaims Will. In a strange voice, as of a trumpet from heaven, it tells a strange story, of which the very essence is that it is made up of Will, or of a free divergence of Wills.

Will made the world; Will wounded the world; the same Divine Will gave to the world for the second time its chance; the same human Will can for the last time make its choice. That is the real outstanding pecularity, or eccentricity, of the peculiar sect called Roman Catholics. And if anyone objects to my limiting so large a conception to Roman Catholics, I willingly agree that there are many who value it so much that they obviously ought to be Roman Catholics. But if anyone says that it is not in fact and history bound up with the Faith of Roman Catholicism, it is enough to refer him to the history and the facts.

Nobody especially emphasised this spiritual liberty until the Church was established. People began instantly to question this spiritual liberty, when the Church began to be broken up. The instant a breach, or even a crack, had been made in the dyke of Catholicism, there poured through it the bitter sea of Calvinism, or in other words, of a very cruel form of fatalism. Since that time, it has taken the much duller form of Determinism. This sadness and sense of bondage is so general to mankind that it immediately made its appearance, when the special spiritual message of liberty was silenced or interrupted anywhere. Wherever that message is heard, men think and talk in terms of will and choice; and they see no meaning in any of the philosophies of fate, whether desperate or resigned.

It is idle to talk to a Catholic about optimism or pessimism ; for he himself shall decide whether the universe shall be, for him, the best or the worst of all possible worlds. It is useless to tell him that he might be more at one with the universal life as a Buddhist or a pantheist ; for he knows that, in that sense, he might be more at one with the universal life as a turnip or a tree. It is his whole hope and glory that he is not at one with the universal life ; but stands out from it, an exception and even a miracle.

There is a great passage in the " Paradiso " of Dante, which I wish I knew enough Italian to appreciate or enough English to translate. But I would commend it to those who may fancy that my emphasis on this exceptional quality is a mere modern whitewashing of a medieval superstition ; and especially to those who have been taught in laborious detail, by learned and very stupid historians, to regard medievalism as narrow and enchained. For it runs roughly like this :

> The mightiest gift that God of his largesse
> Made in creation, perfect even as He,
> Most of His substance, and to Him most dear,
> He gave to the Will and it was Liberty.

A NOTE ON NUDISM

THERE IS one little habit of some of the most intelligent modern writers against which I should like to protest. It consists of flatly refusing to state somebody else's opinion as it stands; and consider it on its own merits. The modern writer must always assume that it is a choice between his own extreme opinion and something at the other extreme. I found a curious example in a very excellent book by Miss Cicely Hamilton called *Modern Germanies*. She was referring to the sect of the Nudists, who have revived the ancient heresy of the Adamites and go about without any clothes, taking themselves very seriously; as if nakedness were a new invention. I think Miss Hamilton really hesitated a little, being moved by her instincts as a civilised person to laugh, and by her instincts as a progressive person to applaud. What then does she do? She immediately repeats the old story that in *Paul et Virginie*, the very artificial sentimental novel of the eighteenth century, the heroine is drowned because she refuses to take off her clothes. She then adds that " if she has to choose " between Virginie and some German flapper who finds it more comfortable to have no clothes to flap, she will choose the latter. But, first of all, why should she " have to choose "? Why should she not consider Nudism on its own merits; and the normal view of clothes, among sane people, also on its own merits? If I have to judge a drunkard, I will judge him without dragging in the comparison of a mad fakir who deliberately died of thirst in the desert. If I have to judge a miser, I will call him a miser; despite the possible existence of an insane and intoxicated nobleman in Vienna, who poured ten thousand gold coins

A Note on Nudism

down a drain. I cannot see why Miss Hamilton should call in one extravagance merely to justify another.

Next, if she really does suppose that normal, traditional or Christian morality are represented by Virginie, she is probably quite wrong. Most Christian authorities would say that her notion of sacrifice came very near to the sin of suicide. For *Paul et Virginie* was not written in a Christian period but in a very pagan period, when pre-Revolutionary France was in love with the pagan Stoics who did not disapprove of suicide. The story itself is largely founded on an old classical romance. It cannot be taken as typical of modern Christianity, or even of medieval Christianity. It is only fair to remember that in this sense Virginie is a heathen heroine ; and Godiva was a Christian heroine.

Lastly, I am not sure I *should* choose the German flapper, even if I were driven to the choice. We may think a sacrifice is made to a mistaken code of honour ; but there is the sacrifice ; and there is the honour. We have no reason to suppose that the Nudist even knows what we mean by honour. We know nothing about her, except that she does not know what we mean by dignity. As a plain piece of practical psychology, I think it extremely likely that the poor mistaken maiden, who would die for her dignity, would also die for her country, would die for her friends, would die for her faith or promise, or any worthy obligation. We know nothing about the other woman, except that (like the pig and other animals), she feels more comfortable without clothes. It seems to me an insufficient basis for moral confidence.

CONSULTING THE ENCYCLOPAEDIA

THE HISTORICAL Student will raise his refined eyebrows if I say that a Catholic is an Encyclopaedist. The name of Encyclopaedism was given in the eighteenth century to the most coldly eager of the enemies of Catholicism. And even now it is generally believed that we bow submissively before the storm of the ephemeral Encyclical, but dare not open the scientific and solid Encyclopaedia—which, by the way, is generally at any given moment much more out of date than the Encyclical.

It is none the less true that the Catholic Church presents itself, though on a higher plane and plan, in a certain double character to which perhaps the nearest natural parallel is the use of an encyclopaedia. For it is the test of a good encyclopaedia that it does two rather different things at once. The man consulting it finds the thing he wants ; he also finds how many thousand things there are that he does not want. It advises the particular man upon his particular problem, though it were quite a private problem, almost as if it were giving private advice. And the man must be so far touched to some tinge of healthy humility, if it be only the admission that he does not know everything, and must seek outside himself for something. Even if he is so ill-advised as to consult a medical work of reference for the proper proportions of hyoscine for the poisoning of an aunt, he must be so far in a pious and respectful attitude and accepting something upon a sort of authority.

I remember a man who told me he never accepted anything on any sort of authority ; I also remember asking him whether he ever consulted Bradshaw, or whether he insisted on travelling by every train first, to see whether it was safe to travel by it. The journey itself might be highly private, the visit to the aunt almost pressingly private, but he would not evolve a railway train entirely out of his private judgment.

But a work of reference works in another way also. It reminds the traveller in the train that there are a good many other trains full of travellers. It reminds the neoethical nephew that there are a good many different words in the dictionary. In his search for hyoscine he will pass carelessly over the honey of Hymettus, and think it needless to dwell on the life of Heliogabalus or the science of hydraulics. And thus he will learn the same lesson in another way; the somewhat difficult lesson that he is nobody except himself.

Those two discoveries commonly combine in a conversion; and this is perhaps the most workable framework in which to state the two chief elements of my own. There was first the relation of Catholicism to my own original and personal problem; and there was a second rather curious and illuminating illustration of the necessity of keeping it in proportion to all the other problems, the problems of all the other people.

Now all the very varied types of people who sooner or later draw near to the Catholic Faith have moved towards it from the most widely different standpoints, across most varying distances, and rejecting or renewing or reshaping the most queerly contrasted types of non-Catholic thought. My own thought, when it was not yet Catholic, was often blasted with the name of Optimist; but it was not quite so bad as that sounds today. It was an attempt to hold on to religion by the thread of thanks for our creation; by the praise of existence and of created things. And the curious part of it is that I found that this piece of private judgment, or private nonsense, was really much more true than I ever thought it was; and yet, if that truth were left to stand alone, it would be a complete falsehood.

For the sake of illustration, or in a rather special sense of illumination, I will take the metaphor of a window; a thing which always had, and still has, an almost weirdly vivid effect on my own imagination. My own original view, which would originally have been an entirely non-Catholic if not anti-Catholic view, might be roughly stated thus. " After all, what could be more mystical or magical than ordinary daylight coming in through an ordinary window? Why should anybody want a new heaven shining on a new earth; why need they dream of strange stars or miraculous flames, or the sun and moon turned to blood and darkness, in order to imagine a portent? The mere fact of existence and experience is a perpetual portent. Why should we ever ask for more? "

There is an old literary joke or game, familiar I think among the transcendental tricks of the Cavalier poets; a game that is called echo verses. It is a sort of punning upon the last syllable of a word; by which Echo is made to answer mockingly the question asked in the line of verse. Thus, to transfer it to a modern topic, the poet might ask, "Say, what high hope is founded on eugenics? " And the obliging echo would answer, " Nix "; or a paean in praise of some Socialist or ex-Socialist statesman would begin with the line, " Labour's great leader; mighty Democrat ", and end with the repetition, " Rat ".

I am haunted by this parallel in the curious logical answer to my own question; which was at once a repetition and a contradiction and a completion. For it seemed to me that when I asked that question, " Why is not the daylight enough?" the ancient voice of some mystery such as an old religion answered my words merely by repeating them, " Why is not the daylight enough? " And when I said, " Why should not that wonderful white fire, breaking through the window, inspire us every day like an ever-returning miracle?" the echo out of that old crypt or cavern only answered, "Why not indeed?"

And, the more I thought of it, the more I thought that there was the hint of some strange answer in the very fact that I had to ask the question. I had not lost, and I have never lost, the conviction that such primal things are mysterious and amazing; but if they were amazing, why did anybody have to remind us that they were amazing? Why was there, as I had already realised that there certainly was, a sort of daily fight to appreciate the daylight; to which we had to summon all imagination and poetry and the labour of the arts to aid us? If the first imaginative instinct was right, it seemed clearer and clearer that something else was wrong. And as I indignantly denied that there was anything wrong with the window, I eventually concluded that there was something wrong with me.

In this case, the divine dictionary had answered my own personal question as directly and even personally as if the answer had been written for me. It justified the instinct that inspired me to accept the daylight as a divine reality; but it also solved the problem that puzzled me about the difficulty of thus accepting the daylight all day and every day. Creation was of the Creator and declared as good; the power in it could be praised by angels forever and by the sons of God shouting for joy. If we were ourselves only occasionally overheard in the act of shouting for joy, it was because we were only partially or imperfectly the sons of God; not indeed wholly disinherited, but not wholly domesticated. In short, we suffered by the Fall or Original Sin; but it is important to note that this is not an answer to the particular question, except in the form of the more moderate Catholic doctrine, and not the old pessimist Protestant doctrine of the Fall.

The Common Man

This particular problem arose entirely out of the fact that man is imperfect; but not, in the pessimist sense, perfectly imperfect. The whole paradox is in the fact that a part of his mind remains almost perfect; and he can perpetually perceive what he cannot perpetually enjoy. I was as certain that existence is ecstatically more excellent than non-existence as I was that plus two is different from minus two. Only there is a practical psychological difficulty about always going into ecstasies over this fact. Man is not symmetrically unsymmetrical; he is a sort of one-eyed creature ever since he fought a duel with the devil; and the one eye sees the eternal light eternally, while the other has grown tired and blinks or is almost blind. Thus the authority solved this private problem, not by denying the truth of my private judgment, but by adding to it the larger and more general judgment of the Fall.

And then, in the very act of understanding my own little private problem, I understood the public authority which I have compared to an encyclopaedia. Here there were thousands of other private problems solved for thousands of other private persons; masses of them had nothing to do with my own case at all; but one of them turned and confronted my own case in a curious way. I began to realize that it would not do to act as so many of the most brilliant men of my time had acted. It was not enough for a man to value a truth merely because he had picked it up by himself; to take it away with him and turn it into a private system; at the best into a philosophy and at the worst into a sect. He was very proud of answering his own question without the help of an encyclopaedia; but he did not even pretend to answer all the other questions in the encyclopaedia.

Now I felt very strongly that there ought to be answers, not only to all the other questions which all the other people were asking, but also answers to other questions which I should ask myself. And the moment I began to think about these other problems I saw at once that I could not even satisfy myself with the solution of one of those problems. The practical example which occurred to me was this. I said to myself; it is all very well to say that the miracle of daylight coming through a window ought to be enough to make a man dance with joy. But suppose another man uses your argument as a justification for putting innocent men in prison for life, in a cell with one window, and then leaving them to dance. What will become of all your own denunciations of slavery and the oppression of the poor, when that highly practical statesman has founded a new commonwealth on your new creed?

And then I think there spread out before me, like a vast dazzling plan with innumerable details, some vision of the thousand things that have to be interrelated and balanced in Catholic thought; justice as well as joy; liberty as well as light; and I felt certain that the mere proportion of all these things, not the negation of any of them, needed, to harmonize it and hold it steady, a power and a presence mightier than the mind of any mortal man.

IF I HAD ONLY ONE SERMON TO PREACH

IF I had only one sermon to preach, it would be a sermon against Pride. The more I see of existence, and especially of modern practical and experimental existence, the more I am convinced of the reality of the old religious thesis; that all evil began with some attempt at superiority; some moment when, as we might say, the very skies were cracked across like a mirror, because there was a sneer in Heaven.

Now the first fact to note about this notion is a rather curious one. Of all such notions, it is the one most generally dismissed in theory and most universally accepted in practice. Modern men imagine that such a theological idea is quite remote from them; and, stated as a theological idea, it probably is remote from them. But, as a matter of fact, it is too close to them to be recognised. It is so completely a part of their minds and morals and instincts, I might almost say of their bodies, that they take it for granted and act on it even before they think of it. It is actually the most popular of all moral ideas; and yet it is almost entirely unknown as a moral idea. No truth is now so unfamiliar as a truth, or so familiar as a fact.

Let us put the fact to a trifling but not unpleasing test. Let us suppose that the reader, or (preferably) the writer, is going into a public-house or some public place of social intercourse; a public tube or tram might do as well, except that it seldom allows of such long and philosophical intercourse as did the old public house. Anyhow, let us suppose any place where men of motley but ordinary types assemble; mostly poor because the majority is poor some moderately comfortable but rather what is snobbishly called common; an average handful of human beings. Let us suppose that the enquirer, politely approaching this group, opens the conversation in a chatty way by saying, "Theologians are of opinion that it was one of the superior angelic intelligences seeking to become the supreme object of worship, instead of finding his natural joy in worshipping, which dislocated the providential design and frustrated the full joy and completion of the cosmos ". After making these remarks the enquirer will gaze round brightly and expectantly at the company for corroboration, at the same time ordering such refreshments as may be ritually fitted to the place or time, or perhaps merely offering cigarettes or cigars to the whole company, to fortify them against the strain. In any case, we may well admit that such a company will find it something of a strain to accept the formula in the above form. Their comments will probably be disjointed and detached ; whether they take the form of " Lorlumme " (a beautiful thought slurred somewhat in pronunciation), or even " Gorblimme " (an image more sombre but fortunately more obscure), or merely the unaffected form of " Garn " ; a statement quite free from doctrinal and denominational teaching, like our State compulsory education. In short, he who shall attempt to state this theory as a theory to the average crowd of the populace will doubtless find that he is talking in an unfamiliar language. Even if he states the matter in the simplified form, that Pride is the worst of the Seven Deadly Sins, he will only produce a vague and rather unfavourable impression that he is preaching. But he is only preaching what everybody else is practising ; or at least is wanting everybody else to practise.

Let the scientific enquirer continue to cultivate the patience of science. Let him linger—at any rate let *me* linger—in the place of popular entertainment whatever it may be, and take very careful note (if necessary in a note-book) of the way in

which ordinary human beings do really talk about each other.
As he is a scientific enquirer with a note-book, it is very likely
that he never saw any ordinary human beings before. But if
he will listen carefully, he will observe a certain tone taken
towards friends, foes and acquaintances ; a tone which is, on
the whole, creditably genial and considerate, though not
without strong likes and dislikes. He will hear abundant if
sometimes bewildering allusion to the well-known weaknesses
of Old George ; but many excuses also, and a certain generous
pride in conceding that Old George is quite the gentleman
when drunk, or that he told the policeman off proper. Some
celebrated idiot, who is always spotting winners that never
win, will be treated with almost tender derision; and, especially among the poorest, there will be a true Christian pathos
in the reference to those who have been " in trouble " for
habits like burglary and petty larceny. And as all these queer
types are called up like ghosts by the incantation of gossip,
the enquirer will gradually form the impression that there is
one kind of man, probably only one kind of man, perhaps,
only one man, who is really disliked. The voices take on quite
a different tone in speaking of him ; there is a hardening and
solidification of disapproval and a new coldness in the air.
And this will be all the more curious because, by the current
modern theories of social or anti-social action, it will not be
at all easy to say why he should be such a monster ; or what
exactly is the matter with him. It will be hinted at only in
singular figures of speech, about a gentleman who is mis-
takenly convinced that he owns the street ; or sometimes that
he owns the earth. Then one of the social critics will say,
" 'E comes in 'ere and 'e thinks 'e's Gawd Almighty." Then
the scientific enquirer will shut his note-book with a snap and
retire from the scene, possibly after paying for any drinks he
may have consumed in the cause of social science. He has got

what he wanted. He has been intellectually justified. The man in the pub has precisely repeated, word for word, the theological formula about Satan.

Pride is a poison so very poisonous that it not only poisons the virtues; it even poisons the other vices. This is what is felt by the poor men in the public tavern, when they tolerate the tippler or the tipster or even the thief, but feel something fiendishly wrong with the man who bears so close a resemblance to God Almighty. And we all do in fact know that the primary sin of pride has this, curiously freezing and hardening effect upon the other sins. A man may be very susceptible and in sex matters rather loose; he may waste himself on passing and unworthy passions, to the hurt of his soul; and yet always retain something which makes friendship with his own sex at least possible, and even faithful and satisfying. But once let that sort of man regard his own weakness as a strength, and you have somebody entirely different. You have the Lady-Killer; the most beastly of all possible bounders; the man whom his own sex almost always has the healthy instinct to hate and despise. A man may be naturally slothful and rather irresponsible; he may neglect many duties through carelessness, and his friends may still understand him, so long as it is really a careless carelessness. But it is the devil and all when it becomes a careful carelessness. It is the devil and all when he becomes a deliberate and self-conscious Bohemian, sponging on principle, preying on society in the name of his own genius (or rather of his own belief in his own genius) taxing the world like a king on the plea that he is a poet, and despising better men than himself who work that he may waste. It is no metaphor to say that it is the devil and all. By the same fine old original religious formula, it is all of the devil. We could go through any number of social types illustrating the same spiritual truth. It would be easy to point out that even the miser, who is half-ashamed of his madness, is a more human and sympathetic type than the millionaire who brags and boasts of his avarice and calls it sanity and simplicity and the strenuous life. It would be easy to point out that even cowardice, as a mere collapse of the nerves, is better than cowardice as an ideal and theory of the intellect ; and that a really imaginative person will have more sympathy with men who, like cattle, yield to what they know is panic, than with a certain particular type of prig who preaches something that he calls peace. Men hate priggishness because it is the driest form of pride.

Thus there is a paradox in the whole position. The spiritual idea of the evil of pride, especially spiritual pride, was dismissed as a piece of mysticism not needed by modern morality, which is to be purely social and practical. And, as a fact, it is very specially needed because the morality is social and practical. On the assumption that we need care for nothing except making other human beings happy, this is quite certainly the thing that will make them unhappy. The practical case against pride, as a mere source of social discomfort and discord, is if possible even more self-evident than the more mystical case against it, as a setting up of the self against the soul of the world. And yet though we see this thing on every side in modern life, we really hear very little about it in modern literature and ethical theory. Indeed, a great deal of modern literature and ethics might be meant specially for the encouragement of spiritual pride. Scores of scribes and sages are busy writing about the importance of self-culture and self-realisation ; about how every child is to be taught to develop his personality (whatever that may be); about how every man must devote himself to success, and every successful man must devote himself to developing a magnetic and compelling personality ; about how every man may become a superman

If I had only One Sermon to Preach

(by taking Our Correspondence Course) or, in the more sophisticated and artistic type of fiction, how one specially superior superman can learn to look down on the mere mob of ordinary supermen, who form the population of that peculiar world. Modern theory, as a whole, is rather encouraging egoism. But we need not be alarmed about that. Modern practice, being exactly like ancient practice, is still heartily discouraging it. The man with the strong magnetic personality is still the man whom those who know him best desire most warmly to kick out of the club. The man in a really acute stage of self-realisation is a no more pleasing object in the club than in the pub. Even the most enlightened and scientific sort of club can see through the superman; and see that he has become a bore. It is in practice that the philosophy of pride breaks down; by the test of the moral instincts of man wherever two or three are gathered together; and it is the mere experience of modern humanity that answers the modern heresy.

There is indeed another practical experience, known to us all, even more pungent and vivid than the actual unpopularity of the bully or the bumptious fool. We all know that there is a thing called egoism that is much deeper than egotism. Of all spiritual diseases it is the most intangible and the most intolerable. It is said to be allied to hysteria; it sometimes looks as if it were allied to diabolic possession. It is that condition in which the victim does a thousand varying things from one unvarying motive of a devouring vanity; and sulks or smiles, slanders or praises, conspires and intrigues or sits still and does nothing, all in one unsleeping vigilance over the social effect of one single person. It is amazing to me that in the modern world, that chatters perpetually about psychology and sociology, about the tyranny with which we are threatened by a few feeble-minded infants, about alcoholic poisoning and the treatment of neurotics, about half a hundred things that are near the subject and never on the spot—it is amazing that these moderns really have so very little to say about the cause and cure of a moral condition that poisons nearly every family and every circle of friends. There is hardly a practical psychologist who has anything to say about it that is half so illuminating as the literal exactitude of the old maxim of the priest; that pride is from hell. For there is something awfully vivid and appallingly fixed, about this madness at its worst, that makes that short and antiquated word seem much more apt than any other. And then, as I say, the learned go wandering away into discourses about drink or tobacco, about the wickedness of wine glasses or the incredible character of public-houses. The wickedest work in this world is symbolised not by a wine glass but by a looking-glass; and it is not done in public-houses, but in the most private of all private houses; which is a house of mirrors.

The phrase would probably be misunderstood; but I should begin my sermon by telling people not to enjoy themselves. I should tell them to enjoy dances and theatres and joy-rides and champagne and oysters; to enjoy jazz and cocktails and night-clubs if they can enjoy nothing better; to enjoy bigamy and burglary and any crime in the calendar, in preference to this other alternative; but never to learn to enjoy themselves. Human beings are happy so long as they retain the receptive power and the power of reaction in surprise and gratitude to something outside. So long as they have this they have as the greatest minds have always declared, a something that is present in childhood and which can still preserve and invigorate manhood. The moment the self within is consciously felt as something superior to any of the gifts that can be brought to it, or any of the adventures that it may enjoy, there has appeared a sort of self-devouring fastidiousness and a disenchantment in advance, which fulfils all the Tartarean emblems of thirst and of despair.

Difficulties can easily be raised, of course, in any such debate by the accident of words being used in different senses ; and sometimes in quite contrary senses. For instance, when we speak of somebody being " proud of " something, as of a man being proud of his wife or a people proud of its heroes, we really mean something that is the very opposite of pride. For it implies that the man thinks that something outside himself is needed to give him great glory ; and such a glory is really acknowledged as a gift. In the same way, the word will certainly be found misleading, if I say that the worst and most depressing element in the mixed elements of the present and the immediate future, seems to me to be an element of impudence. For there is a kind of impudence that we all find either amusing or bracing ; as in the impudence of the guttersnipe. But there again the circumstances disarm the thing of its real evil. The quality commonly called " cheek " is not an assertion of superiority ; but rather a bold attempt to balance inferiority. When you walk up to a very wealthy and powerful nobleman and playfully tip his hat over his eyes (as is your custom) you are not suggesting that you yourself are above all human follies, but rather that you are capable of them, and that he also ought to have a wider and richer experience of them. When you dig a Royal Duke in the waistcoat, in your playful manner, you are not taking yourself too seriously, but only, perhaps, not taking him so seriously as is usually thought correct. This sort of impudence may be open to criticism, as it is certainly subject to dangers. But there is a sort of hard intellectual impudence, which really treats itself as intangible to retort or judgment ; and there are a certain number among the new generations and social movements, who fall into this fundamental weakness. It is a weakness ;

for it is simply settling down permanently to believe what even the vain and foolish can only believe by fits and starts, but what all men wish to believe and are often found weak enough to believe; that they themselves constitute the supreme standard of things. Pride consists in a man making his personality the only test, instead of making the truth the test. It is not pride to wish to do well, or even to look well, according to a real test. It is pride to think that a thing looks ill, because it does not look like something characteristic of oneself. Now in the general clouding of clear and abstract standards, there is a real tendency today for a young man (and even possibly a young woman) to fall back on that personal test, simply for lack of any trustworthy impersonal test. No standard being sufficiently secure for the self to be moulded to suit it, all standards may be moulded to suit the self. But the self as a self is a very small thing and something very like an accident. Hence arises a new kind of narrowness; which exists especially in those who boast of breadth. The sceptic feels himself too large to measure life by the largest things; and ends by measuring it by the smallest thing of all. There is produced also a sort of subconscious ossification; which hardens the mind not only against the traditions of the past, but even against the surprises of the future. *Nil admirari* becomes the motto of all nihilists; and it ends, in the most complete and exact sense, in nothing.

If I had only one sermon to preach, I certainly could not end it in honour, without testifying to what is in my knowledge the salt and preservative of all these things. This is but one of a thousand things in which I have found the Catholic Church to be right, when the whole world is perpetually tending to be wrong; and without its witness, I believe that this secret, at once a sanity and a subtlety, would be almost entirely forgotten among men. I know that I for one had hardly heard of positive humility until I came within the range of Catholic influence; and even the things that I love most, such as liberty and the island poetry of England, had in this matter lost the way, and were in a fog of self-deception. Indeed there is no better example of the definition of pride than the definition of patriotism. It is the noblest of all natural affections, exactly so long as it consists of saying, "May I be worthy of England." It is the beginning of one of the blindest forms of Pharisaism when the patriot is content to say, "I am an Englishman." And I cannot count it an accident that the patriot has generally seen the flag as a flame of vision, beyond and better than himself, in countries of the Catholic tradition, like France and Poland and Ireland; and has hardened into this heresy of admiring merely his own breed and bone and inherited type, and himself as a part of it, in the places most remote from that religion, whether in Berlin or Belfast. In short, if I had only one sermon to preach, it would be one that would profoundly annoy the congregation, by bringing to their attention the permanent challenge of the Church. If I had only one sermon to preach, I should feel specially confident that I should not be asked to preach another.

IF DON JOHN OF AUSTRIA HAD MARRIED
MARY QUEEN OF SCOTS

WHY IS it that the world's most famous love story, after the archetypal story of Adam and Eve, is the story of Antony and Cleopatra? I for one should answer, to begin with, because of the solid truth of the story of Adam and Eve. I have often wondered whether, when the moderns have done playing with that story, burlesquing it, and turning it upside down and tacking on a modern moral like a new tail, or expanding it into an evolutionary fantasia that nobody can make head or tail of, it will ever occur to anybody to see how sensible it is, exactly as it stands. Even if it is an old fable, the old fable is much truer with the old moral. Christians are not constrained, and least of all Christians of my own confession, to treat Genesis with the heavy verbalism of the Puritan—the Hebraiser who knows no Hebrew. But the curious thing is that the more literally we take it the truer it is; and even if it were materialised and modernised into a story of Mr. and Mrs. Jones, the old moral would still be the sound one. A man naked and with nothing of his own is given by a friend the free run of all the fruits and flowers of a very beautiful estate; and only asked to promise that he will not interfere with one particular fruit-tree. If we all talk till we are as old as Methuselah, the moral remains the same for any honourable man. If he breaks his word he is a cad; if he says, " I broke my word because I believe in breaking all limitations and expanding into infinite progress and evolution," he is ten times more of a cad; and has, moreover, become a bore as well as a bounder. But it is this

modern suggestion, that Man was right to be bored with
Eden and to demand evolution (otherwise mere change),
that is very relevant to the question I have asked about
Antony and Cleopatra. It is also very relevant to the question
I am going to ask about two other famous figures in history :
a woman and a man.

For upon this modern theory the Fall really was the Fall ;
for it was the first action that had only tedium as a motive.
Progress began in boredom ; and, heaven knows, it sometimes seems likely to end in it. And no wonder ; for of all
utter falsehoods the most false, I think, is this notion that men
can be happy in movement, when nothing but dullness drives
them on from behind. Children, and such happy people, can
go on from something they really like to something they will
like more. But if ever there was a whisper that might truly
come from the devil, it is the suggestion that men can
despise the beautiful things they have got, and only delight
in getting new things because they have not got them. It
is obvious that, on that principle, Adam will tire of the tree
just as he has tired of the garden. " It is enough that there
is always a beyond " ; that is, there is always something
else to get tired of. All progress based on that mood is
truly a Fall ; man did fall, does fall, and we can today see
him falling. It is the great progressive proposition ; that he
must seek only for enjoyment because he has lost the power
to enjoy.

Now this shadow of failure on all fame and civilisation
which the agnostic poet preferred to call " the something that
infects the world," and I shall cause general pain by calling
Original Sin, does manifest itself markedly in the sort of
historical legends that exist. But I would urge here that it
appears in the historical legends that do not exist. I refer
especially to that grand historical episode of the heroic honey-

moon, otherwise called the marriage of pure minds, which I
study here as closely as is possible in a case that does not exist.
It is a remarkable fact, when we consider how much happiness
love has doubtless given to mankind as a whole, that mankind
has never pointed to any great historical example of a hero and
a heroine wedded in a way entirely worthy of them ; of a great
man and a great woman united by a great love that was entirely
supreme and satisfying, as in the tradition of the gigantic loves
of Eden. Anybody who imagines that I am talking pessimism,
about ordinary people in love, will impute to me the very
reverse of what I mean. Millions of people have been happy in
love and marriage, in the ordinary way of human happiness ;
but then that precisely consists in a certain commonsense
admission of original sin ; in humility and pardon and taking
things as they come. But there has not been any example on
the grand scale, of a perfect marriage—that has remained in
human memory like a great monument. All those monuments,
though often of the purest marble, hewn from the loftiest
mountain, have very clearly across them the crack from the
earthquake in the beginning. The noblest knight of the Middle
Ages, St. Louis, was less happy in his marriage than in all other
relations. Dante did not marry Beatrice ; he lost his love in
infancy and found her again in Paradise or in a dream. Nelson
was a great lover, but we cannot say that his love made him
more great, since it made him do in Naples the only mean
action of his life. These historic examples have become legends
or traditions ; but they have become tragic traditions. And
the central literary tradition of all is that typically tragic one I
have named, in which even perfect love was whimsically
imperfect, and certainly suffered by very imperfect people ; in
which the hero learned no lesson except delay ; in which the
heroine inspired nothing except defeat ; in which romance
made him less than a Caesar and has unkindly compared her

to a snake ; in which the man was weakened by love and the woman by lovers. Men have taken Antony and Cleopatra as the perfect love story, precisely because it is the imperfect love story. It mirrors the thwarting, the unworthiness, the disproportion which they have felt as spoiling so many splendid passions and divine desires ; and mirrors them all the more truly because the mirror is cracked. I imagine that poets will never leave off writing about Antony and Cleopatra ; and all they write will be in the mood of that great French poet of our own time, who describes the Roman warrior gazing into the unfathomable eyes of the Egyptian queen, and seeing beneath a spinning and sparkling light the eddies of a vast sea, filled with the rout of all his ships.

I have here dared to call up out of the dust another warrior, whose destiny turned also with the topsails and high poops of the galleys ; and another woman, whose legend also has been sometimes twisted into the legend of a snake. There was never any doubt about the beautiful colours or graceful curves of the snake ; but, in fact, the woman was not a snake, but very much of a woman ; even by the account of those who call her a wicked woman. And the man was not only a warrior, but a conqueror ; and his great ships sweep through history not merely to defeat, but to a high deliverance, in which he did not lose the empire, but saved the world. Whatever else we may think of the woman, none can doubt where her heart would have been in that battle, or what sort of song of praise she would have sent up after that victory. There was much about her that was militant, though her life might well have sickened her of militancy ; there was much about him that was sensitive and sympathetic with that wider world of culture for which her soul sickened till she died. They were made for each other ; they were in fact the heroic lovers, or perfect human pair, for whom we have looked elsewhere in history in vain. There was only one small defect in their purple and impassioned love story; and that is that they never met.

In truth, this dream began to drift through my mind when I first read a parenthetical remark by Andrew Lang, in a historical study about Philip of Spain. Referring to the King's half-brother, the famous Don John of Austria, Lang remarked casually : " He intended to carry off Mary Queen of Scots," and added caustically : " He was incapable of fear." Of course nobody is incapable of fear. He was certainly, in the common sense, incapable of *obeying* fear : but, if I understand the type, he was not incapable of *enjoying* fear as an element in a mystery like that of love. It is exactly because love has lost that slight touch of fear, that it has become in our time so flat and flippant and vulgar; when it has not become laboriously biological, not to say bestial. And Mary was dangerous as well as in danger; that heart-shaped face looking out of the ruff in so many pictures was like a magnet, a talisman, a terrible jewel. There was, even then, in the idea of eloping with the tragic yet attractive Franco-Scottish princess, all the ancient savour of the romances about delivering a lady from dragons, or even dis-enchanting her out of the shape of a dragon. But though the idea was romantic, it was also in a sense what is now called psychological; for it exactly answered the personal needs of two very extraordinary personalities.

If ever there was a man who ought to have rounded off his victorious career by capturing something more human and spiritual and satisfying than wreaths of laurel or flags of de-feated foes, it was Don John of Austria. Because his actual historical life rises on a wave of conquest in relation to these things, and then sinks again into something less epical and simple, his life has something of the appearance of an anti-climax; and reads like a mere stale maxim that all victories are vanities. He tried to crown his chief exploit by founding a kingdom of his own, and was prevented by the jealousy of his brother; he then went, somewhat wearily, I imagine, as the representative of the same brother to the Flemish fields laid waste by the wars of the Dutch and the Duke of Alva. He set out to be more merciful and magnanimous than the Duke of Alva; but he died in a net or tangle of policies; of which the only touch of poetry was a suggestion of poison.

But in that broad and golden dawn of the Renaissance, full of classical legends, carrying off Mary Stuart would have been like carrying off Helen of Troy. In that red sunset of the old chivalric romance (for the sunrise and the sunset were both in that bewildering sky) it would have seemed a magnificent materialisation of one of those strange and stately public love affairs, or knightly services, which preserved something of the Courts of Love and the pageant of the Troubadours; as when Rudel publicly pledged himself to an unknown lady in a castle in the east, almost as distant as a castle east of the sun; or the sword of Bayard sent across the mountains its remote salute to Lucretia. That one of these great loves of the great should actually be achieved in the grand style, that, I fancy, would have been a wildly popular episode in that epoch. And to the career of Don John it would have given a climax and a clue of meaning which its merely military successes could not give; and handed his name down in history and (what is much more important) in legend and literature, as a happier Antony married to a nobler Cleopatra. And when he looked into her eyes he would not have seen only bright chaos and the catastrophe of Actium, the ruin of his ships and his hopes of an imperial throne; but rather the flying curve and crescent of the Christian ships, sweeping to the rescue of the Christian captives, and blazed upon their golden sails the sunburst of Lepanto.

The converse is also true. If ever there was a woman who

was manifestly meant, destined, created, and as it were crying aloud to be carried off by Don John of Austria, or some such person, it was Mary Queen of Scots. If ever there was a woman who went to seed for want of meeting any sort of man who was anything like her equal, it was she. The tragedy of her life was not that she was abnormal, but that she was normal. It was the crowd all round her that was abnormal. There is almost a sort of antic allegory, in that sense, in such accidents as the fact that Rizzio had a hump and Bothwell some sort of a squint. If her story seems now to be steeped in morbidity, it was because the mob was morbid. Unfortunately for this ill-fated queen, she was not morbid. It is the other characters, each in his own way, which pass before us in misshapen outlines like the dwarfs and lunatics in some tropic tragedy of Ford or Webster, dancing round a deserted queen. And, by a final touch, all these ungainly figures seem more tolerable than the one that is externally elegant, the hollow doll, Darnley; just as a handsome waxwork can seem more uncanny than an ugly man. In that sense she had seen handsome men and ugly men and strong men and clever men; but they were all half-men; like the hideous cripples imagined by Flaubert, living in their half-houses with their half-wives and half-children. She never met a complete man; and Don John was very complete. In that sense she had been given many things; the crown of Scotland, the prospect of the crown of France; the prospect of the crown of England. She had been given everything except fresh air and the sunlight treatment; and all that is typified by the great ships with their golden castles and their leaping flags, that go forth to meet the winds of the world.

We know why Mary Stuart was killed. She was not killed for having killed her husband, even if she had killed her husband; and recent study of the Casket Letters suggests that her enemies are more clearly convicted of forgery than she was ever convicted of murder. She was not killed for trying to kill Elizabeth, even if the whole story of trying to kill Elizabeth was not a fiction employed by those who were trying to kill Mary. She was not killed for being beautiful; that is one of the many popular slanders on poor Elizabeth. She was killed for being in good health.

Perhaps she was the only person who was ever condemned and executed merely for being in good health. The legend which represented Elizabeth as a lioness and Mary as a sort of sickly snake is largely abandoned; anyhow, it is the very reverse of the fact. Mary was very vigorous; a strong rider, and as a dancer almost ready to outrun the Modern Girl. Curiously enough, her contemporary portraits do not convey much of her charm, but do convey a great deal of her vigour. But, as anyone may have noticed in the animal spirits of some of the finest actresses, vigour has sometimes a great deal to do with charm. Now it was essential to the policy of Cecil, and the oligarchs rich with the loot of the old religion, that Mary should die for Elizabeth, and Mary, despite her misfortunes, did not show the smallest disposition to die. Elizabeth, on the other hand, was still dying rather than still living. And when the Catholic heir inherited, it might go ill with the Protestant lords. They therefore applied to Mary, at Fotheringay, one of the sharpest possible remedies for good health, which has seldom been known to fail.

Her energy, which had thus brought her to her death, had also brought her through her life; and may be the key to many of the riddles of her life. It may be that her repeated ill-luck in marriage embittered her more than it might a woman less normal and elemental; and that the very levities, which led to her being painted as a harlot or a vampire, sprang from her primary fitness to be a mother and a wife. It may be (for all I know) that a fairly healthy person, in such a horrible experience, might have wasted her natural instincts on some violent adventurer like Bothwell ; those things are always possible ; but I confess I could never see that in this case they were necessary. I have often fancied that the alliance may have been more politic, and even cynical, than appeared to that fine romantic novelist, the forger of the Casket Letters. Or it might have been surrender to a sort of blackmail ; it might have been many things. Anyhow, being surrounded by brutes, she chose the best brute ; though he is always represented as the worst. He was the only one of them who was a man as well as a brute ; and a Scotsman as well as a man. He at least never betrayed her to Elizabeth ; and all the others did nothing else. He kept the borders of her kingdom against the English like a good subject and a normal soldier ; and she might very well have thrown herself under his protection for that alone. But whether or no she sought satisfaction in such a marriage, I am sure that she never found satisfaction in it ; I am sure she found only a new phase of the long degradation of living with her inferiors.

There was always in her heart a hunger for civilisation. It is an appetite not easily appreciated now, when people are so over-civilised that they can only have a hunger for barbarism. But she loved culture as the Italian artists of the previous century had loved it ; as something not only beautiful but bright and shining and new ; like Leonardo's first sketches of flying-machines or the full revelations of perspective and light. She was the Renaissance chained up like a prisoner ; just as Don John was the Renaissance roaming the world like a pirate. This was, of course, the perfectly simple explanation of her frequent and friendly toleration of a hunchback like Rizzio and a young lunatic like Chastelard. They were Italy and France ; they were music and letters; they were singing-birds from the South who had happened to perch on her window-sill. If there are still any historians who suppose that they were anything more to her than that, especially in the case of the Italian secretary, I can only say that such learned old gentlemen must be pretty much on the moral and mental level of Darnley and his company of cut-throats. Even if she was a wicked woman, there is no sense in supposing that she was not an intelligent woman, or that she never wished to turn from her laborious and life-long wickedness for a little intelligent conversation. The apology for my own (somewhat belated) experiment in matchmaking is that she might have been very different, when married to a man who was quite as brave as Bothwell and quite as intelligent as Rizzio, and, in a more practical and useful fashion, at least as romantic as Chastelard.

But we must not be romantic; that is, we must not concern ourselves with the real feelings of real and recognisable human beings. It is not allowed. We must now sternly turn our attention to scientific history; that is, to certain abstractions which have been labelled The Elizabethan Settlement, the Union, the Reformation, and the Modern World. I will leave the Romantics, those unpresentable Bohemians (with whom, of course, I would not be seen for worlds), to decide at what date and crisis they would like Don John finally to fulfil his design; whether his shining ship is to appear in the wide waters of the Forth as the mad mob in Edinburgh is waving scurrilous scrolls and banners before the window of the Queen; or, on the contrary, a dark boat with a solitary figure is to slide across the glassy stillness of Loch Leven; or a courier hot with haste in advance of a new army hurl a new challenge into the bickering parleys of Carberry, or a herald emblazoned with God knows what eagles and castles and lions (and presumably a bar sinister) blow a trumpet before the barred portals of Fotheringay. I leave that to them ; they know all about it. I am an earnest and plodding student of the dry scientific details of history ; and we really must consider the possible effect on such details as England, Scotland, Spain, Europe, and the world. We must suppose, for the sake of argument, that Don John was at least sufficiently strong to assert Mary's claim to sovereignty in Scotland to begin with ; and, despite the unpleasant moralising of the mob in Edinburgh, I think such a restoration would have been generally successful in Scotland. Professor Phillimore used to say that the tragedy of Scotland was that she had the Reformation without the Renaissance. And I certainly think that, while Mary and the southern prince were discussing Plato and Pico della Mirandola, John Knox would have found himself a little out of his depth. But on the assumption of popular rulers and a strong Spanish backing, which is the essence of this fantasy, I should say that a people like the Scots would have gobbled up the strong meat of the Revival of Learning quicker than anybody else. But in any case, there is another point to be considered. If the Scots did not figure prominently in the Renaissance, they had, in their own way, figured most brilliantly in the Middle Ages. Glasgow was one of the oldest universities ; Bruce was counted the fourth knight in Christendom ; and Scotland, not England, continued the tradition of Chaucer. The chivalrous side of the regime would surely have awakened noble memories, even in that ignoble squabble. I must here unfortunately omit a very fine chapter from the unpublished Romance, in which the lovers ride down to Melrose (if necessary by moonlight) to the reputed resting-place of the Heart of Bruce ; and recall (in ringing phrases) how Spanish and Scottish spears had once charged side by side upon the Saracen, and hurled far ahead, like a bolt above the battle,

If Don John had Married

the heart of a Scottish King. This fine piece of prose must not delay us, however, from facing the next fact; which is that Mary, once safe, would survive as the Queen of England as well as Scotland. It is enough to say that medieval memories might have awakened in the North; and the Scots might even have remembered the meaning of Holyrood.

Don John died trying to keep his temper with Dutch Calvinists, about ten years before the affair of the Armada; and, much as I admire him, I am glad he did. I do not want my individual dream or romance, about the rescue and elopement of Mary Stuart, mixed up with that famous international collision, in which as an Englishman I am bound to sympathise with England and as an Anti-Imperialist with the smaller nation. But, it may be said, how can an Englishman in any case reconcile himself to a romance that would involve the Elizabethan policy being overthrown by a Spanish prince, the throne occupied by a Scottish queen; or some part at least of the Armada's purposes achieved? To which I answer that such a question recoils ruinously on those who ask it. Let them merely compare what might have happened with what did happen. Was Mary a Scot? We endured one in her son. Was Don John a foreigner? We submitted to one when we expelled the grandson of her son. Mary was as English as James the First. Don John was as English as George the First. The fact is that, whatever else our policy of insular religion (or whatever we call it) may have done, it certainly did not save us from alien immigration, or even from alien invasion. Some may say we could not accept a Spaniard, when we had been recently fighting the Spaniards. But, when we did accept a Dutch prince, we had been recently fighting the Dutch. Blake as well as Drake might complain that his victories had been reversed; and that we had, after all, allowed the broom of Van Tromp to sweep not only the English seas, but the English land. A whole generation before the first George came from Hanover, William of Orange had marched across England with an invading army from Holland. If Don John had really brought an Armada with him (and Armadas are often awkward during elopements) he could hardly have inflicted a heavier humiliation on us than that. But, of course, the truth is that I am sensitive on the point of patriotism ; much more sensitive than anybody was in those days. Extreme nationalism is a relatively new religion ; and what these people were thinking of was the old sort of religion. It really made a great difference to them that Dutch William was a Calvinist while Don John was a Catholic ; and that whatever George the First was (and he was nearly nothing) he was not a Papist. That brings me to a much more vital phase of my vision of what never happened. But those who expect me to break forth into thunders of theological anathema, will here be rather abruptly disappointed.

I have no intention, I have no need, to argue here about Luther and Leo and the rights and wrongs of the revolt of new sects in the North. I need not do so, for the simple reason that I do not believe, in the case here imagined, that we should have been primarily concerned about the North. I believe we should have realised instead the enormously important position in the South ; and even more so in the East. All eyes would have been turned to a far more central battle of civilisation ; and the hero of that battle was Don John of Austria.

It has been remarked, and not untruly, that the Papacy seemed curiously negligent of the northern danger from Protestantism. It was ; but chiefly because it was not at all negligent of the eastern danger from Islam. Throughout all that period Pope after Pope issued appeal after appeal to the princes of Europe to combine in defence of all Christendom against the Asiatic attack. They had hardly any response; and only a scratch fleet of their own galleys with some Venetian, Genoese, and others, could be sent to stop the Turk from sweeping the whole Mediterranean. This is the huge historic fact which the northern doctrinal quarrels have concealed; and that is why I am not concerned here with the northern doctrinal quarrels. That age was not the age of the Reformation. It was the age of the last great Asiatic invasion, which very nearly destroyed Europe. About the time the Reformation was beginning, the Turks, in the very middle of Europe, destroyed at a blow the ancient kingdom of Bohemia. About the time the Reformation had finished its work, the hordes out of Asia were besieging Vienna. They were foiled by the stroke of Sobieski the Pole, as a hundred years before by the stroke of Don John of Austria. But they came as near as that to submerging the cities of Europe. It must also be remembered that this last Moslem thrust was really a savage and incalculable thing, compared with the first thrust of Saladin and the Saracens. The high Arab culture of the Crusades had long perished; and the invaders were Tartars and Turks and a rabble from really barbarous lands. It was not the Moors but the Huns. It was not Saladin against Richard or Averroes against Aquinas; it was something much more like the worst and wildest shocker about the Yellow Peril.

I have a great respect for the real virtues and the sane if sleeping virility of Islam. I like that element in it that is at once democratic and dignified; I sympathise with many elements in it which most Europeans (and all Americans) would call lazy and unprogressive. But when all allowance has been made for these moral merits, of the simpler sort, I defy anybody with a sense of cultural comparison to tolerate the image of Europe of the Renaissance given up to Bashi-Bazouks and the wild Mongol mobs of the decline. But it is almost as bad if we consider only the vetoes of primitive Islam; and most of its virtues were vetoes. When all is said, to the eyes of Mediterranean men especially, there passed across their shining sea merely the shadow of a great Destroyer. What they heard was the voice of Azrael rather than Allah. Theirs was the vision that would have been the background of my dream; and lifted all its nobler figures, English, Spanish, or Scottish, into the altitudes of defiance and martyrdom. The dry wind that drove before it a dust of broken idols was threatening the poised statues of Angelo and Donatello, where they shine on the high places around the central sea; and the sand of the high deserts descended, like moving mountains of dust and thirst and death, on the deep culture of the sacred vines; and the songs and the deep laughter of the vineyards. And above all, those clouds that were closing round them were like the curtains of the harem, from whose corners look out the stony faces of the eunuchs; there spread like a vast shadow over shining courts and closing spaces the silence of the East, and all its dumb compromise with the coarseness of man. These things, above all, were closing in upon that high and thwarted romance of the perfect Knight and Lady, which men of the Christian blood can never attain and never abandon; but which these two alone, perhaps, might have attained and made one flesh.

Historians quarrel about whether the English under Elizabeth preferred the Prayer-Book or the Mass-Book. But surely nobody will quarrel about whether they preferred the Crescent or the Cross. The learned dispute about how England was divided into Catholics and Protestants. But nobody will dispute what England would have felt, when told that the whole world was now desperately divided into

If Don John had Married

Christians and Mohammedans. In short, I think that under this influence England would have simply broadened her mind; even if it were only broadened to take in a big battle instead of a small battle. Of that broader battle, and our best chances in it, Don John of Austria was universally regarded as the incarnation and the uplifted sign. Not only the praise due to heroes, but the flattery inevitably paid to princes, would have carried that triumph before him wherever he went like a noise of trumpets. Everybody would have felt in him both the Renaissance and the Crusade; as those two things are warp and woof in the golden tapestries of Ariosto. Everybody would have felt both the rebirth of Europe and its all-but death. Nor need the praise have come merely from any common flatterers. All good Englishmen could have become good Europeans; I should express my meaning better if I said great Europeans. In all that crowd, perhaps, only Shakespeare could not have been greater. And yet I am not so sure; for he might certainly have been gayer. Whatever his politics were (and I suspect they were much like those of his friend the Catholic Southampton) there is no doubt that his tragedies are eternally twisted and tortured with something like an obsession about usurpation and slain kings and stolen crowns; and all the insecurity of royal and every other right. Nobody knows how his heart, if not his mind, might have expanded in that truly " glorious summer " of a sovereignty which satisfied his sixteenth-century hunger for a heroic and high-hearted sovereign. He at least would not have been indifferent to the significance of the great triumph in the Mediterranean. Supporters of the extreme spiritual insularity have often quoted the great lines in which Shakespeare praised England, as something separate and cut-off by the sea. They rather tend to forget what he really praised her for.

The Common Man

This nurse, this teeming womb of royal kings,
Feared by their breed and famous by their birth,
Renowned for their deeds as far from home,
For Christian service and true chivalry,
As is the sepulchre in stubborn Jewry
Of the world's ransom, blessed Mary's Son.

I really think that the man who wrote those lines would have welcomed the victor of Lepanto almost as warmly as he must have welcomed a Scotch Calvinist who was frightened of a drawn dirk.

About Mary I imagine there would have been no difficulty at all. Mary was the perfectly legitimate heir to the throne of England, which is more than can be said for Elizabeth. The general sense of loyalty to the legitimate sovereign, which was enormously strong in England, would have flowed towards her more freely than towards Elizabeth; because she was a more popular and approachable sort of person. She who had so often, and perhaps too often, kindled love even in the very house of hatred, might surely have been loved sufficiently in a happier household of love enthroned; as in the glowing palace of René of Provence. I see no difficulty about her popularity; but even her husband, whether he were called Consort or King, might surely, to say the least of it, have been as popular as any other king-consort. I will not say he would be more popular than William of Orange; for he could not be less. But the English can be polite to foreigners, even foreign consorts. Tennyson, as Poet Laureate, was struck by the resemblance between Prince Albert and an ideal knight of the Round Table. Ben Jonson, as Poet Laureate, would not have to stretch politeness quite so far, in order to compare Don John to an Arthurian knight. At least nobody could say he was a carpet-knight. But, what is much more important, Britain would have been in another and more real sense back in Arthurian times. It would be defending the whole tradition of Roman culture and Christian morals against heathens and barbarians from the ends of the earth. If that had been fully realised, do you think anyone would have gone about asking whether a good Calvinist ought to be a Supralapsarian or a Sublapsarian? It would no longer be a provincial question of whether some Puritan trooper had knocked the nose off a stone saint in Salisbury Cathedral; it would be a question of whether some dervish out of the desert should dance among the shattered fragments of the Moses of Michelangelo. All normal Christians, if they had understood the peril, would have closed up in defence of Christendom. And England would have got glory in the battle, as she did when that ship with crimson sails carried the English leopards to the storming of Acre.

It might, I fear, have meant a certain amount of hostility to France: the rival of the Spanish-Austrian combination; though even here there are reconciling influences and Mary's sympathies would always have been with the country of her youth and her most famous poem. But, anyhow, it would not have been like the hostility to France, or rather blind hatred of France, which we did inherit from the victory of the Whigs. It would have been more like the medieval wars with the French, waged by men who were half French themselves. The English conquests in France were a sort of eddy and backwash of the original French conquest in England; the whole business was almost a civil war. For there was more internationalism in medieval war than there is in modern peace. The same was true of the actual wars which did break out between France and Spain; they did not

273

The Common Man

break the inner unity of the Latin culture. Louis the Fourteenth was guilty of a slight exaggeration in saying that the mountains called the Pyrenees have entirely disappeared from the landscape. Many careful tourists have verified their existence and reported the royal error. But there was this truth in it; that the Pyrenees were in every sense a natural division. The Straits of Dover soon became a very unnatural division. They became a spiritual abyss, not between different patron saints but between different gods; perhaps between different universes. The men who fought at Crecy and Agincourt had the same religion—to disregard. But the men who fought at Blenheim and at Waterloo had this entirely novel feature—that the English had an equal hatred for French religion and for French irreligion. They could not understand the ideals of either side in the great civil war of all civilisation. The limitation was really rather like the Straits of Dover, being both narrow and bleak and dangerous enough to be decisive; bitter as the sea and aptly symbolised by sea-sickness. Perhaps, after all, there was a point in the tale told in our nursery histories—that it was the last Catholic queen who felt the loss of the last French possession, and had " Calais " written on her heart. With her died, perhaps, the last of that spirit which had somewhere in its depths a spiritual Channel Tunnel.

But this linking up of Europe in the Renaissance would have made easier and not harder the linking up of Europe in the Revolution; in the sense of the general Reform that was really rational and necessary in the eighteenth century. It would have been larger and clearer in its tests and ideals, if it had *not* been anticipated by a mere triumph of the richest aristocrats over the English crown. If England had not become entirely a country of squires, it might have become, like Spain, a country of peasants; or at any rate remained a country of yeomen. It might have stood the siege of commercial exploitation and commercial decline, of mere employment followed by mere unemployment. It might have learned the meaning of equality as well as liberty. I know at least one Englishman who wishes to-day that he were as hopeful about the immediate future of England as about the immediate future of Spain. But in my vision they might have learned from each other and produced, among other things, one prodigious consequence; America would be a very different place.

There was a moment when all Christendom might have clustered together and crystallised anew, under the chemistry of the new culture; and yet have remained a Christendom that was entirely Christian. There was a moment when Humanism had the road straight before it; but, what is even more important, the road also straight behind it. It might have been a real progress, not losing anything of what was good in the past. The significance of two people like Mary Stuart and Don John of Austria is that in them Religion and the Renaissance had not quarrelled; and they kept the faith of their fathers while full of the idea of handing on new conquests and discoveries to their sons. They drew their deep instincts from medieval chivalry without refusing to feed their intellects on the sixteenth-century learning; and there was a moment when this spirit might have pervaded the whole world and the whole Church. There was a moment when religion could have digested Plato as it had once digested Aristotle. For that matter, it might have digested all that is soundest in Rabelais and Montaigne and many others; it might have condemned some things in these thinkers; as it did in Aristotle. Only the shock of the new discoveries could have been absorbed (to a great extent indeed it was absorbed) by the central Christian tradition.

The Common Man

What darkened that dawn was the dust and smoke from the struggles of the dogmatising sectaries in Scotland, in Holland, and eventually in England. But for that, on the Continent, the heresy of Jansenism had never so much overshadowed the splendour of the Counter-Reformation. And England would have gone the way of Shakespeare rather than the way of Milton ; which latter degenerated rapidly into the way of Muggleton.

There is perhaps, therefore, something more than a fancy, certainly something more than an accident, in this connection between the two romantic figures and the great turning-point of history. They might really have turned it to the right rather than the left ; or at least prevented it from turning too far to the left. The point about Don John of Austria is that, like Bayard and a few others in that transition, he was unmistakably the original medieval knight, with the wider accomplishments and ambitions of the Renaissance added to him. But if we look at some of his contemporaries, as for instance, at Cecil, we see an entirely new type, in which there is no such combination or tradition. A man like Cecil is not chivalrous, does not want to be chivalrous, and (what is most important of all) does not pretend to be chivalrous. Of course there was sham chivalry, as there is a sham of everything ; and mean and treacherous medieval men made a false parade of it with pageants and heraldry. But a mean man like Cecil did not make any parade of it, or any pretence of it. So far as he knew or cared, it had gone clean out of the world. Yet in fact it had not gone ; and a great rally of it among his foes would still have commanded the natural loyalty of Europeans. That is what makes this story so strange ; that the forces were there for the deliverance. The Romance of the North could really have replied to the Romance of the South, the rose crying to the laurel ; and she who had changed songs with Ronsard, and he who had fought side by side with Cervantes, might truly have met by the very tide and current of their time. It was as if a great wind had turned northward, bearing a gallant ship; and far away in the North a lady opened her lattice upon the sea.

It never happened. It was too natural to happen. I had almost said it was too inevitable to happen. Anyhow, there was nothing natural, let alone inevitable, about what did happen. Now and again Shakespeare, with a horror almost bordering on hysteria, will thrust into the limelight some clown or idiot, to suggest, against the black curtain of tragedy, this incongruity and inconsequence in the things that really do happen. The dark curtains open and there comes forth something; certainly not the Lion of Lepanto clad in gold, nor the Heart of Holyrood, the queen of the poets, who called up the songs of Ronsard and Chastelard; but something quite different and doubtless a sort of comic relief: Jacobus Rex, the grotesque king; clumsy, querulous, padded like an armchair; pedantic; perverted. He had been brought up carefully by the elders of the True Kirk, and he did them credit; piously explaining that he could not bring himself to save his mother's life because of the superstition to which she was attached. He was a good Puritan; a typical Prohibitionist; intolerant of tobacco; more tolerant of torture and murder and things yet more unnatural. For though he shook with terror at the very shape of the shining sword, he had no difficulty about consigning Fawkes to the rack, and when death had merely been attained by the art of poisoning, he was ready with a pardon, as he cowered under the threats of Carr. What things lay behind those threats and that pardon there is here, I am glad to say, no need to inquire; but the stink of that court, as it reaches us through the purlieus of the Overbury Murder, is such as to make us turn for fresh air. I will not say to the ideal loves of Mary and Don John of Austria, which I have merely imagined, but to the very worst version of the bloody loves of Mary and Bothwell which their most furious enemies have denounced. Compared with all that, loving Bothwell would be as innocent as plucking a rose, and killing Darnley as natural as pulling up a weed.

And so, after that one wild glimpse of the possibility of the impossible, we sink back at the best into a series of third-rate things. Charles the First was better, a man sad and proud, but good so far as a man can be good without being good-humoured. Charles the Second was good-humoured without being good; but the worst of him was that his life was a long surrender; James the Second had his grandfather's virtues, so far as they went, and was therefore betrayed and broken. Then came William the Dutchman, with whom there again enters the savour of something sinister and alien. I would not suggest that such Calvinists were Antinomian Calvinists; but there is something strange in the thought that twice, in that time, there entered with that unnatural logic the rumour and savour of unnatural desire. But by the time we come to Anne and the first featureless George, it is no longer the King that counts. Merchant princes have superseded all other princes; England is committed to mere commerce and the capitalist development; and we see successively established the National Debt, the Bank of England, Wood's Halfpence, the South Sea Bubble, and all the typical institutions of Business Government. I will not discuss here whether the modern sequel, with its cosmopolitan trusts, its complicated and practically secret financial control, its march of machinery and its effacement of private property and personal liberty, be on the whole good or bad. I will only express an intuition that, even if it is very good, something else might have been better. I need not deny that in certain respects the world has progressed in order and philanthropy ; I need only state my suspicion that the world might have progressed much quicker. And I think that the northern countries, especially, *would* have progressed much quicker, if the philanthropy had been from the first guided by a larger philosophy, like that of Bellarmine and More ; if it had drawn directly from the Renaissance and not been deflected and delayed by the sulky sectarianism of the seventeenth century. But in any case the great moral institutions of modern times, the Straddle, the Wheat Corner, the Merger, and the rest will not be affected by my little literary fancy ; and I need feel no responsibility if I waste some hours of my inefficient existence in dreaming of the things that might have been (which the determinists will tell me could never have been) and in weaving this faded chaplet for the prince of heroes and the queen of hearts.

Perhaps there are things that are too great to happen, and too big to pass through the narrow doors of birth. For this world is too small for the soul of man ; and, since the end of Eden, the very sky is not large enough for lovers.